Bridget

A Long Way To Nowhere

Anne P. Shirley

To Elias

Lots of love

Anne x

For Linda,
my daughter and best friend.

Contents

Part IV

Part V

Introduction

It's November 1949, on a cold Saturday night, and my grandmother Bridget and I have just left the Low Lane cinema after seeing 'The Al Jolson Story'. I've hooked my arm through hers which, as usual, is bent behind her back. This seems to be the most comfortable way for her to walk. As we pass the Waggon and Horses, an inn midway between the cinema and home, my gran walks me towards the door. On entering the Snug, the room to the right of the entrance, I'm aware that it's almost empty. Perhaps only a few of my grandmother's old pals have dared to venture out into the cold at this hour? I feel the gloom in the room, the only illumination being two small gas lamps positioned on the main wall, each giving out a greenish glow. The once cream walls are now stippled a brown treacle colour, stained from the nicotine tar of cigarette smokers over many years, and they contrast acutely with the new cream paint on the inside of the Snug's door.

My grandmother acknowledges her friends in the semi-darkness and, after a few murmured greetings, orders a bottle of OBJ (Oh Be Joyful) stout for herself and a glass of lemonade for me. As we walk over to the bar to get our drinks, I'm aware of the badly stained wooden floorboards creaking under our feet, our weight adding to the thousand footfalls that have trodden it over many years. There's a blazing fire in the hearth, yet instead of making the room seem homely it merely accentuates the grime. Old church benches, now painted dark brown, sit against three of the walls, and the only two tables in the room, both of which are occupied, are of polished oak with intricately pierced iron legs. These were probably once considered handsome but are now badly scratched and beer-stained, thus adding to the miserable ambience of the surroundings. We remain standing near the bar sipping our drinks, an elderly lady of nearly 70 and a young girl of eight. I drink my lemonade whilst being only slightly aware of the background conversation. I'm thinking about the film we've just seen, imagining as I always did, that I'm the leading lady. Sometimes, I zone into the discussion, listening to my grandmother and her friends chatting about the newly painted door that had been kicked off its hinges the previous Saturday night after a fight had broken out between two tipsy customers. The melee started when the men, who had differing views about which political party should have won the General Election in 1945, began to taunt each other. As expected, we don't stay at the inn for very long; my grandmother prefers to drink at home in quiet solitude. We finish our drinks and my gran puts our empty glasses back onto the bar. She buys two further bottles of OBJ stout and a small bottle of Irish whiskey which she puts into the large blue cloth bag she always carries. After a few murmurs of farewell, we leave the bar, and slowly continue our journey, heading for the shiny cobblestones of The Hill, and home.

My gran's old tomcat is already sitting waiting in front of the closed door and, on seeing me, shows his pleasure by winding his thin body between my legs making me laugh. As my grandmother opens the door, he squeezes through the gap, rushing in before us, taking his favourite place on the warm hearthrug. Following the cat into the semi-darkness, my grandmother hurries over to the fire, avoiding the cat and the furniture. Picking up a spill of rolled-up newspaper from an old mug kept on the shelf above the fireplace, she puts this to the fire, blowing gently on a small glowing piece of coal until the spill catches light. Moving over to the gas light in the ceiling, her movement causing the flame to reach out for her fingers, my grandmother draws over a wooden stool and, standing on it, she pulls one of the delicate chains that hang down on each side of the mantle. Pausing a few seconds until she hears the gas hissing from the pipe, she then touches the lighted spill to the gas gauze. I hear the plop as the flame ignites the gas. Gradually, a dull glow fills the room. The paper spill has almost burned to the end, touching my grandmother's bony fingers once more, but she seems oblivious to this. Stepping down from the stool, she throws the remainder of the spill onto the fire and, in doing so, tiny specks of burning paper fall onto the home-made woollen rag rug, quickly burning themselves out. My grandmother doesn't notice this either.

I give her my coat, and she walks off to the cellar to hang it up on the large hook hammered into the wall. Returning to the fire, banked up earlier with slack (coal dust), she magics the flames back to life with the poker.

Once the gaslight is fully burning, I can see more. I drag two wooden stools over to the fire and put cushions on each of them. Grandmother places the two bottles of stout she bought earlier on the hearth to warm, and then, opening the wall cupboard beside the fireplace, she picks out a large glass and a bottle opener before sitting down beside me. Picking up one of the bottles of stout, my gran opens it and pours some of the contents into her glass, placing the now half-empty bottle onto the overhanging arm of the grate, nearer the fire, for later. Savouring the taste, she offers her glass to me and I take a sip but pull a face and hastily return the glass to her. The raw liquorice flavour is too bitter for me.

These were precious nights and, if I close my eyes, I'm still there, in my gran's scullery, listening to her talking.

Sitting in the dimness, I notice that the only sound in the room is the purring of the old cat, and the voice of my grandmother who is now telling me another story about her childhood.

Picking up the cat, I sit him on my knee, hoping he'll stay, but he doesn't, preferring his usual spot on the rug in front of the fire, between my gran and me. Occasionally, my attention wanders as gran talks. I've heard the story before, and anyway, I'm listening hard for a particular sound; I'm listening for the click of the catch on the gate outside, a sign my Aunt Alice is back from work. Time's getting on now though, so she must be working late.

'Well now, it's time for bed, Anne,' my gran is telling me.

The story is finished, and I've had my milk and Garibaldi biscuit. Before turning out the gaslight, my gran lights the candle in the candle holder, then together, we slowly head for the stairs. Glancing at the walls as we climb, I again notice the words running down both sides of the sheets of wallpaper saying: 'Made in England'. My mother tells me that my aunt doesn't know how to hang wallpaper, that she should have cut these advertising strips off before she put the paper up. It looks alright to me!

We reach the top of the stairs and turn left. The three bedrooms are divided by thin wooden partitions, and we walk through Uncle Cormac's bedroom to gain access to gran's room. Of course, my uncle is out, most likely at the Irish Nash, drinking with his friends. It will be hours before he gets home, and gran and I will be asleep by then. Gran's small double bed is on the far side of the room, tucked into a corner between the outside wall and the unused fireplace. It is wooden with a spring base and there is a flock mattress on top. The flocks easily stick together, making lumps that need separating with fingers each night before the mattress can be made comfortable. The sheets are home-made and probably from the rag mill. They often have a seam down the middle (or maybe two seams) if they are pieces of sheeting my gran has sewn together. The sheets are greyish because they are only ever washed by hand in the bathtub, in water previously used for bathing.

Before climbing into bed, I kneel down beside my grandmother and close my eyes to say my prayers. Then, getting into bed first, I move to the dip in the flocks that gran has just made for me at the far side of the mattress. She gets in after me. Before my gran blows out the candle, I take a last look around the room. On the wall beside me I see the photograph of my granddad, Nicholas. Gran says he is wearing his tram driver uniform, but my mother has told me stories that he was once a dock policeman, and a bad one, so this is what I believe him to be in the photograph. A double row of silver-coloured buttons lines the front of his heavy-looking dark double-breasted jacket, which is fastened up to the neck. His hat is flat with a shiny peak and, on the front, is a badge. He is a big man with a mass of dark tight curls springing out from under the hat. He isn't smiling.

Under the window is a gramophone player; it must just be a piece of furniture because I've never heard any of the records kept inside it being played. It is a floor-standing wooden cupboard with a box on top with a lid that opens to reveal the record deck. There are only a few records inside, and each has the words 'His Master's Voice' and a picture of a Jack Russell dog on the label.

I'm always happy at my grandmother's house, and particularly happy that my Auntie Alice still lives there.

My grandmother's name is Bridget. At the time of this recollection, she is still working full time in the mill, which is good for me as the rag mill is the place where I get most of my clothes. My name is Anne, and I am the second child of Winifred, the eldest daughter of Bridget.

Prologue

The sun was high in the sky as Michael reached the top of the hill, and the mist that had travelled with him since he had alighted the horse and trap on the Ballincrea road had, by now, almost evaporated. His bag was heavy, and he stopped to take a breath, reflecting that the hill seemed steeper than he remembered.

Looking out onto the world, he saw the creek, formed millennia ago, as it meandered its way through fields, the route often being deflected by boulders sending it off on another tangent. The path leading down to the meadow below was badly overgrown, and Michael wondered how many people had passed that route since last he travelled along it. Lifting the bag onto his shoulder, he began his descent. The grass, stained with morning dew, was slippery and he occasionally stumbled.

Reaching the bottom of the hill, the path took him close to the creek and, nearing it, he was surprised to see his youngest son, Martin, sitting on a large stone, his bare feet dipping carelessly into the brook. As he passed by he called out, 'Come on home wi' me now, Mart'n, or yer mother'll wonder where ye are.' But although Martin smiled at his father, he didn't move from the boulder. Ah well, thought Michael, sure, it's been so long since he last saw me, maybe he doesn't recognise me.

From time to time, Michael glanced back, but Martin still had not moved.

Continuing his slow journey, he arrived at fields which long ago had been fertile with crops, but on which only the cows now ambled leaving their tell-tail tokens like calling cards. Soon he was lost in thought. His father would turn in his grave if he knew how the farm had become neglected. It had been handed down to generations past and should have been successfully passed to many more, but times had changed. Now, in reality, it would never be anything other than a smallholding though he easily convinced himself that he still had great plans for it. When the children were old enough to take charge, things would be good again.

He was brought out of his reverie by the sight of the low house in the distance, noticing that even the sun didn't brighten the drab exterior walls, and even the smoke from the chimney seemed to curl a melancholy greeting to him. As he went by the old sheep dog drinking from a dis-used trough into which water from the well had been pumped, it momentarily interrupted its thirst, wagging its tail lazily in silent greeting.

Shaking his head to rid himself of his melancholy he murmured, 'Nothin' is goin' ter spoil this day fer me. Just the thought of Ireland and home makes me happy. By God, I'm lookin' forward to drinkin' the beestings again after the watered-down milk ye get over there". He always wished at times like this that he didn't have to traipse over to England to earn a living. But it couldn't be helped. Now the anticipation of spending a few weeks visiting and drinking with friends gave him a surge of adrenalin and, suddenly feeling happier, he took on a jaunty step.

Reaching the farmhouse, Michael quietly opened the door. His senses were instantly struck by the smell of newly baked bread, sending his taste buds into ecstasy. Mary, his wife, was bent over the earthen pot skimming the barm from the next batch of rising yeast. She hadn't been expecting him; but then, she never did. Apart from the money he cabled, he didn't communicate with her from one trip to the next. Michael was his own man. He didn't feel it necessary to explain his actions to anyone as, to him, in many ways, a woman's feelings weren't of much importance. Their marriage had been a strange union. From the time he was a young man, Michael had spent many years back and forth to England, and the pick of the bunch had long ago been fought over and won. By the time he had thought of settling down, the choice had been very limited. Now, the way he looked at it, she had been on the shelf when he met her, so wasn't she lucky that he had plucked her from the drudgery of her father's house? And didn't he regularly cable her money, instead of squandering it on drink and women the way some of his friends did.

The boy was the first to see his father. 'Oh goodness, Mammy, isn't it me dada come home?' he shouted, although he didn't make a move to greet him.

Making his presence felt, his heavy body still blocking the doorway, Michael said, 'Now when ye've all finished what ye're doin', I think one of ye should go down to the creek, as I've just seen Mart'n down there. I told him ter come on home, an' he all but ignored me. Ye know, Mary, he's far too young to be so far away from the house on his own. Now go on, woman, get the boy to fetch him. It's gettin' cold, it is.'

For the first time since he entered the door, Michael noticed he had gained the full attention of his family. The room had gone quiet. The children, who had initially begun talking excitedly about their father's return, were suddenly silent, looking at their mother.

Mary stopped what she was doing and, slowly turning to look at him, her face now ashen, said: 'What did ye say? That ye've seen Mart'n down at the creek? Oh man, ye must be mistaken; ye can't have seen Mart'n. Oh God, I've had no way of tellin' ye up till now, but Mart'n's dead. He's been dead and gone these many months. The poor bairn caught a chill and he never rallied.'

Part One

1899-1918

Bridget's Story

1899 to 1905 - The Early Years

AS SHE GREW OLDER Bridget began more and more to dislike her father's infrequent trips back home to Ireland. Although she didn't see a great deal of him during his stay, his time being taken up with places to visit and friends to see, nonetheless, his return interrupted the routine of the house and caused an atmosphere. However, her father was not immune to feeling the miserable mood in the house himself. Having been away so often he felt like a stranger and, in the close confines of the small farmhouse, knew that everyone was ill at ease in his company.

'Sure, I'm goin' down to the bar, Mary. I'll be out of ye'r hair for a while at least.' Michael was putting his coat on as he spoke.

Bridget and her mother were standing at the kitchen sink hand-washing clothes. As he left the house, they both sighed in unison and, had he turned around, he would have seen them laughing at their own angst.

There had been six children in the family. Maggie, Bridget's older sister, had left Ireland as soon as she was 17, and was now working in Liverpool. The other children, Thomas, Mary and Catherine, were younger than Bridget and, for the most part, looked up to her following her lead, except when she was being confrontational, which was a tendency she was learning with a vengeance. Martin, their youngest brother, had died of fever at the age of four.

The smallholding generated a lot of work for Mary, particularly when the lambs were in season, but from being small, the children had been given their own jobs to do. As they got bigger, they had taken over more of the essential work, though naturally, this interfered with their schooling. The village school took children from the ages of four to ten or eleven, but there were now so few families in the locality that all the age groups were taught together in the one classroom, by the same teacher. They sat doing their three Rs on rows of roughly constructed forms, balancing their slates on their knees. In winter the only heating in the large room came from an open fireplace in the corner of the room which burned turf, and on cold winter mornings the children would rush to sit on the seats nearest the fire only giving up their position to a child younger than themselves.

A blackboard and easel rested beside the wall near the one window, and each child was provided with a small slate and a piece of chalk with which to work. At the end of the day, the slates were wiped clean in readiness for the following day.

Bridget left school when she was ten as, by then, all her siblings had started school, and her mother needed help during the day.

She had mixed feelings about leaving school. She was happy to be growing up, but sad that she was leaving behind the books she so loved, particularly the poetry into which she could escape for a time.

Her favourite poem, and the story relating to it, was *The Rose of Tralee,* written by William Pembroke Mulchinock.

William met a girl called Mary O'Connor, the daughter of a shoemaker and a dairymaid, and began writing the poem 'The Rose of Tralee'. Mary at 17 was very beautiful; she had long dark hair and soft, shining eyes and William was madly in love with her. The Mulchinock's were a rich family employing many servants, and Mary had become a maid at the grand Mulchinock house. However, William's family didn't approve of the relationship and, the story goes, William was sent to join a regiment in India.

Some years passed before he returned to Ireland and Tralee. On his way to see Mary, he stopped off at an inn in the town. Whilst drinking there, he saw the landlord begin to draw the curtains, which was the rule in those days to mark the passing of a funeral cortege. On asking who had died, William was told that it had been a beautiful young lady named Mary O'Connor - the Rose of Tralee - who, he had been told, had died of a broken heart. William was devastated to learn this.

Though he eventually married, and he and his wife emigrated to America, he never forgot his first true love. Unfortunately, his marriage didn't last.

In 1855, William returned to Ireland where he sought solace in alcohol. The last thing he did before he died was to pen a final verse to his love story. William died in 1864 aged forty-four and was buried beside his true love, Mary.

FOR AS LONG AS SHE COULD REMEMBER, BRIDGET HAD daydreamed about going 'over the waters' to work, like her father, and sister Maggie, and over the years she had constantly badgered her mother with questions she couldn't possibly have known the answers to.

One day, she asked, 'Are the streets of London really paved in gold? One of me friends told me they were. And if they are, d' ye think the streets of Liverpool will be paved in gold too?'

Mary had laughed at that and, shaking her head said, 'Now, Bridget, ye know that's silly talk. Sure, if that really was the case, then why on earth isn't yer sister, Maggie, rich? An' me an' yer daddy too, fer that matter?'

Of course, there was no reply to the silly question. But Bridget felt she needed to go to see for herself anyway and couldn't wait for her younger siblings to leave school so that her mother wouldn't need her help anymore.

Maggie had left for England when Bridget was only fourteen and hadn't been back home in the four years since then. Although she would be following in her footsteps, Bridget had very little notion of what life was like in England because, sadly, she had never had the chance to ask her sister. But she was confident she would find work, even if it was menial work only available to unskilled hands.

When the time came, and with her mother's blessing, Bridget wrote to Maggie telling her of her future hopes and plans but got no reply which upset her very much. Mary suggested she wait a while before contacting her sister again. She had an idea. Unbeknown to Bridget, her mother wrote to Maggie telling her that, as it was now time for Bridget to leave Ireland and make her own way in the world, she thought it would be nice of her sister to answer the letter that had been sent, pointing out that their father had initially looked after her those few years earlier when Maggie had first left for England; and so Mary expected Maggie to do the same for Bridget.

When it came, the surprise reply to Bridget from Maggie had been brief and to the point. In effect, she said yes, she would be met, and yes, she could stay with her for a while.

Reading and re-reading the short letter, Bridget's heart was heavy. It was obvious that her sister was not at all happy at her coming and perhaps she was just doing her duty as a sister. But the decision had been made and now she needed to move before Maggie changed her mind.

Writing once more to Maggie, Bridget told her of her travel plans, though in her heart, she wasn't at all sure her sister would be there to meet her upon arrival in Liverpool. But she dared not mention this to her mother who had enough worries of her own.

THE TIME TO LEAVE CAME QUICKLY ONCE THE DECISION WAS made, but Bridget was shocked at the unexpected and overwhelming pull of Ireland she now felt on leaving the country of her birth. Holding back tears as she walked along the familiar lanes leading away from home the day she left at the beginning of life's long journey, she dared not allow her mind to dwell for too long on what her future might be. Having bidden her siblings farewell, her last words to her mother had been that she would return to Ireland to see them when she had saved up enough money.

By now, she knew that the streets of Liverpool would not be paved with gold. To confirm what her mamma had said, Bridget had also asked the question of her parish priest after confession one day. But Father Cronin had laughed, saying 'Oh Bridget, who on earth told ye that? Of course, they aren't. Sure, I wouldn't be sittin' here wi me feet feelin' like lead in the bog if they were. I'd be scrapin' the pavement wi me shovel.'

Sadness had overwhelmed Mary also. She wondered if she would ever see her strong-willed, sensible, daughter again. The village contained mostly old people and children, the young men and women having long departed to a 'better land'. If there was any consolation for Mary, it was that her daughter was going to England and not America; the stretch of water between Ireland and England was short and navigable.

After weeks of planning, Bridget had thought she was fully prepared for the long journey to Cobh, County Cork, yet found herself both mentally and physically exhausted on arrival after days of travelling. But now, to add to her fatigue, she had arrived at the docks a day early and needed somewhere to stay for the night.

The area around the docks was dingy and the intermittent gas lamps, which jealously hugged the pavement, appeared loathe to show Bridget the way as she searched for a vacancy sign. From time to time, a transient girl of the night would shout a cheery hello, and it did cross her mind that perhaps the young lady would know where she could get cheap accommodation. However, she sensed somehow that anywhere recommended would not be suitable lodgings for her, and so continued searching. The accommodation Bridget eventually found was cheap, in keeping with the area, but it was clean and comfortable enough.

Lying in bed that night, Bridget felt a great weight on her chest. She worried about what lay ahead of her and wasn't at all sure she would be able to sleep peacefully. Nonetheless, exhaustion took hold and eventually she fell into a restful sleep. Though vaguely aware of the sounds of comings and goings during the night, the noises didn't disturb her too much, and the next morning she awoke feeling more cheerful than on the previous day. Laying there, her eyes rested on the ceiling, and she noticed that someone had haphazardly scratched words into the plaster: "Don't go where the path may lead. Go instead where there is no path and leave a trail." Reading the message, a number of times and not quite understanding the meaning, she wondered if perhaps it was confirmation that her journey to another kind of life was the right thing to do, though she wasn't at all sure what kind of path she would find herself on.

After a brief wash with cold water from the only tap in the bathroom on the floor below, she gathered her packages together and left the boarding house, walking the short distance to the docks. It was a cold November morning and the ships moored along the wharves were being bumped backwards and forwards against the sea wall by the heavy swell. Seeing the movement, Bridget worried that she would be sick on the journey, imagining that the feeling would probably not be dissimilar to the feeling she had at that very moment.

With time to spare, she meandered along the quayside. One of the ships was already loading passengers and goods for Ellis Island and, for a second, seeing the excitement on the faces of the passengers, she got caught up in the thrill of the moment. What must it be like to sail to New York? she wondered. Perhaps the Irish fared better there in the great new land with new people?

By the time Bridget too found herself on board ship, the delight and elation of earlier had left her, being replaced by a strange feeling of foreboding. Laying her packages on the floor underneath a weathered bench bolted to the deck, she took a moment to look around.

The deck of the ship was thronging with people, and she wondered if it was as busy as this on every weekly sailing. Ladies of elegance wandered casually by in their fur coats and muffs, whilst other ladies, gripping their thin shawls tightly across their chests, frantically breathed on an exposed hand in the vain hope of keeping warm. But it was the din that surprised her most! The noise of people shouting to each other mixed with the crying of the babies, and the harrying of the young children, very nearly deafened her.

Some of the passengers' luggage, which had been lain on the ground, was getting kicked about by people as they dashed across to the portside of the ship to bid a final farewell to family and friends on the quayside. The sights and sounds were all so new to Bridget who suddenly smiled to herself, remembering the message on the ceiling in the boarding house.

Bending down to collect her bundles, she was shocked to see that the butter she had cosseted for so long had seeped through its packaging, leaving a greasy stain on the wooden deck. Picking up the bundle containing all that remained of the butter, she pushed through the mass of people to make her way to the starboard side of the boat. Leaning over, she threw the dripping greasy parcel into the murky waters, and watched as the butter began to disappear, leaving behind a yellow cloud of floating grease. Sadness abruptly enveloped her, remembering how hard her mother had worked to prepare the butter, it being the only present she could give Maggie for initially taking care of her younger sister. Bridget lay her forehead on the ship's rail and sobbed.

The sudden movement of the ship brought her back to her senses and, wiping away the tears, she retrieved the rest of her packages and quietly watched as the ship left the quayside.

Amid the general noise of the excited passengers there was now another noise, much shriller this time. Someone was shouting through a loudspeaker. Bridget didn't understand what the invisible voice said, but in what seemed like an instant, people quickly began moving across the deck towards some open doors.

'Come on, dear, you can slip in here in front of us.' A kindly lady was encouraging her to join the queue, but Bridget hesitated, not knowing what the queue was for.

'Where are we goin'?'

'Didn't you hear the loudspeaker just now telling steerage passengers that we have to leave the upper deck and move to the deck below? Come on, give me one of your packages as I have a free hand.'

Handing over one of her parcels she allowed herself to be propelled across the deck and down a set of corroded metal steps. At the bottom, Bridget had no choice but to go along with the flow, the mass of people behind her pushing her forward seeming to sense that the floor space was rapidly becoming occupied.

The old boat creaked and smelled badly of burning diesel and the thought raced through her mind that she might never see the light of day again; only the silent Our Father's and Hail Mary's prevented her from panicking.

Seeing an empty space, Bridget took back her parcel from the kindly lady, and quickly claimed the spot. People had already begun creating small areas in which to sit or lie down, and some were using their packages to ease their discomfort in the cramped space. Copying them, Bridget settled her few packages around her then, laying down, she rested her head against the softest one and, closing her eyes, fell into an exhausted sleep. Occasionally, the rolling of the boat caused someone to step on her in their eagerness to rid themselves of their last meal, but Bridget was mostly oblivious to the distress of the other passengers.

When she opened her eyes again, she noticed the atmosphere had changed. Some of the passengers were quietly speaking with their neighbours, the initial inhibition of meeting strangers for the first-time giving way to friendliness and occasional shy laughter. People had begun walking around the lower deck, checking their fellow passengers to see if there was anyone they knew from their hometown, and an occasional whoop of pleasure rang through the deck when someone familiar was discovered.

Sitting up and stretching to remove the kinks in her body Bridget looked around. People were eating the food they had brought with them and, seeing this, for the first time since leaving the boarding house that morning she felt hungry. Quickly feeling into her coat pocket, it was comforting to know that the leftover piece of dry bread a guest had left on a table, and which she had picked up, was still nestling there. But no matter how hungry she felt, it was important that she resist the temptation to consume it at the beginning of the voyage.

The air was getting stale below deck; people were coughing and sneezing, and the thought occurred to Bridget that perhaps diesel fumes were leeching through the floorboards. In need of some fresh air, she decided to take a walk above deck.

Before leaving, she spread out her bundles reserving the place on the floor, hiding everything underneath her coat. It was going to be a long night and she needed to protect her place.

Leaving the musty lower deck, she took a deep breath and was glad of the chill in the night air. Looking out to sea, the moon appeared to be draped across the waves like slashes of molten gold, and at that moment, it was difficult not to feel at peace with herself.

Wondering if her mother was looking up at the stars too, a thought that was the only parallel she could think of to bring them together, Bridget desperately wanted her to know that everything was all right now; there was no longer any need for her mother to worry. The breeze was blowing away any fears, giving her the strangest sense of wellbeing,

THE BOAT DOCKED AT LIVERPOOL MIDDAY ON 27TH November 1900, and the day would be etched on her memory for the rest of her life.

Many of the passengers had already gone onto the upper deck in anticipation of the ship's arrival, and picking up her remaining packages, Bridget took her place alongside them. The town could be seen from the deck. Church spires, large buildings and warehouses, mingling with narrow streets of terrace houses, all leading down to the dockside.

As their boat approached a mooring on the quayside, other ships, tenders, cranes and derricks all fought for the small space, appearing to leave very little room for each vessel to dock. Some of the ships already moored were being loaded with goods that, as Bridget later learned, was probably cotton and woollen cloth from the north of England. There were stations at all the quays for goods and rail connections for the large railway network that had grown up around the docks. Coal was being loaded onto larger ships, probably in readiness for their long journeys across the seas to America and the rest of the world.

When Bridget's vessel was safely moored to the quayside, the passengers prepared to disembark, although she chose to stay on deck until the crush had subsided. Idly watching people on the dockside waving to friends still on board, she unexpectedly felt the ship reverberate to the sound of a small explosion. Falling to her knees in fright, she hid her head in her hands. A passing sailor laughed. 'It's only the gunships giving the time of the day. It's one o'clock, if you didn't already know.'

Clambering to her feet Bridget shook off the dust from her coat and feeling embarrassed, she shyly took her place in a queue that had begun to form on the deck, making sure her few bundles were still intact. Some passengers were ignoring the line of waiting people and were pushing their way through to the gangplank, but the general atmosphere was so happy that very few passengers complained.

Assembling the passengers into groups of five or six as they arrived at the bottom of the gangplank, officials were then leading them into the Customs House, where each passenger was instructed to place their packages onto trestle tables, behind which stood grim-faced men. Every parcel was opened and fingered and squeezed and pushed and then left in a miserable heap for them to sort into a proper bundle once more. There were lots of mutterings from the passengers, but these were low. On board the warning had gone around that .... 'this is the Englishman's country and it's best for the Irish not to complain too loudly.'

Following the method of the other passengers, Bridget put her belongings onto the table and removed her long coat, placing this on the table beside her possessions. To her disgust, the Customs man didn't pick up her coat to inspect it, instead he merely poked it with a pencil before ordering her to remove it from the table. Having donned her coat once more, she waited patiently whilst he also dissected her goods.

With his task complete, the man directed Bridget towards a queue of people being ushered between barriers. Standing in line, her mind began to wander. Would Maggie be waiting outside? She was in a strange country with very little money, and it hadn't entered her head to make note of the address from her sister's letters. What if Maggie wasn't waiting outside? Would she be able to cope on her own? Her heart began beating so fast it made her tremble, and she closed her eyes trying to control the anxiety.

The sudden instruction shouted in her ear made her jump. 'Will you get a move on, woman? You're stopping others from entering the barrier.' The voice had come from an official-looking man in a uniform. Quickly moving forward Bridget closed the gap that had opened up.

As they left the Customs shed, people initially began to assemble on the quayside trying to gauge which way to go, eventually moving towards large gates at the end of the dirt road leading away from the docks. As she walked along on the edge of the crowd, Bridget searched for her sister. The road was bumpy with large rocks embedded in the soil making it difficult to walk, but on the few occasions she left the path, her legs were stung by nettles peeping through the grass and she wasted time looking for dock-leaves to rub through her stockings to take away the pain.

The dirt path led through huge open gates onto a busy road and, exiting, Bridget looked around to see if her sister was waiting there; but she wasn't. Forcing down the urge to panic, she knew there was nothing she could do but wait, hoping her sister had merely been delayed and had not changed her mind after all.

To take her mind of the immediate problem, she leant against the pillar connected to the gate, and watched, in fascination, as the passing horse-drawn carriages bounced along the uneven cobbles, most of the occupants sitting frozen faced, bracing themselves against the sides of the carriages to minimise the jarring bumps.

What was the draw to this alien country other than work, she wondered? Everything was so different. Where were the fields? Where was the silence she craved for? But most of all...., where was her sister?

In her daydream, Bridget had been unaware of Maggie coming towards her until she heard her name being called. On seeing her sister, Bridget was so happy that, when she was within arm's length of her, she fell into an embrace, an action so unexpected of herself that she was suddenly embarrassed. Thankfully, Maggie seemed not to notice. Taking a step backwards to untangle herself from Bridget's clasp, she turned towards a man who appeared to be loitering nearby.

'This is John, me intended. He came t' help with yer luggage, Bridget, though I see ye don't have much!'

John was a tall, dark-haired young man, wearing a coat that seemed too short in the sleeves and too tight around the shoulders, giving him the look of a boy who had unexpectedly matured into a man. John took Bridget's hand and shook it, a gesture quite unfamiliar to her.

Picking up her packages, she noticed that John had bitten fingernails like her brother, Thomas, and it made her smile for the first time, inwardly remembering all the scolding mother had given her brother.

'I bet the journey over from Ireland was grand,' John said cheerfully.

Slightly embarrassed at the attention she was getting, unused as she was to the company of men other than her father and brother, she answered, 'No, sure t'wasn't too bad.' But even to her own ears she sounded altogether too meek.

'Well, that's good. Then ye won't mind the next part of the journey as it might be grim,' he said with a grin, leaving Bridget to ponder what he meant.

'Come on wi' ye,' said Maggie tartly. 'I've got better things to do wi' me time than stand here fiddle fartin' about.'

Maggie scurried along the cobbled road in front of them. 'Come on, come on, ye two. Ye can take in the scenery some other time.'

John was still buoyant as they boarded the horse-drawn tram waiting at the end of the road, but he managed to mortify Maggie by getting the few packages he carried jammed on the bend of the stairs as he headed up to the top deck.

The journey was slow, and initially, Bridget was excited to take in the view. It was only when they reached the outskirts of town that her sadness returned. Everything was grimy – the houses, the roads, the pavements, even the dirt itself was black, so unlike the lovely reddish coloured soil of her homeland.

Alighting the vehicle outside the tram depot, Maggie and John took off along the street at a pace, leaving Bridget following behind. The cobbles hurt her feet; the shoes she had worn for the last 24 hours were now tight, and the soles were thin and worn, and it was a relief when they eventually slowed their walk, reaching what she assumed was their destination. But the road they entered came as a shock to her. The rows of houses on both sides of the street looked almost derelict; impoverished even. Dirty, torn curtains hung from windows, some of which were broken and had been repaired with rags stuffed into the holes in the glass. The windows of others were covered with pages of newspaper probably salvaged from the porch of a nearby church. People were sitting outside these poor dwellings, on chairs or wooden boxes, but they seemed happily unaware of their poverty.

Walking along the street, Bridget inwardly shuddered when she noticed that some of these poorer houses were actually exhibiting signs above their doors advertising themselves as Boarding Houses. How on earth could anyone charge to stay in a hovel?

Catching up with Maggie and John as they reached the end of the road, a cul-de-sac, she was about to ask her sister in which house she lived, when she spotted the 'ROOMS TO LET' sign above the door of a house her sister was heading towards. Before she could ask a question, Maggie was already ringing the doorbell.

The old lady who answered the door was holding a piece of rag to her nose and appeared to be trying to absorb repeated sneezes into it. Each time she removed the rag, an orange nicotine outline of dried snuff was revealed to be running down from her nose to her top lip, immediately giving a clue as to the cause of her sneezes. Peering at them through wet eyes, the old lady exclaimed, 'There'll be no men allowed in the women's rooms in this house, d' ye hear me? I'll have none of it,' before stepping aside to let her guests enter.

The entrance lobby was large but dark and gloomy, the only light coming from a small window above the outside door. Walls, which would once have been a pleasant red colour, were now darkened with age. The badly worn linoleum on the floor was cracked and faded, but here and there, yellow coloured flowers seemed to fight their way through the cracks looking for daylight as though they had been planted in spring and were just awakening. Now, the cracks gave their own patina to the flooring.

Once inside, Maggie briefly explained to the landlady that they weren't all seeking accommodation – no, not at all. Only one room was required, and this was for her young sister, (pointing at Bridget), and it would only be for a short time. Bridget was dumbfounded; she certainly didn't want to stay here on her own. Silently praying the accommodation would be too costly, she kept her mouth shut, but unfortunately, the old lady 'only had accommodation for one person left and would need a deposit to secure it'.

Without asking Bridget's opinion, Maggie opened her purse and counted out the money. Then turning to Bridget, she said, 'Be good, and we'll be back to collect ye soon.'

Standing in the hallway watching her sister and her sweetheart disappear into the street Bridget wondered what on earth had just happened!

With a satisfying nod, the old lady closed the door. Smiling, she looked down at her half-closed hand and counted the money once more, before putting it into her apron pocket. Bringing out the piece of rag, she again gave her nose a hard blow before putting the cloth back in her apron on top of the money. The skin on her bony hands was transparent and reminded Bridget of the china statuette of St Bridget that stood on a table inside the porch of her parish church back in Ireland.

Having secured the funds for the room, the old lady was now in a hurry to settle her visitor into the accommodation. Gathering up her long skirts, she bent an arthritic finger gesturing for her guest to follow, leading the way towards the staircase. Walking down the hallway, Bridget surreptitiously ran a finger along the dado rail and was slightly relieved to see that it was a relatively dirt-free finger that she removed; the house was cleaner than at first imagined. On the other hand, her senses were being attacked by a strange smell of beer and cabbage which seemed to fill the air.

At the bottom of the stairs, the old lady stopped and, holding onto the baluster, lifted her eyes upwards towards the top landing. Then, with a heavy sigh, she began to slowly climb the steps with Bridget unhurriedly following behind. The noise coming from the woman's throat as they mounted the stairs was alarming and it was obvious she was having trouble breathing; however, stopping every two or three steps to take a pinch of snuff seemed, even for a brief moment, to give her enough energy to continue the ascent.

Seizing the chance to view her surroundings during these rests, Bridget glanced around. The stair carpet had an overall bluey polished glazed look, probably the result of dust trodden into it over the years, although in places, some of its true colours still showed through faintly. The walls and stair bannisters were painted dark green, which seemed to match the sentiment of the faces of the angry-looking relatives staring out from photographs hanging on the walls. She didn't bother to compare the similarity between the old crone and the photos as she could well guess the relationship.

Reaching the top of the stairs, the woman shuffled over to a chair that was placed against the wall and sat down with a bump. Her breathing, now obviously distressing her greatly, was taking an eternity to stabilise. Bridget stood and waited as there wasn't anything else to do.

Strains of music coming from the passageway leading from the stairs was intriguing. From where she was standing, Bridget could see five or six doors along the hallway, the doorknobs progressing along the wall like a series of semibreves on a sheet of music, and she was tempted to investigate the noise. But a deep sigh from the old lady brought her back from her thoughts.

Having now recovered somewhat, the woman had risen from the chair and was standing beside it stretching her back. Satisfied she was over her minor trauma, she then slowly moved down the corridor with her guest in tow, past the 'music room', stopping at the door at the end of the corridor.

Knocking on the door once, and without hesitation, the landlady opened it and walked in. Naturally, Bridget followed her. But on entering, she was shocked to see a young woman of her own age already occupying the room. By the startled look on her face the young woman was equally surprised at the intrusion, though she didn't make any comment.

Surreptitiously surveying the room, Bridget noticed that there was only one large bed.

During this time, not one word had been spoken. To an outsider, it would have looked like a meeting of friends where words were not needed yet, ten minutes earlier, the three people had been total strangers.

Her job now done, the landlady turned on her heels to leave but then stopped and almost as an afterthought said, 'Bridget, this is Marie. She's from the same part of the world as yerself, I think.' Then she disappeared.

Placing her bags on the floor Bridget said to the young woman standing looking at her, 'Well, I have absolutely no idea what just happened. Me sister picked me up from the boat an hour or so ago, an' she's just dumped me here. I thought I was bein' taken' ter her place but instead, I'm left in a boardin' house wi' someone I don't even know, and wi' only one bed to share.'

Suddenly, the bizarreness of it all hit them and they started to laugh, Marie adding her own analogy. Soon they were both in hysterics.

Marie had only arrived at the boarding house earlier that same day but, unlike Bridget, had been advised that there was only one room available, and it was a double. That, if she wanted the accommodation, she would have to accept to share it if the need arose. Of course, she had hoped the need wouldn't arise, but here was Bridget!

It was Marie who suggested they explore the house. But not knowing who the other lodgers were, they thought they should first hide their scanty possessions as there was no key in the lock so the door couldn't be secured. Reasonably happy with the hiding places they found, they left the room and retraced their steps back down to the hallway. The smell of cabbage escaping from some unknown kitchen was now overpowering, but they were both hungry. A badly printed sign on the wall indicated that the dining area was outside and there they found an outer building, the double doors of which were wide open.

Approaching cautiously, the girls were met by a cacophony of sound. Thankful at last to discover the source of the food, they entered the building and found themselves in the centre of what appeared to be a mini league of polyglots; the air was filled with foreign languages: Russian, Chinese, Polish; there was even the odd Irish accent.

'What're we goin' to do now?' asked Marie.

Bridget smiled. 'Oh, don't worry, we'll find a way. Me mother used to tell me "ye'll never be lost so long as ye have a tongue in ye're head", an' she was right. Why don't ye sit down at the table over there an' I'll look around.' So, Marie sat at the table whilst Bridget began to do a tour of the room.

Interrupting two men who were getting up from a bench, she asked what the rule was for getting food and, without a word, they pointed towards a trestle table at the far side of the building.

Nearing the table, Bridget saw it held two huge cast iron pots which were standing with their lids slightly askew, long handled spoons preventing the lids from being closed properly. Lifting the lids, she peered inside and saw they both contained the same delicacy – potato and cabbage hash. It was the most unappetizing food she had ever seen, but she and her friend both needed to eat. Picking up a large empty dish she filled it with the food, collecting two slices of bread from the end of the table as she passed, and returned to Marie. Catching sight of the meal being placed on the table in front of her, Marie began to laugh; now they both knew the cause of the bad cabbage smell. However, surprisingly, they both ate the food from the shared dish with relish.

The girls didn't speak much as they returned to their room after the meal and, once there, were both silent. Bridget began busying herself, tidying up her packages and, in the process, picking out something to wear in bed. She was now keenly aware that they were two strangers after all, even though they had spent the last few hours together. Bridget was about to break the silence in the room when she caught of Marie, through the mirror, kneeling on the floor furtively trying to undress. Oh dear. It occurred to Bridget that, if she now did the same, it would embarrass Marie, so instead she turned her back, quickly undressing down to her shift. Clambering into the side of bed nearest the door, she waited for Marie to turn off the small gas lamp and climb into bed beside her. They both said 'goodnight' before turning their backs to each other but, lying there in silence Bridget felt she needed to say something more. However, exhaustion was creeping up on her and suddenly she just wanted to go to sleep. Her main worry as she drifted off was that Marie might snore!

THE TWO GIRLS VERY QUICKLY BECAME FAMILIAR WITH THE routine. Getting up early in the morning, they washed, made the bed, and then left the boarding house for the day, returning each evening to repeat the process of sitting at the trestle table in the outer building, eating their potato and cabbage hash.

By pooling some of their money, they found that, with care, they could manage to stave off hunger with a daily visit to the bakery to get broken offcuts of warm fresh bread, which they would eat as they walked around the streets.

On the second day, they took a tram ride into town where, again, Bridget was shocked at the noise and bustle. Everything was so new.

With a mixture of admiration and envy, they gawped at the rich ladies emerging from the dress shops and milliners, carrying bags and boxes conveying the names of the stores, declaring to the world they had enough money to shop at *Andre Galerie* and *Madame Katrina*. They sometimes playfully copied the elegant stroll of the long-skirted ladies walking along the street, exaggerating how one lady gracefully buttoned her cape at the shoulder, and laughed at the man in the dark three-piece suit who habitually removed a timepiece from his waistcoat pocket to check, and double-check, the time. This particularly amused the girls, having only ever before seen timepieces on buildings; the sight of these small clocks fascinated them.

By the fifth day, having not heard from Maggie since she left her at the boarding house, Bridget had begun to wonder if she would ever see her again. Perhaps her sister had never been in a position to look after her in the first place, yet Mother and she had hardly given her a chance to refuse. However, if this was the case, then Bridget thought it would have been kinder for Maggie to just say so, or even to have ignored the letters. She worried too how far the deposit on the room would last as her personal money was fast dwindling away.

Marie and Bridget talked constantly about their problem. With shrinking funds, they would both need to find jobs sooner rather than later, and certainly before their money ran out completely.

When, at long last, Maggie reappeared, Bridget had terrible mixed feelings; She was relieved she was here but sad and very worried for her friend, knowing it would be almost financially impossible for her to manage alone. Bridget asked Maggie if she could bring her friend along with her, but she just said, 'No!'

Leaving the boarding house that day, her heart felt like lead, and it was difficult to hold back the tears.

Maggie and Bridget walked along the road in silence. Not surprisingly, it was proving awkward to have a conversation as they didn't know each other very well. But Bridget was glad her sister had arrived alone so at least she could talk without John gawping at her. As they walked, she rehearsed a few sentences in her head, blurting them out as they occurred, 'I'm so glad ye're here, Maggie. To be honest, it's been frightenin' not knowing when ye would be back to collect me. Me money's almost gone an' Marie and meself 've been spendin' our days walkin' around the streets just lookin' in the shop windows, an' wonderin' what we'd do when we had no money left fer a tram ride, or to buy the baker's bread titbits. Also, the soles of me shoes are getting' worse. Do we have far to walk?'

But Maggie seemed in no mood for talking allowing Bridget to speak her piece in silence, only responding to the last question: 'Wait and see.'

At the end of the street, they caught the open-topped tram again, staying downstairs this time. When the tram eventually stopped and they alighted, Bridget knew they had only travelled a short distance and she was puzzled as to why Maggie had not collected her sooner? However, not wanting to really know the answer in case it hurt her feelings, this time she kept her own counsel and didn't ask any more questions.

After a short walk, they stopped in front of dingy, double-fronted, two-storey accommodation and, as usual, old newspapers covered most of the front windows. On entering, the first thing Bridget noticed was the smell; again, a pungent smell, but this time of rotting food mixed with another smell she didn't recognise, though which she was later to learn was the odour of beetles.

Maggie passed along the hallway and walked towards the stairs. 'We're up on the next floor, and the house is shared with three families. As ye'll learn soon enough, accommodation isn't easy t' find.'

On the upper landing there was a sink under a small window, and alongside that, a one-burner paraffin hob balanced on top of a wooden crate. The landing was dark and dank, the grimy wallpaper so wet it was peeling away like the rag ringlets on a little girl's head.

Maggie walked on ahead towards the door at the end of the upper hallway which, to her surprise, was partly ajar. 'We're here, then,' she said, and pushed the door open fully to reveal a room almost depleted of furniture. The double bed, which seemed to have a secondary use as a wardrobe, was pushed up against one wall, and two badly scuffed wicker chairs, also draped with clothes, were placed against the opposite wall. A cord had been strung across the room and this too was heavy with paraphernalia.

Bridget's heart sank. The room was so small there was nowhere to put anything out of sight. Was this what she had dreamed of leaving her beloved Ireland for? It was now obvious to Bridget why Maggie had left her at the lodgings for so long - she was embarrassed. Hiding her disappointment, she walked into the room, parting some of the hanging clothes to get near the bed.

'Sure, it's not too bad, Maggie; we'll make it work. Which side of the bed d' ye sleep on then?' Holy Mother of God, she thought. What have I done?

It took a few weeks to accept that this, or something very much like it, was going to be her life if she stayed in this country. But with her money dwindling away Bridget knew she must begin looking for work; but what sort of work could she do with no experience other than helping her mother at home? More than once Maggie had suggested millwork alongside her, but the thought filled her with horror. She would be confined in a large room with noisy machines all around her. How could a farm girl who was used to running around the fields in bare feet cope with this? However, with no other choice, eventually Bridget had reluctantly agreed to at least try the work.

As she had expected, the noise was horrific, and she hated it from the very first day. Maggie had no sympathy though – no-one from the old country lived the life of Reilly, and the sooner her younger sister learned that lesson the better for her.

Eventually Maggie began hinting strongly that Bridget might be happier in her own rented room. Of course, she was right – Bridget would prefer more space, but what would she pay the rent with? She hardly earned enough to buy food and pay the small amount she gave her sister each week towards the room. Oh, she knew well enough that she was in the way, but thought it was only because Maggie and she were fighting for space. Amazingly, it hadn't occurred to her that John and Maggie were actually courting, even though John had been introduced as her sister's 'intended'.

Yes, she most certainly was in the way; not once had she left them alone in all the weeks she'd been staying with her sister! However, Bridget only realised it was time to go out into the world on her own when, one day, Maggie jokingly said, 'John's been sayin' he doesn't think there'll be enough room in the one bed fer the three of us when we're married, and he's gettin' worried.'

That was it! Time to move on. With the next phase of her life approaching, Bridget had to re-think her future.

The perfect solution was to seek work at one of the 'posh houses' owned by the many millowners in the area because those jobs usually offered accommodation as part of the job. Walking back to the room after work one evening, she saw an advertisement in a shop window for someone seeking a resident domestic helper. Nearly beside herself with excitement Bridget hurried back to Maggie's and, finding a piece of paper, wrote down the lady's name and street address that she had memorised from the advertisement. Exchanging her old work shawl for her coat and putting the note with the address of her hopefully future employer safely into a pocket, Bridget left a brief note for her sister telling here what she was doing and then started out in search of the house.

It was a long walk, much further than she had anticipated, and was in an area unknown to her. However, she thought that perhaps the priest back home in Ireland had been wrong enough - the houses were amazing, and so maybe the streets were paved in gold after all. If she got the job, at least Bridget felt she would be close to the richness. Smiling to herself at the thought she stopped and, bending down, scratched the pavement with fingernails. But instead of gold dust, she merely collected dirt. Rubbing her hands together to rid them of the dust she continued walking along the avenue, counting down the house numbers.

The number and name of each house she passed was skilfully painted on either side of the double columns that supported the ornate metal gates, and she found the address she was seeking without too much trouble.

Peering through the gates, Bridget was awestruck. The house in the centre of the driveway looked like a huge lopsided dolls' house with towers and turrets and wraparound porches. It was magnificent and was surely the house of a lord and lady.

Her heart involuntarily skipped a beat. 'Goodness, what do I know about housekeeping? Maybe it would be better to save meself the embarrassment of bein' told I wasn't suitable and walk away right now; it wasn't too late,' she thought. But remembering the tiny room waiting for her at her sister's made her reconsider. Still contemplating what to do, she saw the bell-push. Ah well, it's now or never, she thought, and pressed the bell twice.

A man in work clothes appeared from the side of the house and, seeing her standing at the gate, walked down the driveway, an irritated look on his face. At the gate, he pulled back the two heavy bolts that locked the main section, leaning so close to the bars as he bent down that Bridget could smell his sweet breath. However, he totally ignored her presence as he did so – it was as if she was invisible. Then, having unlocked the gate, his job done, he turned tail and walked back up the drive, leaving her to push the heavy gate open herself. In her wisdom, she took the unlocking of the gate as an invitation for her to follow him, and so she did.

There was no-one in sight save the insolent man in front of her and she was tempted to play hopscotch along the York stone flags. But what if the mistress of the house was watching, what then ...? Thinking better of it, Bridget continued walking sedately. The gardens were beautifully laid out and spread as far as the eye could see. It must surely take a number of gardeners to keep the grounds looking so spick and span, she mused. Ah, yes, perhaps she had already met one of them! Oh dear, she thought, smiling to herself.

The 'gardener' stopped at the side of the house and waited for her to catch up. As she neared him, without a word he pointed towards a door, then disappeared behind the house.

Assuming it to be the kitchen, Bridget lifted the door knocker and, after striking the plate a few times, waited. When the door was opened, the person standing there dressed in work clothes actually seemed happy to see her.

'Oh, hopefully you've come in response to the advertisement. Madam will be really pleased. We're all finding the work heavy-goin' at the moment.'

Stepping aside, the domestic signalled that Bridget should enter. Then, like the gardener, she too disappeared without a word, leaving Bridget wondering what to do next. What was it about her that made people disappear?

Noticing two small girls busying themselves at a very long kitchen table in the middle of the room, Bridget went over to see what they were doing and learnt they were making 'bread men' from leftover dough. The room was hot and smelled of freshly baked bread, and the faces of the two girls were a lovely pink colour from the heat.

The kitchen was huge with a purpose that seemed practical rather than attractive. Pans with brass bases hung from large hooks along the main wall and a dresser was filled with matching crockery. There was a double stone sink under the large window, stacked high with pots and pans and crockery already washed and drying. Beside this was a copper sink, which Bridget was later to learn was for washing delicate things like fine bone china, the surface of this sink being softer, making it safer from clumsy hands, like hers, that might chip the tableware.

'Madam will see you now.' The servant had re-appeared, indicating that Bridget should follow.

Out in the main hallway, the sun was shining through the stained-glass windows on the landing of the upper floor, sending sunrays rippling down the walls of the staircase. Ahead of them, the drawing-room door was open, and as they walked towards it Bridget could see that everything inside was either pale blue or dark blue and cream: the carpet, the two settees, the chairs, the curtains, even the picture frames. The thought of having sufficient funds to be able to gather together the same colours was a bewilderment to her in her poverty-stricken world.

Stopping at the door the servant indicated that Bridget should enter and, on doing so, she saw the lady of the house sitting on one of the blue settees, nursing a new-born baby. For a brief moment, it was mesmeric; the thin covering protecting the lady's chasteness had moved and she could see the baby suckling. Embarrassed, and looking away, she remembered how her own mother had protected the children from anything that was considered rude. But the mistress didn't appear to notice Bridget blushing, merely indicating that she should sit on the blue settee opposite, whereupon the she then began asking questions about her previous employment.

Though Bridget answered truthfully, after a few minutes, it became obvious that it didn't really matter how she answered, as some of the questions being asked didn't have any relevance to her previous employment. After a short silence, when the only sound to be heard in the room was that of the baby quietly feeding, madam finally said, 'Well then, Bridget, I think you will be suitable for the post and I would like you to start straightaway if that's at all possible.'

Maggie was ecstatic when, rushing home to the room, Bridget told her of the job she had found and, not surprisingly, helped pack her few possessions into a small bag, even insisting on walking her back to the big house. At the gates they said their goodbyes and Bridget, striding back up the long driveway, turned around a few times, noticing that Maggie was still standing watching her.

The imposing six-bedroom home was set in more than an acre of land and required two gardeners for the upkeep of lawns, flower beds and the vegetable garden. The house itself had been lavishly furnished, and on her first day, Bridget had to walk around the house twice before finally believing that she was working and living in such beautiful surroundings.

It didn't take long to settle in and at first everything was wonderful. She preferred her own company when not working so was pleased to have been given her own little room in the garret, up in the roof space; the other servants were housed on the floor below.

The head gardener, who could often be found in the kitchen talking to Cook, was a jovial old man whom Bridget liked from the moment she met him. But the assistant gardener, the man who had brought her up from the gate, was a bruiser of a man who, when he spoke, had a foul tongue. But his main talent was mocking the staff every chance he got. Bridget put him in his place right away when, alone in the kitchen one day, she came across him stealing biscuits that Cook had just made for afternoon tea. Showing she wasn't afraid of him, she made it clear she knew where the pans were, and how to use them if needed.

The working hours were long and arduous, but she accepted this knowing it was part of the job. However, the lady of the house had absolutely no concept of fairness, often insisting that Bridget help the other two domestics with their jobs if she had completed her own tasks too quickly. It took her a while to realise that the boot was never on the other foot, that perhaps the other staff worked slowly on purpose.

One Monday morning, after being off for the weekend, Cook sent a message to Madam saying she was feeling ill with a bad cold and would not be at work for a few days. To her shock, Bridget had then been told she would be required to do the cook's work until she returned. However, it wasn't until the assistant gardener had joked that Cook was probably suffering from a hangover, that Bridget realised she was being taken for a fool.

That evening guests were expected and, shortly after telling Bridget she would be acting-cook, Madam gave her a recipe sheet to look at. Never in her life had Bridget been interested in cooking; even a simple meal was almost beyond her abilities. Trying to impress her cooking frailties on Madam, it fell on deaf ears, Madam seemingly being indifferent to any staffing distress.

Silently taking the recipe sheet from her employer, Bridget made the decision that she wasn't going to worry too much if there were complaints; the guests would just have to understand. However, to add insult to injury that day, she was told the house must also be spick and span for the guests, and she would need to complete her own tasks before going down to the kitchen to prepare the meal.

Bridget was furious at everyone – with Cook for taking advantage, with Madam for assuming it was all right to put on her, and with the assistant gardener for pointing all this out in the first place!

The day didn't go well. She had been told to clean the silver before setting the table, but Bridget knew she wouldn't have time to do this and had merely wiped the finger marks off the knives and spoons before covering any tarnish on the forks by placing the serviettes slightly over them; however, she had forgotten the Mistress had the eye of an eagle. To add to this blunder, the potatoes got slightly burnt so they had to be mashed up with the end of the rolling pin. Adding some milk and butter to take away the burnt taste didn't help as, apparently, they still tasted bad.

All told, the day was a disaster and, after the guests had left, Bridget had a ferocious argument with Madam, eventually walking out into the evening air leaving her job and the accommodation that had been her home for over eight weeks.

With no alternative but to return to her sister, she slowly retraced her footsteps along the streets now paved in misery.

Of course, she wasn't welcomed back with open arms; and it was understandable why. Now jobless, and almost penniless having only the two shillings she had earned for her eight weeks' work, to add to this misery, she was in the way.

Something had to be done and, bless her, in the end it was Marie who unintentionally solved the problem. Having remained good friends since their first meeting, Bridget was eager to tell Marie what had occurred since they last met, but she waited until the weekend, and then took a tram to the rooming house where Marie now lived.

Most of the buildings in the street were tenements containing immigrants not unlike herself. But it was seedy, even during the day, and a hugely risky place to walk at night. Each time she visited her friend, Bridget worried about her, though on reflection at least Marie had somewhere of her own to live, whereas she didn't. That day, nearing Marie's building, Bridget heard a hullabaloo coming from somewhere inside; the language was appalling. Quietly venturing up the stairs to the landing and discovering Marie in tears, her neighbour yelling obscenities like a fishwife, her heart leapt.

Quickly moving to Marie's side, Bridget blurted out, 'Now that she's not alone, maybe we can both clean the filth from yer mouth, lady!'

The woman stopped shouting and turning, walked back into her own room. But before she closed her door, she had one last snipe at Marie, 'Ah, yer won't always have yer friend wi' yer, and then we'll see who's smilin' best.'

Relieved that the argument was over, the two girls went back into Marie's room but as soon as they closed the door, they both exhaled before exploding into quiet nervous laughter.

'Oh Bridget, thank you for that. I don't know what I'd have done had ye not arrived when ye did. Me back was really up against the wall, so to speak, as she frightens me. But I'm sick and tired of her comin' into me room an' takin' me food whenever she feels like it. I'd get a lock put on me door if I could afford to.'

Marie's face was still red with tears, but she tried to look cheerful. However, they both knew the consequences of the little spat. Marie's life would be hell from hereon in, and the bully certainly wouldn't stop raiding her food. The room was silent as they both tried to gather their thoughts. It was Marie who ended the silence.

Turning to her friend, she put her arm around her shoulder and said, 'Ye know Bridget, we don't have to stay here in Liverpool. Before I came to this Godforsaken place, I was given the address of a family friend who lives near Manchester. Sure, I've written to her a couple o'times since I arrived an' she knows about ye, of course. She would love to see us; she always tells me so. Why don't I write again and ask if she could take us in fer a few weeks? I've heard there's plenty o' work in the mills around Manchester an' we could get a place to live together. I'd be in me element!'

Maggie was right. It was perhaps the opportunity she had been waiting for. And just two weeks later, the friends were on their way to Pendleton, a town near Manchester that Bridget had never heard of before. They were both excited and apprehensive. Would they find anything different to what they already knew?

But goodness me, what they actually found on arrival was better than either of them could ever, in a million years, have expected. Walking just a short distance from the tram station, they discovered the quaintest little town. There was a market in progress along Towngate, the main street running through the centre of the square, and people were selling homemade goods, particularly jams and cakes, the stalls all ablaze with colour. Towards the end of the street, the area gradually opened out onto a meadow where some animals were grazing in enclosures, held in readiness to be sold.

Walking through the market square, they met a small group of young children playing with spinning wooden tops, the multi-coloured chalk patterns drawn on the tops becoming a kaleidoscope of shapes when the tops had been whipped once or twice. Bridget and Marie had never seen such things before, and stood watching whilst the children played, occasionally having to jump out of the way when the spinning top skimmed their shoes.

The fruit and vegetable sellers had set up stall on the pavement near the end of the street and displayed their wares on small framework tables standing alongside the railings leading onto the meadow. But the most surprising feature of all was the sight of cows roaming around the square, sniffing the displays as though inspecting the merchandise; obviously they were escapees from the meadow corral.

Standing in the midst of all this, Bridget wondered if her heart would burst she felt so contented. The town was everything the city was not. Taking a deep breath of fresh air, and gently exhaling the sweet smell of happiness, she remembered once more the peacefulness of her lovely village back home in Ireland.

BRIDGET'S LIFE WAS DEVELOPING IN STAGES, EACH ONE different and happier. As Marie had said, her dear friend Dorothy and her parents were more than happy to meet her. These kind people, who had never seen her before, accepted Bridget like a sister and daughter, giving her free board and lodgings until she found work. She was to never forget them.

The girls found jobs in one of the cotton mills in the area, and though it was noisy and dirty, being together probably gave them some of their happiest memories. However, they only stayed together for 18 months. Marie had met a young man at work, and became very fond of him, and Bridget, anticipating they would soon want to marry, thought she should move on. You see, she was in the way again and, anyway, something was pushing her to move.

Having kept in touch with her sister Maggie, who was now married to John, Bridget was at first tempted to return to Liverpool to seek work there again, but it was Maggie who suggested she get in touch with Kathleen, a cousin who lived across the Pennines in Yorkshire. She had heard that Yorkshire was overflowing with woollen mills and jobs. Initially Bridget saw there would be a drawback, as she knew the work in the cotton mills of Lancashire was going to be different to the application in the woollen mills of Yorkshire, and she wasn't very confident that she would be able to make the change. So, it was with slight trepidation, that she sent her cousin a note asking if she could help her to find accommodation, but she didn't get a reply. It was

Maggie who again suggested she should just pack up her few possessions and go.

When the time came to leave her good friend, she was both happy and sad. Happy that she had made a friend for ever, but sad that another episode of her life was ending.

Little did she know that this was the beginning of both the good times and the bad times for her.

SHE LEARNED HER PLACE

'HOUSE TO LET - No Irish Need Apply' read the sign in crude print. This was the second window Bridget had seen with the same information prominently displayed since crossing over the border from Lancashire into Yorkshire. Of course, she had been warned before arriving in England that the Irish were treated with hostility here, though personally she hadn't met with any antagonism apart from what she had seen that first day on arrival in Liverpool. Consequently, this notice came as a surprise.

As the tram moved slowly along the middle of the road, she looked through the window again searching for more warning signs that perhaps she would be unwelcome in the town but didn't see any more. Reaching her stop, alighting the tram near the coal depot, she felt a small shiver down my spine. What do the Irish look like, she wondered? Putting her worries to one side, she walked back along the pavement towards the police station, a building she had noticed from the tram window.

At least this was her destination and she now only needed to find her cousin Kathleen's house. Instructions from her sister Maggie had been to go to the police station along the road from the coal depot, and from there she would get directions to The Hill.

The pavement was busy with people pushing old prams and hand-made carts, totally oblivious to anyone or anything in front of them, and she had to dodge this way and that to avoid getting her clothes dirty.

Stopping at the open gates of the coal depot she looked in and was fascinated to see people shovelling coal dust into their home-made implements. The coal dust was piled high against a wall and appeared to be detritus, the dust that remained after the bags had been filled with coal. She occasionally had to move aside to allow a horse and cart to pass into the depot yard, the horse happily skipping along with an empty cart completely unaware that, in a short time, its strength would be required to pull another burden out through the gates again.

The horses and empty carts were lined up near the far side of the yard against a huge mound of coal lumps. From this mound, men were shovelling the coal into sacks and heaving the sacks onto the carts. On top of the carts, men, their faces streaked with perspiration and dirt, were neatly stacking the bags upright.

Realising she was wasting time Bridget resumed her trek towards the police station. Now that she was on the last leg of her journey she wondered if she was doing the right thing. Maggie's suggestion, that she could try Yorkshire, had appeared a good one at the time, but now she was here she wasn't so sure. Although having written to their cousin, she hadn't received a reply, and now had a nagging feeling that maybe she wasn't going to be welcome. Was this to be the story of her life?

Notwithstanding, Bridget continued her journey, finding that, as the town was small, the directions she got from the police station proved to be correct, and in a short while she came upon The Hill. The houses were built haphazardly with no thought of planning, and every conceivable space was occupied by a dwelling, every door of which opened onto a dirt road, the roads darting to left and right to spawn further dwellings. It was a warm afternoon and people were sitting on chairs outside their houses which, being so close together, were all within bellowing distance.

Bridget was immediately aware of the familiar accents of 'home'.

'Who're ye lookin' fer, lass?' asked an obese lady sweating profusely and mopping her face with a piece of cloth.

'Oh, I'm lookin' fer Kathleen Kenny. She's me cousin from Mayo.'

'Sure, ye'll find her in the house around the corner; the one up the steps.'

With that, everyone appeared to lose interest in the visitor and resumed their chattering. As directed, Bridget walked around the corner coming into a small dirt yard. There was a wall to the left, which seemed to be the back of a house that had been built on a slope, and to the right of this, in the far corner, were the steps. Below the steps and to the side was another door which was wide open. Picking her way over the sharp stones and dry mud, she was about to mount the steps when a voice rang out.

'Who's that?' An old crone, dressed in a black shawl despite the summer heat, appeared at the opening. 'Do I know ye?'

'No, I'm afraid ye don't, I've come t' see Kathleen. I was told she lived here.' Bridget said pointing up the stairs.

'Now what d'ye want wi' her? She didn't say she were expectin' anyone, though I do remember her sayin' she had a distant relative livin' somewhere in Lancashire who had written, botherin' her. Anyway, ye won't find her in as she's down at the convent cleanin' and doesn't get back till around five.'

'But I've come all the way from Manchester ter see her.' Bridget was irritated that Kathleen had discussed her letter with a neighbour but hadn't bothered to reply to her.

'Well then, ye'd better wait wi' me till she gets back home.'

The old crone stepped aside bidding the stranger enter. Stepping over the threshold, Bridget entered into a small dark room, the only light coming from the fire. The floor was bare stone except for two clip rugs, one on the floor in front of the fire and the other beside a bed in the far corner. Covering the bed was a patchwork quilt made from an assortment of brightly coloured fabrics cut into small patches and hand-stitched together haphazardly.

Completely ignoring Bridget now, the old lady began busying herself. Taking hold of the poker which had been leaning against the wall, she loosened the coals on the fire until they caught alight, sending strange shadows around the dark room. Appearing happy that the fire was burning well enough, she lifted a heavy kettle from the grate with two hands and shook it gently. Hearing the shushing noise of water coming from the kettle, she seemed satisfied it was full enough for her purpose, smiling as she lay it on the lighted coals. The kettle would soon boil. Bridget watched in fascination as the years of soot on the bottom of the kettle began to spark and crackle, spitting tiny particles of burning soot onto the hearth.

The old crone continued busying herself; her visitor was totally ignored. The pot of tea was a serious matter and nothing and nobody could distract her from the chore. Reaching up to the shelf over the fire-place she lifted down a square tin, myopically peering inside until she located the small spoon, which she used to carefully scoop two measures of loose tea into a teapot that had been warming on the shelf above the oven. She smiled to herself again; maybe she was now contented that she was prepared for the occasion. Placing the tin of tealeaves back on the shelf, the old lady turned her attention to the kettle once more, glaring at it, perhaps daring it to boil more quickly.

During this ceremony Bridget had been sitting on the side of the bed, grateful for the rest, but the silence began to make her feel ill at ease and it was a relief when she heard footsteps in the yard. Maybe recognising the footsteps, the old lady rushed over to the door, her long skirt skimming the cat awakened by the noise outside, and which had been in the process of stretching after a long sleep.

'Ye've got a visitor,' she told the approaching footsteps, moving aside to let Kathleen know the visitor was inside her house.

Kathleen stood in the doorway with a puzzled expression. Peering into the room, she glanced at Bridget, continuing to move her eyes around the small room, seemingly expecting to see someone else, someone she knew perhaps? On finding there was no-one else there but Bridget, her eyes once more rested on her. It was the old lady who spoke first.

'This is yer relative from Manchester.'

'I'VE NO PLACE HERE FOR YE TO SLEEP – CAN'T YE SEE HOW small me little room is?' We had climbed the steps and were now in the room above the old crone. Kathleen seemed upset. 'I didn't expect ye to just turn up.'

'Well I'm sorry Kathleen but if ye had replied to me letters, then maybe I wouldn't have just turned up.'

'I didn't reply because I have nothing to offer ye. If ye stay here long enough, ye'll soon find out how difficult it is living in England. Ye'll find that there's plenty of work to do but the pay is terrible and don't ye expect to keep ye'r hands clean. But we daren't complain. After all I'm sure ye've heard by now how badly we Irish 're treated. We're Catholics livin' in a Protestant country an' don't forget, plenty of people around here think we Irish 're beneath them because some of us like a drink.'

As she spoke, Kathleen had been busying herself removing some of the bedding on the small bed in the corner and putting it on the settee.

As she watched, Bridget knew it would be difficult for the two of them to live in the same room for very long, and not just because of the small space.

Fortunately, she only had to stay with Kathleen for a few weeks although, during that short time, they had almost come to blows more than once. Two women with strong views were never going to agree on much. When a one-roomed cottage nearby became empty after one of Kathleen's neighbours had passed away, Bridget rushed to see the landlord. On meeting her, he wasn't too happy letting the accommodation to another Irish woman, but he knew by now that no English person would want to live amongst these 'backward lazy people' and, as long as he got his money every week, why should he worry?

KATHLEEN WAS RIGHT; THERE WERE PLENTY OF JOBS, AND Bridget was happy when she found work in the rag mill. Even on the first day she felt at home where she was amongst her own Irish community.

'Now sit yerself down, Bridget,' said the woman who seemed to be in charge, and who introduced herself as Lizzie Murphy. 'Just turn one o' them baskets upside down an' I'll show ye what t' do.'

Doing what she had been told, she then watched as Lizzie continued her instruction.

'Sithy, all these baskets 're full o' materials which 'ave already been sorted by other workers. There are baskets for cottons and woollens, and baskets for mixed fabrics. It'll all be used again fer either clothes or textiles, but the material must be completely clean - no buttons or double thicknesses. Look here - this basket is full o' cotton rags but, take this shirt fer example, it has buttons down the front on one side and buttonholes down the front of the other side. Then ye have the cuffs in double material. It's the same with the collar. Well, ye have to cut all this extra stuff off the shirt leavin' only the pure clean single thickness of material. Ye start to do that an' I'll examine it when ye've finished. But make sure it's clean don't forget.'

After a few minutes working on the shirt, Bridget was left with only a small piece of cloth, but this seemed to please Lizzie, and she handed her a pair of trousers next with the same instructions, but with a final comment: 'Don't ye leave any shite on it anywhere.'

By the end of the day, Bridget's hand was swollen from gipping the large shears, and her back ached from bending over, but at least she had a job and so could pay her way. Every now and then she would see something her own size; a skirt or a blouse, or even a shift to wear in bed, and she would furtively put it into her bag when no-one was looking. But mostly what she took home was fleas, though she felt it was a small price to pay.

'Will ye come fer a drink wi' me, Bridget?' said Lizzie one night as they walked back to The Hill where they both lived. 'The smell o' filth off old men's britches is stickin' in me throat and the fleas 're drivin' me mad.'

Bridget smiled to herself. Yes, she understood the smell of the britches, but she suspected there were more fleas in Lizzie's house than down at the rag mill. She was tempted to suggest they get a jug of beer from the bar and drink it at home, but, as she was sick of seeing the same four walls, she agreed.

Once back home, she quickly washed her hands and face with cold water then, donning her shawl over the black work pinafore she was wearing, she went to meet Lizzie at the bottom of The Hill, and they set off together on the short walk to the inn.

The room in the bar was dark, lit only by fly-spotted, smoky oil lamps which hung low from the beams. Cobwebs dangled from every protrusion and the walls were brown from the customary nicotine staining. There was a long rustic elm bar table resting against one of the walls, its surface worn into grooves by the constant spillage of beer, and on this table sat a number of stoneware casks from which hung metal measuring vessels of varying sizes. Arranged beside the casks were several pewter mugs.

The ancient woman leaning against the table nodded to them as they walked in. Picking up a mug, and without asking, she proceeded to carefully fill a measure of beer from one of the casks, her shaking hand making sure she spilled any beer back into the cask. Once she had filled the measure, she then poured the beer from the measure into a pewter mug. If she spilled any beer at this stage, which she often did, she need not make up the loss. Her way of thinking was probably that, as she had carefully measured out the beer having filled the measuring vessel to the top, then whatever happened after that was not her business. This way she knew she would never be out of pocket. Apparently, this anomaly went unnoticed as nobody ever argued with the lady, not even the most inebriated Irishman.

From time to time, a muted ping could be heard from someone who, having coughed up phlegm, had then directed this at the spittoon. But, just as often, only the sound of the cough-up would be heard, the emission landing silently in the sawdust on the floor. The sawdust was kicked into small heaps around the spittoon, and it was always wise to avoid standing on these mounds.

Lizzie and Bridget picked up their drinks and looked around for somewhere to sit. Over in the far corner were a couple of men, the tall one with fair hair was talking loudly, causing his stout companion with dark curly hair to laugh vigorously. The men were making so much noise that people, having trouble hearing themselves talk, began moving away leaving empty tables nearby. Settling themselves at a table furthest from the men, Bridget sat with her back to the noise. But Lizzie was in her element facing the men; usually on the lookout for a free drink this gave her the opportunity to smile at them, letting them know she was interested in their conversation.

Suddenly, a shadow appeared at Bridget's elbow and, looking up, she saw it was the loud fair-haired man. 'Oh no, what is this imbecile going to do now,' she thought. As she was wondering how to tell him to go away without too much offence, he interrupted her thought and, leaning on her, his hand resting on her shoulder to keep himself upright, he smiled at Lizzie and asked, 'Well then, what would this pretty lady like ter drink?'

Swearing under her breath Bridget shrugged the hand away. They had come for a quiet drink and talk, and not to be burdened with drunks.

But with enthusiasm, Lizzie placed her order for a drink, smiling back at the fair-haired man to let him know she was interested.

Then, without warning, a second voice was saying, 'My, ye're a pretty lass, what're ye called then?' Bridget had been about to get up to leave the table but turning, saw the curly-haired man standing beside her.

'Sit down, lass, I'm sure ye have time fer another drink.' But before she could answer he had moved forward onto the bench confining her between himself and the wall and was continuing the one-sided conversation: 'Me name's Nicholas, by the way, an' me friend there is John.'

Sighing, Bridget thought, 'show me yer company an' I'll tell ye what ye are. 'What else could she expect? Wasn't she with Lizzie, who was always on the lookout for a man? And, of course, she would be cast in the same mould.

'We're just over from the old country, lookin' fer work,' he continued, 'an' I've left me brother lookin' after the farm. We're doin' very well over there, so work isn't a priority fer me just now, and when me father passes over an' we sell the farm, there'll be more money than we can spend in a lifetime. Ah, sure, me brother isn't interested in farmin' and intends going to America. He says life is much better there.'

Realising he hadn't had a response, he glanced at Bridget. 'But never mind me, lass, what's yer name, what do ye do fer a livin'?'

Smiling, she looked at him. 'Oh God, ye do make me laugh with all yer stories o' wealth. If life is so great in Ireland, what're ye doin' sittin' here in this grubby place, drinkin' this sour beer, and tryin' to pick up poor workin' women then? An' as fer what I do fer a livin', what do most Irish women in this town do? What work is there fer us other than the rag mill? Ye see, I don't have the luxury of a farm ter fall back on. Mind ye, there is one thing ter say about being poor an' workin' in the rags – we're never short o' clothes.'

Ignoring the hostility from her, Nicholas droned on hoping to hold her attention, though if he had been sober, he would have realised the conversation was boring her.

Although it took some time, it did eventually dawn on Nicholas that he wouldn't get very far with Bridget this night. Making eye contact with John, the conversation between him and Lizzie quickly ended. Without another word, the two men left their seats and headed back towards the bar, maybe hoping to spread their nets over two more unsuspecting women.

However, even though she had determined to ignore the men in future, the next time she and Lizzie went for a drink, she found it impossible to ignore them. They had taken a pitch near the bar table, and the old crone serving the beer was certainly enjoying their company if her ear-splitting laughter was anything to go by. The merriment became almost magnetic and people near the three 'comics' began joining in the fun. Unfortunately, Lizzie didn't have the same attitude towards men that Bridget had and decided she would like to make herself known to the two Irishmen once more, knowing full well what her work friend would say.

'Now, Bridget, I know ye aren't too convinced about John and Nicholas, but I've been thinkin''. Ye know there aren't too many single men in the town, an' our two seem to be uncommitted an' are good-lookin' men into the bargain. I quite fancy John an' he keeps lookin' at me, so I think he might be interested as well. What do ye think then?'

By the end of the oration, Bridget's face was red with anger.

'Lizzie, I'm not yer keeper an' ye can do whatever ye want. Sure, I wouldn't dream o' standin' in the way o' yer love life which seemin' is so important that ye would demean ye're self with the man. Well, ye go on then. I'm on me way home.'

Holding back tears, Bridget got up and pushed her way towards the door through a small group of people. At the door, she turned around to see if Lizzie was watching, but she was nowhere to be seen.

At work the following day, Lizzie didn't mention anything about the previous night, much to Bridget's relief. Again, she was reminded of the saying she had remembered the previous evening, and no, the company she kept wasn't always the best, but most people couldn't afford to be choosy. Everyone had their faults, she supposed.

Yet, strangely, over time, Bridget began to be intrigued by the two Irishmen; they had apparently appeared from nowhere, and because of their innate ability to be friendly with everyone, they had immediately become accepted as part of the Irish clique living in the area. Nicholas always had money to throw around, and it occurred to her that perhaps he was being truthful when he said the family had a large farm, presumably from which the profits were distributed.

His hair was neatly cut, and his clothes were decent. What if she was making a mistake? What if he was a catch, after all? As Lizzie had said many times in the past, there weren't too many unattached men around. Yes, it was true, he was a fine-looking man.

As the weeks passed to months, she realised she was mellowing more and more towards Nicholas, sometimes even getting butterflies in her stomach on seeing him in the bar. But one thing bothered her – whenever she called into the bar, whether during the day or in the evening, whether to stay a while or to collect a jug of ale to take home, he was almost always there already, and she always left him there afterwards. So, when and where did he work? And where did he live? Was there a grand old house hiding somewhere in the town that she didn't know about?

One day, neighbours nearby Lizzie did a moonlight flit, furtively vacating the house during the night to avoid paying money they owed. Hearing about it afterwards, no-one was particularly surprised, as there had been talk that no money had gone into the house for some time. The rent was collected weekly and was a small amount considering it was only a one-room cottage. But, of course, it didn't matter how little the rent was if you were too poor to pay it.

The neighbours around wondered how long it would be before a new person moved in, knowing that whoever it was they would probably be Irish. But, when Lizzie told Bridget the cottage had quickly been let, she was stunned to hear that the new occupant was Nicholas himself. Now why on earth would he, with all his so-called wealth, want to live on The Hill with its dirt roads and cockroaches? There would now be no way she could avoid seeing him, although she quietly felt some pleasure at the thought that Lizzie would be green with envy that it wasn't John who had moved there.

Nicholas and Bridget passed each other on the road from time to time, acknowledging each other briefly, but they didn't really meet again until they saw each other at the bar several weeks later. That day, Bridget and Lizzie had had a hard day at work and Lizzie wasn't feeling too well. On their way back from work, Bridget had an idea. 'Now then Lizzie, why don't I get a clean jug from home and go down t' the bar an' buy ale t' bring back. We could then drink it in the warmth of the fire, and maybe it would make ye feel better.'

Having made sure Lizzie was settled, she collected a jug and walked the short distance to the inn.

It was another busy night in the bar and, of course, Bridget expected to see Nicholas somewhere around. And she did. He was leaning on the bar, laughing and holding court with friends. To reach the serving table she had to push her way through the throng of people standing in groups, and as she handed over her jug to the old dear serving the beer, she was shaking.

Bridget had donned her black shawl which covered her from head to knees, though she was still wearing her old work clothes underneath and hoped that no-one, and in particular Nicholas, would notice the dirty old dress hanging below the shawl. However, there was no need to worry because Nicholas was too drunk to notice much of anything that evening. He seemed to be talking in riddles most of the time, much to the amusement of the people around him.

Once back home, Bridget regaled Lizzie with a blow-by-blow account of the brusque Irishman, and Lizzie admitted afterwards that she felt much improved after an evening of laughter. The beer helped, of course!

But it was only a matter of time before the two Irish exiles began bumping into each other in the street. Getting off the tram one Friday evening after work she accidentally collided into Nicholas and, as he was walking towards The Hill, she had no choice but to walk along the road with him.

'How are ye then, Bridget? Sure, I don't see ye often enough these days – ye must be hidin' yerself from me view. I've got an idea - now why don't ye bring ye're friend along an' I'll see ye this evening for a drink.'

It wasn't normal to go out at night very much during a normal week, it being too much trouble to wash the smell of the rag mill away and change out of my dirty clothes. But having told Lizzie of their meeting, this day Lizzie was adamant the friends must accept the 'invite' even if it was only for one drink.

'Oh, Lizzie, how many times do I have to tell ye, I really don't want to spend the night drinkin'. I do have other things to do.' Bridget tried several times to say 'no', wishing she hadn't mentioned the accidental meeting of earlier with her friend. But Lizzie was having none of it, insisting they would only stay a short time. When she eventually ran out of excuses, Bridget had to concede it would be good to draw a close to the week with a glass of stout before the weekend onslaught of the usual drudgery of washing and cleaning.

Hastily eating a meal of bread and cheese as this night there wasn't going to be time to eat a proper meal – she realised that a flutter in her chest was already making her feel full.

Putting on her only respectable dress, she looked at her reflection in the mirror which sat in the corner of the room and immediately felt irritated; she could only see herself in detached fragments as the mirror was losing its silver backing. Standing on tiptoe, she twisted around, trying to dodge the dark spaces. It was a false smile that was returned to her from the mirror ... 'oh dear, how I wish I had good teeth as me smile spoils me face.' She said to herself. 'Maybe the hat will help as I'm always wearin' the old shawl when I see Nicholas an', indeed, sure hadn't I been wearin' it when I had first met him. But he might be impressed this evening if he saw me wearin' a hat, as I'm sure me rag of a shawl makes me look older than my twenty-three years.'

The reflection of the room in the mirror was depressing – not just the image of herself, but indeed the appearance of everything she could see in the reflection behind her. The single bed was covered in old clothes which she had brought back from the mill, though by now they were clean. She had begun making a bedcover by hand many months ago using pieces of various coloured cloth brought back from work, though there wasn't much for such 'ladylike' pursuits after working all day. And so, the bedcover was still only partially completed. The floor was bare, except for two rag rugs which she had found time to make, purely because her feet were usually cold when she got into bed. The rugs were the first things she had made on being given keys to the little cottage. The rest of the floor was bare flagstones which she had to admit didn't get cleaned very often. On the few occasions that she had gone down onto her hands and knees to wash the floor with soap and water, it had taken days to dry because of lack of heat and general dampness in the house. It had also taken weeks to remove the grit and dirt from her fingernails, which she had then been loath to bite for quite a while afterwards.

On turning slightly, Bridget could see the reflection of the old divided orange box beside the bed, which was functional in that it contained a spare under-shift and a few pairs of stockings in the upper part, and a pair of winter boots in the bottom part. Glancing to the top of the orange box she caught sight of the glass dome containing the Virgin Mary, and automatically crossed herself saying, 'Thanks be to God'. At least she had somewhere reasonably warm and clean to live in.

Taking down her coat, which was draped over a piece of string secured across the alcove at the right-hand side of the fireplace, she held it up to the light to make sure it was clean before putting it on. The coat was one she had managed to save up for and buy, and it would have to last a long time. Her hat hung from one of the nails holding the string and was usually only worn on high days and holidays, but tonight Bridget certainly wasn't going to wear a headscarf with her best coat. Putting on the hat she secured it carefully with a hatpin.

The fire had caught a draught as she walked past it earlier, and now its fingers were gaily climbing up the chimney, making sparks in the soot that had fused to the brickwork over many years. Going to the fire, she stooped to collect a shovelful of coal dust from the bucket at the side of the fireplace, making sure her coat didn't sweep across any coal dust accidentally spilled on the hearth. Throwing the dust on the fire, she waited until she was satisfied it was beginning to dampen down.

Folding back the rug away from the hearth, Bridget was reminded of the terror felt by a neighbour the previous winter. The young mother kept her new-born baby in a drawer that she was using as a cot, and she had placed the drawer onto the rug in front of her fire to keep the baby warm while she quickly went outside in the yard to the toilet. The little mite had been swaddled in a cotton sheet and surrounded with rolled-up cloths to keep him from rolling over. Although the mother was only gone for a few minutes, by the time she returned it was too late: the baby was engulfed in flames – the sheet and cotton cloths surrounding the baby were on fire. The poor child didn't stand a chance. The eerie thing was the child had not cried out, not once; there had not been a murmur from him. Oh God, the pain she had felt for the mother as well as the child. The police had agreed that it had just been an accident and that a piece of coal had probably fallen from the fire onto the baby's blanket. Now, in her head, Bridget could still hear the mother's screams.

Shaking her head to rid it of the distress she still felt about the accident, she walked out through the door, locking it behind her.

The pub was quiet when she arrived, so she didn't have to look very far to notice Nicholas. He was standing at the far side of the bar, leaning against the wall talking to Paddy Halloran and Jimmy O'Grady. Glancing around the room, Bridget couldn't see Lizzie. How unusual, she thought, as Lizzie normally arrived early to get an extra drink down her before her real drinking began. Standing there, smiling inwardly, she wondered if Nicholas had noticed her yet, especially as she was probably looking the best she had ever looked.

There were some empty tables dotted about and noticing one in the corner, away from the general noise of the bar, she began walking towards it but had only taken a few steps when she realised she was being manoeuvred away from her path and towards a different area of the bar.

Only one person would dare do this to her.

'What're ye doin', Nicholas? I'm expectin' Lizzie and need to save the table.'

By now, Nicholas was leaning heavily on her, and at close range, looked inebriated. Not wanting an argument so early in the evening, Bridget allowed herself to be shuffled along. Taking her around the far corner of the bar to the side room she was amazed to see Lizzie sitting with John; and they already had drinks in front of them.

Trying to ignore Nicholas's beer breath and hoping he wouldn't want any more drink that night, Bridget accepted his offer of a small glass of beer. Having put her into a chair near her friend, he staggered back to the bar, plaiting his legs as he walked along the room, now and then grabbing the shoulder of someone standing in his way to get his momentum once more, no doubt using the occasion as an excuse to divulge some dirty or sarcastic comment. When he returned, he was carrying a tray containing large glasses of beer and small glasses of whiskey, all of which were now sitting in a river of brown foam.

The conversation didn't flow very well between them. The men, already inebriated, were slurring their words and guffawing when they couldn't be understood, which frequently left Lizzie and Bridget talking quietly between themselves.

'Why on earth did we come tonight?' Bridget whispered, trying to hide her anger. But Lizzie was looking at John with unconcealed affection.

'Well, to be honest, Bridget, John thought it time ye and Nick got together.' She crossed two fingers and put them under her friend's nose, laughing as she did so.

'Oh Lizzie, the difference between us is that ye obviously wanted to come tonight whereas I didn't, and ye could at least have warned me of yee'r intentions.'

She felt deceived by her best friend. How did Lizzie not understand that if she and Nicholas were to ever get together, it would have to be on their own terms?

The intermittent talk continued, and drinks were replenished, although Bridget didn't much feel in the mood for drinking this night. When eventually the conversation began to fade totally, with both Lizzie and her friend now feeling they'd had enough to drink, Bridget broke into the conversation between the men telling them, 'Well, thank ye for the drinks, but me an' Lizzie will be headin' for home now.'

With that, they both stood up and turned towards the door.

'Wait a minute, wait a minute,' Nicholas called loudly to them, 'I'll walk ye home.'

Bridget would probably have been thrilled had Nicholas said this to her at almost any other time, but now she was feeling so manipulated that she wasn't going to give him the satisfaction of a response and continued walking towards the door, encouraging Lizzie to follow. But the men were behind them, and once out on the street, John took hold of Lizzie's arm, steering her away from Bridget's side and along the road ahead. Bridget felt the heat from Nicholas's breath as he moved closer, trying to kiss her, his arm resting on her shoulders. Doing her best to ignore the attention she was getting, following Lizzie, she headed off towards The Hill, a five-minute walk from the bar.

On reaching her home, she shrugged Nicholas off. 'Goodnight, Lizzie. Goodnight, John. Could ye both make sure Nicholas gets home? I think he's had too much ter drink tonight and might end up in the gutter without some help.' But Lizzie and John merely stood watching the scene unfold.

As Bridget unlocked the door, Nicholas strode past her, moving into the room and, with a smile, turned and called out 'G'night' to

Lizzie and John who, with a knowing look, had by now resumed their walk up the road.

With dread, Bridget realised Nicholas's intentions, but at that very moment was feeling too much guilt to tell him she was uncomfortable being alone with him in her house. Oh yes, he had bought drinks for her most of the evening, and they would certainly have cost him a good part of his wages if he was working, and this she didn't know, but all the same, she was beginning to feel alarmed.

Without another word, Nicholas retrieved the key from her clenched hand, and she watched in silence as he re-locked the door. Walking over to the fireplace he then placed the key on shelf above the glowing fire. Suddenly, the room felt very cold.

'C'mon, lass, ye know yer feelin's fer me,' he slurred.

Bridget had remained standing near the door, wondering what to do, but seeing she hadn't moved, Nicholas walked over to her, putting his arm around her shoulder, guiding her further into the room. Suddenly shivering with distaste, she began to see that she had done the wrong thing in letting him walk her to the door. How could she have been so naïve?

The smell of beer, cigarettes and sweat was overwhelming in the close confines of her small room. Turning away from him she gulped down fresh air. He instantly began pawing her, trying to kiss her. My God, how sick she felt! But she was afraid of his strength. He was such a big man, and everyone knew of his many fights at the inns in town, though he bragged about everything from the size of the family farm in Ireland to the jobs he had turned down because he had been too good for them. Bridget didn't really know what to do. Was the loss of her virginity to be the cost of a few drinks of alcohol?

Breaking away from him, she walked towards the bed alongside the wall at the far side of the room. It was a cold night and the bed looked warm and inviting, but she knew that this night she was going to hate every minute that lay ahead of her.

Turning her back to him, she began to slowly undress, leaving on her vest and pantaloons. No matter what was going to happen this night, she didn't intend getting pregnant. Failing to notice that she wasn't receptive to his 'sweet-talk', he continued to tell her how much he loved and admired her, although by now he was beginning to slur his words. With both relief and fear, Bridget realised he was more inebriated than had first appeared. The relief was that he might fall asleep soon, but the fear was that he might turn nasty if provoked.

Getting between the covers, Bridget made room for him and he slipped in beside her. Nausea hit her quickly; he smelt disgusting and his naked body was repellent to her. She held her breath waiting for the nausea to pass. Putting his arms around her, he began fumbling with her clothes talking sweet-talk as he did so, but Bridget lay there quiet, and still, and rigid, waiting for the nightmare to end.

Thankfully, his efforts were feeble, made even more so by the number of garments he was having to navigate, but his final sigh was released as he reached his goal. She would always remember those mad, sick minutes.

This wasn't what she had expected from her first union with a man. Her stomach heaved as she lay on the bed, bile rising in her throat. Her mind raced ahead with the problems his violence could create. Then, without warning, his breathing changed from fast to rhythmically slow and then loud, as his snores rang out.

Slowly rolling away from him, Bridget sat on the side of the bed and carefully stood up. Her feet on the cold flagstones felt good. Picking up her dress from the floor, she draped it over the back of a chair before going over to the sink near the window. The moon was shining through the window and she stared at it for a few moments remembering how, in the silent film she saw, the moon had been a symbol of love. Oh, not so tonight.

Although not sure what she expected to happen at this moment, she did know that she desperately wanted to wash away the terrible feeling that now pervaded her whole body. Removing the remainder of her clothes, she quietly turned on the water tap and, wetting a cloth with the icy water, she ran it over her body for several minutes hoping the cold would wash away the memories along with the obscenity.

After drying herself, and feeling a bit better, she put on a clean shift. The smell of his filth and sweat was still in the air but she daren't open the window as the noise might waken 'him' (she could hardly bear to think he had a name). For a while she sat on the wooden chair beside the window, listening to his snoring, which now and then fluctuated, making her heart sink when it momentarily went quiet! After what seemed like minutes but was in fact only seconds, he would give out a loud gasp and the snoring would begin once more.

Sitting there pondering, it occurred to Bridget that after the heavy drinking he had done, he would probably sleep through the night. Maybe she could get a few hours' sleep too if she remained quiet. Looking over to the small armchair near the fire, she noticed with horror that her best coat had carelessly been thrown over the arm. It annoyed her that the one thing she cherished had been unthinkingly discarded in her urgency to manage her predicament.

Settling herself on the armchair Bridget drew her nightshift up underneath her legs and, covering herself with the creased coat, she finally settled for the night. It wasn't very comfortable, and she couldn't fall asleep hearing his breathing. Every few minutes there would be silence and her heart would give a jump wondering if he was waking up. Then the sound of snoring would again reverberate around the small room. Looking over at his body lying comfortably in her bed, Bridget accepted she would probably just lie awake, waiting for the day to break and for him to leave.

It was still dark when she got up from the chair. Her head was thumping, and her eyes were sore. She felt sick but wasn't sure whether this was due to lack of sleep or the thought of the monster sleeping like a baby in her warm bed.

Giving herself another quick wash, she caught sight of her reflection in the mirror as she pulled on her work-dress. Was this really her? Had she actually allowed herself to be picked up by this man, who she had only ever spoken with briefly, mostly in the bar, and permitted him to utterly degrade her like this? What had she been thinking? It was then anger kicked in. Bridget wanted him out of her house at any cost, and right now!

Going over to the bed, she shook his shoulder. 'Nicholas, ye have to get up now. Me sister's coming from Lancashire this mornin' an' I'm picking 'er up from the tram depot.'

Nicholas opened his eyes trying to focus. She could see he was trying to gather his wits, taking a few seconds to realise where he was. Then slowly slipping out of bed, he stood; Oh God, his body was even more repulsive in the light of day.

Bridget had already decided on a plan and immediately put this into action.

Turning away, she walked towards the fireplace, calling back over her shoulder that she needed to leave the house within the hour. Overnight, the fire had settled into a volcanic glow and she prodded the mass until it ignited into low flames. Putting the kettle on the flare, she waited for it to boil, thinking, one mug of tea, that's all he'll get, just one mug of tea. The noise of the bubbles bursting inside the kettle was a comfort; it brought some normality to the situation.

Forcing down her fury, she managed to make small talk with him as he dressed, whilst at the same time, busying herself to convince him she was about to leave the house. As he took a few sips of tea, Bridget went to get her coat, noticing again that it was crumpled. She felt so angry, and it was all his fault!

'Ye'll have t' go now as I need t' clean up before I pick up me sister. I don't want her t' know that I've had a man in me home,' I said.

He seemed confused but he complied with her request, going towards the door which was now wide open. Bridget managed to get there before him, stepping outside to encourage him to leave. On passing her, he hesitated and, sensing he was about to kiss her, she quickly stepped back into the room, closing the door and locking it behind her. Then she waited! Was he standing outside, hoping she would change her mind? Listening for any noise, she tiptoed over to the window just in time to see him walk past.

Her heart was beating almost out of her chest. Did anyone see him leaving, she wondered, knowing she would be the talk of The Hill if they had. Oh, the shame of it, yet none of it had been of her making.

Looking over at the bed with disgust, Bridget ran to it as fast as her legs would take her and began stripping off the bed covers, leaving them in a pile on the floor. Only when she had finished, did she realise the hairs on the back of her neck were standing on end. Shivering, she thought, 'What in God's name had just happened? What will the priest say to me the next time I went to confession?'

Shaking such thoughts from her head and forcing herself to concentrate on the here and now, she whispered, 'The bathtub. I need the bathtub; but I'll have to open the door again to get it from outside.' Gritting her teeth, she quietly turned the large key in the lock and slowly opened the door a crack. Seeing that no-one was passing by, she lifted the old tin bath down from the large hook in the wall and brought it back into the room. Now she needed to boil water, and lots of it.

It took most of the day to heat the water and wash the bedding, and as the minutes ticked away, Bridget grew angrier. Washing bedding wasn't her favourite job anyway, particularly as the old mangle needed all her strength to turn the handle to get the rollers moving, and it meant she would have wet clothes hanging around the room for days. But by mid-afternoon she was feeling a little better. As she washed and scrubbed the clothes, it was easy to persuade herself that she was also washing the terrible episode out of her life, hoping she could quickly forget it.

But that wasn't to be.

THE FOLLOWING DAY WHEN SHE MET LIZZIE, SHE NOTICED how cheerful she looked. It was obvious that, unlike her, Lizzie had enjoyed a happy evening with John. This peeved her even more as it was in some part due to Lizzie's involvement that she had ended up as soiled goods. However, despite her feelings, she needed to tell someone of the nightmare of the previous night. To her surprise, Lizzie appeared to understand, commiserating to the extent that she even suggested they should find a new drinking place in future to spend their money. That appeared to close the matter. However, a few weeks later when they discussed having a drink again, Lizzie said she would like to go back to the old place, saying they could always keep away from 'him' if she wanted, but that she wanted to see John again. What could Bridget do but agree?

Opening the pub door in front of Lizzie, Bridget took a step backwards as the acrid smoke and deafening noise of the packed bar steam-rolled over her, deafening her senses. A small group of people followed them in, causing a draught which, for a few seconds, cleared the atmosphere. She could see John and Nicholas sitting at their usual spot, talking to some friends. Noticing the two women standing at the door, John beckoned them over, and much to her horror, Lizzie nearly fell over herself in her eagerness to reach him through the crowd. As Bridget took in the scene, she saw that three of the tables had been pushed together and two seats had been left empty near the men, presumably in expectation of their arrival. Had Lizzie already spoken with John? Well, Bridget certainly had no intention of sitting with the group.

Glancing around, she searched for a spare seat, noticing one at the bottom side of a table occupied by a small group of noisy people she didn't know. Excusing herself she asked the man sitting on the stool next to the empty one if the seat was taken. He had been in conversation with his friends when she interrupted him, but he smiled and indicated that the seat was hers before turning back to his colleagues. Bridget sat down with relief, happily aware she couldn't see Nicholas, although she could hear his voice occasionally.

Interrupting the man once more, telling him she was going to the bar, she asked if he could make sure no-one took her seat. Without waiting for a reply, she got up and threaded her way through the crowd, picking up her skirts as she walked to avoid mopping up the wet beer deposited on the stone flags by careless customers.

Picking up her drink, she put the glass to her mouth and took a long slow sip, turning around as she did so, thus giving her chance to scan the room. Nicholas and John were getting louder, which was a good thing so far as she was concerned, as it meant they had other things to talk about. With her now half-empty glass of stout in one hand, and her skirts in the other, Bridget wound her way back to her seat.

Once more seated, she became aware that the conversation between her neighbour and his friend had stalled so, leaning across, Bridget took the opportunity to thank him and his friend for looking after her seat, at the same time exchanging a few pleasantries. As she was doing so, out of the corner of her eye she saw a movement and, looking up found John standing alongside her, his face like thunder. Suddenly, without warning, John threw his fist into the face of the man seated beside her, the unexpected force lifting the man off his stool and knocking him back onto the stone flags. All the time, John was shouting at the guy telling him to 'Fekkin leave me friend's lady-friend alone'. The innocent man's legs were somehow trapped between the stool and the table, and he tried desperately to unravel his legs and upright himself before the anticipated next blow, aimed at his head, hit its mark. Bridget pushed John sideways, shouting at him to leave the man alone, that he'd done nothing wrong. How in God's name could Nicholas ever think she was his lady-friend?

As she watched, unable to stop the turmoil, it began to dawn on her that she must have been set up by John from Day One, and that he was merely 'protecting' her for his friend Nicholas. Bridget felt sick. What power did this despicable man have over people?

When he felt he had taken enough revenge out of the innocent man, John then turned on Bridget, calling her a 'fekkin bitch' and a 'slag' who took great pleasure out of hurting people.

John was triumphant. Everyone in the bar was looking at him with what he believed was respect. He strode back to Nicholas, who had been standing watching the action and, putting his arm protectively around Nicholas's shoulder, gave him a bear hug. But Nicholas seemed to be having trouble concentrating; from time to time he veered off, only to be brought back to a standing position by John who still had a few last words for Bridget. As she walked towards the door, he shouted, 'Don't forget me words, ye slag. Ye'd better change yer ways, otherwise ye'll not be accepted into this group again.'

The harsh words rang in her ears. Even if she and Nicholas had willingly spent the evening together, it still wouldn't have given either him or John the idea that Nicholas owned her. After all, she had only been speaking with the stranger and it upset her to think he had been so viciously attacked for nothing, the poor man.

But apparently, Lizzie had also been shocked at the turn of events and told John she was truly sickened by his behaviour.

THE INEVITABLE HAPPENS

Although she stayed away from the bar, it was inevitable that Bridget would occasionally see Nicholas wandering around the neighbourhood. Each time they chanced to meet, she felt both shame and anger, particularly as this big man had added insult to injury by allowing his friend to offend her in front of everyone she knew. Nevertheless, Bridget knew she needed to accept what had taken place, partly persuading herself it was her own fault to some degree. After all, knowing that Nicholas drank heavily, maybe it would have been possible to stop him from walking her home that night. However, she certainly felt manipulated as she hadn't willingly allowed any of it to happen. Oh, she had learned a lesson, a hard one too, but now it was time to get on with the rest of her life. But little did she know that the rest of her life was going to change, and not for the better.

It wasn't long before she began to worry that she might be pregnant as she was a few days 'late', although she didn't really see how that could be as nothing had happened ... well not really. But as the days went by, she became more and more concerned. What in God's name was she going to do?

Feeling the need to speak with someone of her foreboding, and with reluctance, she eventually discussed it with Lizzie, asking her to please not tell anyone else as she needed time to think.

'But how could it happen like that?' queried Lizzie, 'Particularly as you said you had avoided actually connecting with "him"?' This was said in a tone indicating that she didn't really believe her friend, which sent a knife through Bridget's chest. If her friend didn't believe her, then how could she ever expect acquaintances to do so? Unfortunately, there was no answer.

Of course, Lizzie couldn't keep the secret for very long - it was tantamount to a coin burning a hole in her pocket - and she went straight to John, passing on the good news to convey to Nicholas.

NO MATTER HOW HARD SHE TRIED, BRIDGET WAS UNABLE TO stop her heart from sinking each time she went back over the events of that night – it was like the horror movie 'Bluebeard' but without the happy ending. She had held the key to the forbidden door but had handed it over to a man she hardly knew and was now soiled goods.

Leaning over the washtub scrubbing her work clothes, her mind muddled with thoughts, she pounded the cloth against the rubbing board, metaphorically beating the man out of her life. Suddenly she heard a loud crack and, looking down, saw she had dislodged the wooden frame from the metal core. Wiping the perspiration from her forehead with the back of her wet hand, she looked at the broken board lying on the floor. Oh, what I wouldn't like to do to that man with this piece of board! she reflected, immediately dismissing the evil notion from her mind with a quick sign of the cross. Fighting back tears, she went to her small cellar to find something suitable to repair the appliance. The cellar was merely a tiny extension to the one-room cottage, accessible by two steps down into a dark, dingy subterranean area. Searching in the dark and locating a hammer she returned to the bottom of the steps, gripping the implement in her hand.

Stepping out of the darkness, Bridget was alarmed to find Nicholas standing near the open doorway of the storeroom, looking down at her.

'What the hell d' ye want?' she shouted.

Seeing the implement in her hand, Nicholas began backing away, moving over to the far side of the room.

'What d' ye want? What d' ye think ye'r doin' bargin' into me house? Ye've no right comin' in here.' As Bridget was saying the words, it was dawning on her why he was there. He would never just walk into her house without a good reason; Oh, he already knew, didn't he? Oh my God, what had Lizzie done?

Ignoring Nicholas as much as she could, Bridget walked over to the shallow sink and began repairing the broken rubbing board, her ears ringing with anxiety. She had nothing to say to him so why didn't he just go! But he spoke first.

'Bridget, if ye have a minute, I'd like to talk to ye. I've now been told the news, and I know me duty. I'll stand by ye if that's what ye want, though it wouldn't have been me first choice to marry like this. And whilst I'm here, I'd like to tell ye also that I was very drunk that night at the bar an' it wasn't my idea to start trouble wi' ye'r friends like that. But I couldn't stop John in the state I was in. I hope ye'll forgive us.'

Shocked to the core, Bridget wondered if this was his way of making an apology. And surely, he wasn't offering to marry her?

'Please, Nicholas, I'd like ye to go. I need ter think this thing through meself first without committin' to anything.'

Turning, Nicholas left without another word.

Though still wary of him, she had mixed feelings. She didn't want to marry this man but, at the same time, didn't want to be classed as a whore, as someone who gave her pleasures for free outside marriage.

Over the next few days, Bridget tried to collect her thoughts, putting her confused worries into separate boxes inside her head. 'If he means what he says, and if I am pregnant, then of course I would need to get married at some point, and really before I begin to show, although with all the clothes I wear that would be covered up for a while. But if Nicholas backs out of his promise to look after me, and I'm not sure whether it's him talking or the drink, then I can always go back to Ireland and make up a decent lie to suit the occasion. If I'm bein' honest with meself, then I suppose he's a fine-looking man when he wants to be, and yes, I am a little bit flattered at the attention he's givin' me'.

But it was somewhat of a surprise, some six weeks later, that Bridget found she wasn't pregnant after all. Had she known better, she would have realised it was an impossibility from the start but unfortunately, with her strict Catholic upbringing, she knew very little about lovemaking, readily accepting that this is what carnal knowledge was.

Feeling stupid for having mentioned it, her first thought was that she should tell Lizzie as, although still unhappy with her friend, nonetheless she probably meant well.

Putting on her shawl and smiling to herself, Bridget walked the short distance to Lizzie's house. Finding the door wide open on her arrival she went in and saw her friend sitting emptying the contents of a jug of beer into a glass, whilst at the same time trying to focus on her visitor.

'Oh, Lizzie, sure I've got good news fer ye.'

Seeing it was Bridget, she chortled, 'Well, Bridget, what good news could ye possibly have fer me, apart from the news that the mill had burnt down and that we'd still be gettin' paid?'

Going over to her to keep the news from the rest of the street, despite knowing full well that Lizzie had probably already broadcast the news, she whispered: 'I'm not pregnant after all'.

'Well now, don't ye tell him,' she whispered back, pointing her thumb out in the direction of Nicholas's street. 'Let him go on thinkin' ye're pregnant. Ye can think of some excuse once ye're married.'

Bridget was horrified. Was Lizzie being serious? Of course, she would have to tell Nicholas; why wouldn't she? And what kind of a life would she have knowing she had trapped some man into marrying her. And did she really want to be married anyway if she didn't have to be? With Lizzie's remarks still ringing in her ears, Bridget left for home. She wasn't sure if her friend really meant what she had said; perhaps it had been the drink talking. No doubt that would become clear soon enough.

However, back in the quietness of her own home, Bridget started to turn the situation over and over in her head. Lizzie's comments were beginning to bother her. On the one hand, if it hadn't been for Lizzie telling the tale to John, she would have been able to get on with her life and no one would have been any the wiser; then again, if she hadn't told Lizzie in the first place...! Her head was spinning.

However, when she visited Bridget later that evening, not only had Lizzie sobered up but she alarmed Bridget by saying, 'Ye know, I've been thinkin'; I'm glad ye aren't havin' his child. If I was ye, I'd ignore the man from now on.'

'But I thought ye wanted me to marry him, Lizzie. At least that's what ye were tellin' me earlier in the day.'

'Well now, Bridget, I can change me mind, can't I? And t' be honest, I've never really taken to the man. As me old mother used to say, 'Never judge a book by its cover and never judge a man by his garments!' In my view, he hasn't changed one little bit, no matter what ye say; once a bully always a bully and ye would have had a miserable life with him.'

This change of attitude amazed Bridget. Perhaps her friend was jealous?

The following day, Nicholas appeared at her door once more. 'Oh no! Lizzie has done it again; she had given Nicholas the news. What kind of friend is she?' Bridget felt betrayed a second time, but there was nothing she could do but explain her side of things to Nicholas.

Hating having to ask him into her home, Bridget stood aside, indicating she expected Nicholas to enter. He was polite enough and, on passing through the door, found an empty chair and sat down, immediately making her feel a little better.

Whilst trying to explain the situation to him, he frequently interrupted her, telling Bridget he was drunk at the time, that he didn't remember very much about what happened, even having the nerve to ask if she had enjoyed the evening in general! She was disgusted at his manner, but as usual, could smell alcohol on him.

Initially, it was difficult explaining the sequence of events without actually saying the words, 'I now feel soiled by what you did', but she did her best to express her feelings, taking the opportunity of also telling Nicholas that she had asked Lizzie to keep her counsel in the first place until she knew for sure, but of course, Lizzie was like a foghorn blaring out everyone's business except her own. In the end, it nearly burnt her tongue when she had to tell him she was sorry the matter had come out and that it had all been a big mistake.

To her surprise, he wasn't annoyed; at least he didn't appear so.

'Ah well, Bridget, sure it's good news for ye. But I must admit, I had begun t' get me mind around it and was warmin' to the situation. Anyway, what do ye want ter do now?'

What on earth did he mean by that? So far as she was concerned, the matter was over. Good God, she thought, don't tell me he's serious when he says he will look after me?

Carefully putting her thoughts into words, Bridget said, 'Nicholas, you aren't too bad a man when ye aren't drunk, but when the drink is in ye, then ye are the devil incarnate. I'm still smartin' at the incident an' I just don't trust ye. But who knows what the future holds? I'm sure I'll see ye about anyway.'

Standing up, Nicholas walked towards the door saying, 'I'll talk with ye some other time, Bridget, when I'm fully sober.' And with that, he disappeared, leaving her pondering.

Having already let her cousin Kathleen into her confidence about the fateful night, she felt she now had to reverse the situation. Later that day, when she told her about the conversation with Nicholas, Kathleen had laughed. 'Well, you certainly seem to have snared the man. But do be careful, there seems to be something undesirable about him. I've spoken with people about him and been told he's a chameleon and can change his colour at the flip of a coin.'

Bridget continued going to Mass each Sunday after that fatal night but had stopped short of going to Holy Communion as she hadn't felt able to first go to confessions to admit to her sins. Perhaps it had partly been her own fault, which she couldn't explain to the priest who, in her belief, took the place of Christ in the confessional. In fact, she stopped doing much of anything after that night, other than going to the rag mill and home.

It took her a few weeks to realise she was punishing herself by isolating herself from people. Everyone had their own business to think about, so why would they care about her? Of course, she was embarrassed whenever she thought about the incident with John and the young man he had a skirmish with and wondered how many of their friends blamed her. However, putting herself into seclusion wasn't going to make any difference to what had happened. So, maybe the time had come to forgive herself and forget.

The next time Lizzie asked her to spend an hour at the inn, Bridget didn't say no. Donning her coat and hat, and joining Lizzie, they walked the short distance to the place. It was a quiet evening in the bar with very few people drinking; there were plenty of empty tables to sit at and, as she chose one, Lizzie disappeared to the far side of the bar, presumably to say hello to her John, who was with Nicholas of course. She returned to the table carrying two glasses of beer which she said had been paid for. Knowing by whom, every sip of the stout reignited Bridget's anxiety. The last time 'he' had bought drinks for them there had been a consequence for her. Would it be the case this evening also? But the evening turned out to be uneventful and, after a second glass of stout which they each paid for, the two women left the bar and walked slowly back to their homes.

Nevertheless, fate seems to have a way of dealing with our expectations, sometimes turning them into a destiny we would prefer to avoid. Having already broken the ice, so to speak, Bridget now felt able to visit the bar alone, and it was during one of these lone visits one night that Nicholas came to sit with her. They both talked of Ireland and about their families, and he told Bridget of his expectations for the future. For the first time ever, she thought she saw the real person. He even apologised again but, of course, blamed the drink once more. Oh, you could say she was flattered by the attention he gave her, and she would have to agree with you. And wasn't Nicholas a handsome man!

She saw him often after that day; he kept his promise to treat her kindly, and she felt happier in his company. He began to visit her for an hour or so occasionally, and she would make a meal for the two of them, which she didn't often do when it was just herself. Bridget soon began looking forward to his visits.

One day she heard through the grapevine that there was to be a two-roomed house nearby available to rent in the near future, and so Bridget decided to speak with Nicholas about it the next time he visited. However, he was in a bad mood when he arrived that evening and she realised she needed to tread carefully, knowing that Nicholas wasn't the kind of man to be pushed into things. Waiting until they had finished the meal and when he was about to leave, she took a deep breath and said, 'I don't want ye to be annoyed wi' me, but I've just heard there's a nice house goin' for rent nearby which won't be there for long. What d' ye think about lookin' into the possibility of takin' the house? An' then perhaps we could speak wi' Father O'Dea at the same time?' She watched his face to see if there was any sign of rebuff. He didn't answer at once, though he stared at her for a long time, possibly weighing up the consequences of 'making her an honest woman'. When he did respond, it wasn't exactly what she wanted to hear, although she was nonetheless relieved that he hadn't actually rejected her suggestion. 'Well, Bridget, ye know now what I'm like an' I can't change me nature. It's up to ye what ye do, I'll leave it to ye. But don't expect me to do anythin' that could be considered woman's work.' Bridget took this to mean that she had been given the go-ahead.

The following evening, she made arrangements to see the landlord of the property to rent and secured the house on the spot.

Having begun the process, she then needed to speak with the priest. So, before work the next morning, Bridget attended the six o'clock Mass. When Mass was over and, after waiting a suitable time for the priest to take off his robes, she quietly crept into the sacristy to speak with Father O'Dea about their wedding. She arrived a little too soon and caught him just as he was removing his vestments. Standing soundlessly in the doorway watching, she was mesmerised at the ritual. The priest was softly murmuring prayers as he took off the Roman chasuble, a square piece of ornamented cloth with a hole in the centre through which a priest's head passes. Bridget knew she was intruding on a sacred ceremony and didn't want to interrupt in case the moment was lost. She continued watching as he carefully folded and kissed the chasuble before laying it down on a side table. It was as he was removing the white cotton Alb that he noticed her standing in the doorway.

'Now, Bridget, what can I do fer ye? For God's sake, don't say ye're about to tell me ye're goin' to stop cleanin' the presbytery on Saturday?'

'Oh, no, no, Father, sure I wouldn't be doin' that. No, I'm askin' what the route is if I want ter get married.'

Father O'Dea paused, giving her a stern look. 'Bridget, is this a good Catholic man ye're talkin' about?'

'He's from Ireland, Father,' she told him. 'His name's Nicholas

Kelly, an' me cousin seems to like him, which is praise enough don't ye think?' She hoped the small lie wouldn't go against her with God.

On hearing her proposed spouse's name, Father O'Dea went very quiet and continued busying himself, neatly laying the Alb on top of the chasuble. When he looked at her again his face seemed sad. 'Well, I have to say, I'm surprised at ye, Bridget. I would have thought ye could have found a man other than this Kelly. Oh, I like the odd pint of beer meself and have no problem with other men doin' the same, but I've come across this man whilst on me rounds and I don't like him. He's brash and offensive, and too fond of usin' his fists in an argument, especially when drunk. I fear for ye, lass, as ye are just a simple girl from the old country. Oh, I know, I know, ye can't stop the heart from choosing the wrong man.'

But he must have thought he could delay the inevitable giving her time to think again, because he suddenly said, 'Ye know, Bridget, I don't ever see this man at Mass, an' I believe ye know the rules of the church, don't ye? I can only marry a Catholic to a Catholic, an' I need to know that he really is a Catholic. He'll have to come to church on Sundays for the next three months before I can sanction any marriage between ye, and of course, I'll have to have a talk wi' him to make sure he understands the implications of marryin' in the Catholic church.'

Bridget didn't remember the walk to work that morning as she was feeling very worried. Going over and over what the priest had said, it bothered her what she would need to tell Nicholas knowing full well that he didn't go to Mass anymore. However, Bridget need not have fretted as, on passing on the information from the priest, he assured her he would do whatever Father O'Dea said would be required of him to marry her, though he did warn her he had no intention of doing one iota more than what was needed. Nonetheless, over the next few months, she saw Nicholas at Mass from time to time, which pleased her, but at the same time it put her off-guard.

Not very long into the new relationship Bridget began to notice a change in him. He developed the habit of brushing her off with a sharp remark when she spoke, or he would just ignore her completely which was embarrassing when he did this whilst in the company of others. When the time came to speak with him about money for the wedding, because of his manner, she now dreaded bringing up the subject. And it was at this time that Bridget realised what an inveterate liar Nicholas really was. It turned out the money he had bragged about was never forthcoming but, if she was honest, she knew this in her heart almost from the beginning. Yet somehow, despite what she knew him to be like, she couldn't walk away, and their relationship continued, possibly because they were two lonely people away from their homeland, without many friends. Or perhaps it was desperation on her part?

The wedding service, when it happened, was short and simple, but little did Bridget know the marriage was to become a protracted life sentence for her. Wearing her best coat and with a second-hand gold ring, she vowed to love, honour and obey this man and to live with him for better or worse for the rest of her life.

There were only four other people at the wedding: Kathleen, Marie, Lizzie and John, the last two being witnesses at the ceremony. The date was to stick in Bridget's memory forever: Tuesday, 10th January 1906. She was twenty-three years of age and Nicholas was twenty-four.

After the marriage ceremony, the six of them made their way to the inn for a celebration drink, but Nicholas was already winding himself up. He hadn't liked the way Father O'Dea had spoken with him before the service reminding him about his obligations to Bridget, to their future children, and to the church.

'Who in hell does the man think he is, tellin' me how to look after a woman. And as for warnin' me that I would suffer the fires of hell if I didn't continue going to church on Sundays....! Who does the imbecile in the fancy frock think he is?'

Without too much persuasion, Nicholas convinced John to join him in some heavy drinking, leaving the four women to watch from the side-lines.

'Oh, Bridget, what in God's name have you gotten yerself into?' Lizzie whispered, but Bridget laughed telling her Nicholas was just celebrating their marriage and that everything would turn out all right in the end.

Her sister Kathleen, weighing up the consequences of a bout of heavy drinking, excused herself after only one drink, saying she was leaving, and Bridget's friend Marie, who had been quietly talking with Kathleen, did the same, saying her train was due soon and that Kathleen had offered to take her to the station so she didn't get lost. This confused Bridget as she had expected Marie to stay a few days and had even arranged with her sister that she would be accommodated.

The men continued celebrating well into the afternoon, with Lizzie and Bridget having to half-carry the men home after their binge. However, as soon as Nicholas and his new wife entered their new home, closing the door to the world, Bridget knew she had made an horrific mistake and should probably have listened to the priest. Out of sight of everyone, Nicholas immediately sobered up – his acting would have won an award – and he now reverted to type, his anger at boiling point. The first words that came out of his mouth were to tell her that she was now his wife and he had rights over her. He told her to get on with the meal as he intended going out again as soon as he had eaten, to meet up with his other drinking friends.

THE CHILDREN

That was the beginning of a harrowing period in her life. Nothing she did was ever right for Nicholas. If he didn't like what she cooked, he would pick up the plate and throw it at her face, following on with his fists. He would mock her abilities at anything she did, leaving her feeling ashamed. And this became a way of life for Bridget.

Their first child, Winifred, came into the world on 10th December 1906, ten months after their marriage. Unfortunately, an unsettled homelife had already begun by this time as Nicholas, in debt up to his eyes and hoping to evade the tallyman, had insisted they leave The Hill and their friends, and move to a one-room cottage amongst the concealed rubble of a back alley in the next town.

Bridget hadn't been able to work for a number of weeks before the birth, being struck down with daily sickness, and so their funds had dried up. The occasional labouring work that Nicholas did helped to pay off some of the rent arrears, but he had a problem keeping any job, his brusqueness and temper leaving many a boss quaking in his shoes.

Thankfully, they were soon on the move back to The Hill and Bridget was relieved to be with her old friends once more, but it was proving impossible to find anyone already nursing a baby to look after Winifred, which would enable her to return to work.

Not wanting to rile Nicholas, Bridget wasn't brave enough to ask outright if he intended finding work, instead she would from time to time cautiously mention their lack of money, particularly if something was needed for the baby. However, the man had a knack of turning almost anything she said into a complaint. When she did ask one day if maybe he could find a local labouring job so that they had a bit of money to pay their way, he menacingly whispered, 'What'r ye playin' at woman – I think ye'r trying to take me confidence away by stompin' on me testicles. Well, it won't work. I'll get a job when I find one that I like, and not before. So, shut up.' And, of course, Bridget did shut up.

Oh, how she hated the man. She lived in fear, afraid to open her mouth in case she used the wrong word or had the wrong expression on her face when she spoke to him. And she dreaded him coming near her, always demanding his conjugal rights, even more so when he was drunk. His lovemaking was harsh and sinful, but she was too afraid to open her mouth to complain in case of further punishment, which is what she felt of his compassion towards her: a punishment.

It was John, his friend, who suggested work at the Tramway Company which had a depot in the town. Nicholas, the big man, had the gift of the gab, but even so, it took all his powers of persuasion to get the tram company manager to give him a trial as a tram driver. He was intelligent enough to pick up the rudiments of driving a tram; however, driving a tram and drinking beer didn't mix, and the job lasted less than six months.

In June 1909, Cormac was born, and for some reason, this birth seemed to exacerbate the cruelty Nicholas had begun exhibiting. Bridget was not well enough to cope with the new birth on top of physical and mental abuse but didn't have the courage to answer back as that would be an excuse for him to 'chastise' her even more.

Bridget had eventually managed to acquire the services of a neighbour to look after Winifred but now, with a new baby, the neighbour was going to have to look after two babies, with the additional cost that went with them once Bridget was feeling well enough to resume working.

There was never enough money, especially after Nicholas had taken his share of her wages, and more often than not, Bridget would take her 'best' coat to the pawn shop on the Monday on her way to work to be collected on the Friday night after she had received her wages. Astonishingly, with only one exception, she had always managed to retrieve her coat for Sunday Mass, and would have felt embarrassed that the coat had sat in the pawnbroker's shop all week, except that she knew for a fact that many other women's coats were hanging there beside hers; in church she could smell the mothballs!

Often Bridget saw Lizzie at Sunday Mass and, after the service, they would stand talking for a few minutes, although Bridget daren't spend too much time away as Nicholas wanted his meals at a set time and woe betide her if she was late.

'I don't know how ye can put up wi' the man,' said Lizzie one day. This from the woman who always gave the impression, to anyone who would listen, that she had herself married a 'good' Irishman.

'Instead o' takin' the blows, ye should give him some,' she continued, putting up her fist like a prize boxer. 'My John daren't put a finger wrong, otherwise he'd know what day o' the week it was.'

Bridget had to smile to herself. This from the woman who couldn't go out for days on end because 'her John' would take her only pair of shoes with him when he went to work, to make sure she was there when he got home and hadn't run off with the tallyman. The only difference between them was that 'her John' brought money into the house, whereas Nicholas took it out.

THEY MOVE TO MANCHESTER

With his feet beginning to itch, Nicholas decided it was time to leave Yorkshire particularly as, through the grapevine at one of his drinking holes, he had heard there was plenty of work going at the busy Manchester Ship Canal Docks where they needed men to 'police' the sprawling wharfs.

Initially, Nicholas went alone, leaving the family behind in Yorkshire until he was sure he had a job and Bridget joined him with the two children a few weeks later, by which time the shipyard company had given him accommodation near the docks.

Oh, wouldn't life have been different if she had refused to go with him! She certainly didn't need the man. Nonetheless she had taken her vows, and in the eyes of God, would be the wife of Nicholas until either one of them died. But why mull over this question now? She must be dreaming if she thought, for one minute, that she could have gotten away from Nicholas so easily. He would have found her and blackened both her eyes, and the few teeth she possessed would have been sitting out on the floor in front of her if she had even dared to suggest that the family didn't follow him.

Of course, they moved across the Pennines as instructed.

The new accommodation was better than the rented house on The Hill and for a while Bridget felt some happiness. There were plenty of jobs available in the mills too and soon she was bringing home a few extra pence.

Nicholas also appeared happy. He had quickly found new friends, and in his spare time, of which he had lots, had resumed his drunken ways, often becoming a public nuisance and needing the police to bring him home. They came to know him well. Several of his drinking pals were working on the docks with him, so life, as he had always known it, continued.

He was a vain man and would parade himself around the streets in his docks uniform, reminding people he was a dock policeman and not just a navvy like most of the Irishmen in the area. Seeing him like this, Bridget had to admit that he did indeed look handsome when he brushed back his dark curly hair and donned his cap. She had hoped that maybe this new job would change things between them, that it would be a new start, but that hope was soon shattered.

'D'ye want a baytin, woman?' he demanded one day after Bridget had asked him for some of his wages so she could pay some urgent bills. 'Twould do ye no har-um to get me fist from time to time – tis a good thumpin' ye need to keep ye in yer place, woman!'

She knew not to ask again but needed to wait until he had fallen into one of his deep, drunken sleeps so she could go through his pockets to look for some money. But this time, when she eventually got the chance to search his clothes, she found only a few coppers, which she knew to leave well alone, fully knowing the consequence if his pocket contained only thin air when he was paying for the next round of drinks once he had sobered up enough to go out once more. Ah well, t'would be the pawn shop again on Monday!

. . .

A ROUTINE QUICKLY FORMED IN THEIR LIVES. BRIDGET WAS working and looking after the children and Nicholas was working and drinking. She looked forward to the nights when he was on the graveyard-shift as she would be free of him for a few hours giving her chance to do some household jobs without worrying that she was going to say something to antagonise him. Each morning when he got back from work, he would eat a quick meal, and was usually in bed before she left for her work.

But one morning he arrived back from his job a little later than usual. Bridget was getting the children ready to go off to the childminder, and as soon as he walked through the door she sensed trouble. Instead of being tired and slightly inebriated as was often the case, he was just so angry.

Recoiling from every swearword he shouted at her, fear pulsated every pore in her body. His anger seemed more powerful because, she gathered, the dock police had caught him before he'd even had chance to open a bottle of whiskey, so he was probably feeling withdrawal symptoms on top of everything else.

Dodging a flying mug that had been laying on the table ready for his first drink of tea, and the tin plate that bounced off the wall just skimming her arm, Bridget wondered what to do.

'Why me? Why me?' he shouted as he threw the articles about. 'Why did the idiots pick me out? Sure, I was only doin' what everybody else was doin', an' the whiskey is there fer the takin. I swear t' God, from the highest to the lowest man, the drink is bein' taken in abundance. I've seen crates of it bein' carried out of the yard to waitin' transport. Sure, I only took one crate, and it would have lasted me till the middle o' next week. An' it isn't as if they don't claim fer the losses back on the insurance.'

To add to his frustration, it would seem the long, dark night had given him chance to reflect on his life, and he must have hated what he saw. Bridget knew from previous outbursts that he felt trapped; that he was living in the midst of a domestic world which, although he had helped to create, he now loathed and detested.

Sensing there was going to be a big problem that day she frantically looked for a way out. Keeping her back to him so that he didn't see the fear in her eyes, she began preparing some food, hoping he would eat and then go to bed as he usually did. But this morning he was too wound up pacing the floor like a man possessed.

Trying to protect the children, Bridget kept them near her. They were always fearful of the loud voice of their father, so she put her arm around her two children drawing them close to her. Cormac was still a baby, but Winifred was old enough to know that her father's shouting would get louder and louder, and only stop when she would hear her mother weeping, as she usually did.

Glancing out of the window, Bridget saw that the commotion indoors had spread to a show outside, some of the neighbours having gathered into small groups. She shuddered. God only knows what they must think of the Kelly family as there seemed to be constant noise coming from their house. Seeing that her next-door neighbour was standing with one of the groups was, in a way, a relief, as she would surely know she wouldn't be needed to childmind this day as Bridget probably wouldn't be going to work.

As she was preparing a meal for Nicholas, the dock police came knocking at the door and, to her shock, they arrested him on the spot. Once handcuffed, he didn't argue, leaving the house without a murmur. Though once outside in the street, she watched him grinning at the groups of people assembled, swaggering past them, and turning around to show them his hands cuffed at the front of him.

'See, they've had to cuff me in case I turn on 'em, the fecking idiots,' he said as he was led towards the police van parked in the roadway.

En route to the van he bent pretending to tie an already-fastened bootlace, before forcing a detour onto the road where he purposefully stepped into a pile of horse dung, taking the horse muck into the van with him, no doubt intending to clean his boots on the floor.

Knowing Nicholas as she did, Bridget imagined his anger would have dissolved once at the police station; he was a coward at heart and, of course, he wouldn't have an audience there. The man could turn it on and off like a tap. Then, being the consummate liar that he was, she would expect him to use his Irish guile to talk himself out of trouble. But it seems the offence proved to be too critical for just a slap on the wrist, and Nicholas came back home with his tail between his legs though angrier than ever.

The following day he was ordered to hand in his uniform. His good job on the docks was at an end, so too was the accommodation that went with the job. They were left with nothing but the clothes on their backs as they walked away from their home, not knowing where they would lay their heads that night.

Nicholas's job at the Docks was never going to last very long in any case. So far as he was concerned, any job he got must fit in with his work principle, which was zero. In the long run, he had no intention of working for a living, although he had come to a sticky end this day.

The Docks Managers had been aware for a time that goods were being stolen from the wharf, somewhere between unloading and registering with the Port Authority, and they had employed a Security Officer to bring the thieving to a halt. It didn't take the officer long to find a suspect as, checking the records each morning, he noticed that there were usually more irregularities whenever Nicholas Kelly was working. There was only one way to be sure, and that was for the officer to go undercover and work the night shift.

'I'm sorry, Nicholas, but this job on the docks is a good one and I'm not about to lose it, man.'

The plan was working as, within weeks of the 'new security guard' commencing work, Nicholas had already begun trying to involve him in his illegal activities.

'Ah, get 'way wi ye, Jim. Don't be such a simpleton; nobody is goin' ter notice us 'ere. Sure, there's plenty of booze an' nobody would dare to come onto the docks at this 'our, what wi' us actin' as guards. Hahaha. I've put the box wi' the whiskey under the tarpaulin over here. When the lights go out, I'll open a bottle. I've done this many time before. Ye jist need ter know the ropes.'

Rolling a cigarette from one of the packets he had pilfered previously, Nicholas was about to pick up the end of the tarpaulin when strong torchlight immediately put him in the spotlight and a voice in the darkness commanded, 'Stay where you are. This is the police.'

Freezing, not sure what to do, he shouted, 'What's the matter? Sure, I'm jist about ter start me nightly walk ter make sure the docks are quiet.'

'It's no use trying to bluff your way out of it, Kelly. We know about the whiskey stashed away as we've been watching you for a long time, haven't we Jim?'

It occurred to Nicholas that he might have time to run, but his weight would be no match for the lithe guard who, by now, had moved out of the darkness and was standing so close he could smell his breath.

'Bastards! Why're ye worryin'? Nobody loses out. Sure, they claim fer any loss from the insurance company an' don't lose anythin', an' anyway everybody does it, I'm not the only one.'

'Yes, we know you're not the only one, and you'll be sitting on the same bench, at the same police station, with the rest of the thieving bastards!'

After his arrest, and overnight stay in jail, he had been released the next morning, together with a group of men who had also been caught stealing that night.

Reluctant friends took the family in for the first few days, and through some of Nicholas's drinking chums, they found a small cottage which they made into a home for an unpredictable future.

Nicholas found odd jobs here and there, but his reputation had gone before him and people were wary of him. Now, with time on his hands, his drinking became worse.

Unfortunately, Bridget fell pregnant for a third time, and Mary Teresa was born in June 1911. Then, on 16th August 1913, Alice was born and, fortunately, this would be the fourth and last child.

Bridget had breastfed all the babies for as long as had been possible and she had intended doing the same with Alice but had found a job in the meantime, so that now wasn't achievable. Then a neighbour offered to take care of the children for a small payment which was a Godsend to her.

She breastfed Alice each morning before leaving for work and again in the evening on her return, but during the day the childminder fed her 'pap'; this was a mixture of bread soaked in hot milk. (Oddly at the time, money for medication being scarce, a similar mixture of bread soaked in warm milk was used to bring out the soreness in boils and to ease the aches and pains of everyday life. Similarly, a mixture of breadcrumbs and water was used as wallpaper paste. It was no wonder so many houses were infested with bugs).

As Cormac grew, so did the loathing Nicholas seemed to have for his small son. Maybe he was jealous of the attention Bridget gave to the child which, of course, she needed to give whilst Cormac was just a small boy.

The poor child was always the target of his father's abuse. Occasionally, and without any explanation other than that he hadn't liked the way his son had looked at him, Cormac would be made to stand on the fireside hearth facing the fire until his little face was red and he screamed with pain, after which he would then have to endure further physical abuse at the hands of his father for crying. Bridget tried her best to intervene, but because she was afraid of the man herself, there was very little she could do. When he was in the mood for total respect, Nicholas would stand all four children beside the table to watch him eat, laughing and talking with them as he ate his meal. Oh, how she hated the man.

BACK TO YORKSHIRE

Being unable to find permanent work in Manchester, Nicholas got in touch with a friend back in Yorkshire and got the promise of a job back there. Once more, against all her instincts, she prepared herself and the children for another move, incredibly back to The Hill.

The Hill was a mix of roads entirely constructed of dirt and cinders; consequently, the area was a breeding ground for bugs. It was assumed that every house on The Hill was alive with either roaches, bedbugs, black clock beetles or mice, and some houses even had all four. Bridget made this assumption early on as, over the years, the family had lived in at least three different houses, all of which had such combinations, and No. 54 on The Hill was, unfortunately, infested with a particularly nasty form of black clock beetle which had a terrible smell they would never get used to.

Over the next few years, life took on habitual drudgery. The three older children were accepted into the local Catholic school, and Bridget found someone to take care of Alice until she was old enough to go to school with her siblings. She herself returned to the rag mill for the much-needed wage.

From an early age, each child was allotted a job helping in the household, and Cormac, who was now almost six, had the job of making sure all the shoes were clean. If Winnie wasn't too busy doing her own chores, she would take pity on him and would help with the shoes, as his small hands could become raw and sore from the cloth that needed constant wetting to clean off the dirt. Winnie would tell Cormac to leave Nicholas's big pair of shoes for her to clean. But Nicholas hated his orders being flouted and would rant and rave at Winnie if he found out she had changed the rules. But he never touched her; instead, if his rage had reached a climax before he fell asleep from the drink, he would attack Cormac for not doing his job properly.

After drinking heavily one day, he came home in his usual bad mood. Looking for Cormac and finding him playing in the street, he grabbed the child by the arm and pulled him back into the yard.

'Where 've ye been? Didn't ye hear me callin'? How many times do I 'ave ter tell ye ter stay around the yard so I know were ye are? Ye little bastard, ye never do as ye're told, look at these fecking shoes – d'ye think I can stand wi' me mates an' not 'ave em snigger at me? I should 've smothered ye at birth.'

This time, taking hold of Cormac by the hair, he dragged him towards the outside toilet, screaming obscenities all the time. In his terror, Cormac thrashed about, kicking his father's legs.

Bridget rushed outside but was too late to stop Nicholas who, having pushed his poor son's head down into the dirty toilet water, was now pulling the hanging piece of string to flush it. Cormac was gasping for breath and choking. In between the sobs and screams, he was saying, 'No, no, no more... please, Mammy!' but by now Nicholas was enjoying himself, throwing his son onto the floor and gearing himself up for a final thump. Bridget screamed at Nicholas to stop but was so shocked by what was happening that she was frozen in horror.

It was Winifred who reacted, running past her mother towards her father, and standing between him and her small brother who was sobbing bitterly. Her eldest daughter had a great deal of courage for an eight-year-old but was too small to have any effect on the monster who was still winding himself into a frenzy. Catching several blows herself as he flailed around with his fists, she didn't stop screaming at the tyrant.

EXAMINING HER FATHER ONE DAY, THIS MAN WHO WAS supposed to be her protector, Winnie recognised the ugliness of him, which shocked her for she had never actually 'looked' at him before for fear of what she would see. In one of those rare moments of understanding, though not quite realising what she was seeing, Winnie knew that one day she would make her father suffer for all the pain he had put the family through. She understood why her mother remained silent as, more often than not, she and her siblings could hear the blows being rained down on their mother. But the thing she could never understand was why, when her friends asked Bridget about the black eye or why her arm, or chest. was so bruised, her mother always told them she had fallen. Surely, they would have helped her if they had known what was happening.

ANOTHER DAY, ANOTHER WEEK, AND YET ANOTHER argument. Bridget was dismayed to think that her life was going to continue like this until either Nicholas or she took their last breath. Life was too cruel for words. Nicholas had been in one of his drunken moods the previous night, having spent the day with friends, and had been in a stupor when he went to bed. He was still hungover the following morning when Bridget was getting the children ready for school.

Nothing seemed to be right for him; there was too much noise, not enough tea in his cup or it wasn't sweet enough, there wasn't enough coal on the fire; on and on went the complaints. The whole family were walking on eggshells around him and were in a hurry to leave the house. As she walked past him, Nicholas lashed out at Bridget and, although she had been quick enough to dodge the blow, she felt the wind as his hand slammed past her face.

She was in a dark mood herself when she left the house. The two older children had already left for school so, taking the hands of the two younger ones, she crossed the street to Clara, her kindly neighbour who was willing to look after the children whilst she was working. Bridget didn't need to say a word to Clara as she, and probably the rest of the neighbours, knew of her situation. Once the children were safely with Clara, Bridget walked past her home without a second glance, and down the hill towards the main road.

The morning was bleak and cold with the strong winds that were usual for that time of year, but the cobbles were icy, and she felt her feet slide over them. Unable to steady herself, Bridget hit the floor hard. Her tote bag lay on the ground and everything it contained was scattered. As she lay there, she remembered it was her birthday, the fifth of November, though only rich people celebrated the day of their birth. She was thirty-three years old but looked and felt like sixty.

With an effort, she managed to get onto her knees, tentatively getting up onto her feet. The pain in her ankle was excruciating but she felt some relief that she didn't have a broken leg. Looking around, and seeing that there was no-one to help her, gasping with the pain, she bent down and started picking up the bits and pieces. Once she was sure everything was in her bag, Bridget cautiously hobbled over the cobbles and onto the flat pavement. The pain almost took her breath away.

The gaslight was on in the back room of the grocer's shop on the corner, and she pictured Mr Pickles busy filling up boxes of orders ready for them to be delivered by his young helper on his bike. Bridget leant against the door to catch her breath, glancing through the glass between all the advertisements pasted on the door, but she didn't knock for help. What had she been called in the past? 'A hard, old bugger?' Well then, she'd show them what she was made of! With that thought in her mind, Bridget set off at a very slow pace towards the marketplace, hopping when the pain compelled her to do so.

There was a tram waiting as she reached the stop, and, with an effort, she managed to pull herself up onto the platform.

'Ah yer all reight, love?' The conductor gave her a sympathetic look as he helped her to a seat. Bridget nodded but didn't answer; not because she was rude (although she could be that) but because she was in so much pain.

It took almost twenty minutes for the tram to reach her stop, and every second of those twenty minutes she spent imagining the agonising walk she would have before she reached the mill (some quarter of a mile), remembering every incline and mound on the rough pavement.

Getting off the tram, and sweating with the effort, Bridget eventually reached the mill gates. The structure she worked in felt like a hundred miles away, though she could see clearly it at the far end of the yard. Just one last surge of energy will get me there, she thought, as she hobbled along the hard mud path towards the shed that would eventually give her some respite. The structure ahead of her was windowless and, to a great extent, door-less. It was simply a huge, cold, stone-sided shed with wooden beams and whitewashed walls. As she neared it, Bridget could see the door was already open, and huge bales full of old clothes were almost blocking her way.

Passing through the door into the shed, pacing herself, she limped over to where her work friends were sitting talking. Hoping her limping didn't prompt too many questions, she was relieved to see they were too busy talking to even notice. Joining them in the semicircle of large, upturned baskets, in the nearly empty space in the middle of the floor, Bridget picked up her cutting shears and waited to begin work.

The young labourer had been standing on top of one of the bales as Bridget entered, and was now busy cutting the ties holding the bale together. Working quickly, he pulled open the now freed covering and began distributing the reclaimed clothes into several wicker baskets at the foot of the bale; his accurate throw would have been the envy of many a cricketer. When all the wicker containers were full, he climbed down from the now receding bale of rags and dragged the containers to the middle of the floor.

For the next few hours, there was only sporadic conversation, the main sound being the clicking of shears with just an occasional chuckle.

The first thing Bridget picked out of the basket was an old pair of men's trousers. One of the older ladies sitting nearby, mistaking the look on her face for one of disgust, said, 'My God, Bridget, why don't they use more than one-piece o' newspaper to wipe themselves down?' But for once she didn't chuckle as agony had taken over her normal feelings.

Pushing the pain aside for a while, she attacked the welt and buttons of the trousers from the front first, before cutting down the thick seams at both sides of the legs, inside and outside; then the waistband, pockets and cuffs from the bottom of the leg. Each time she cut off waste, she threw it into the basket in the middle of the group. When all the seams and thicknesses had been cut away and all that remained was two long pieces of clean woollen material, Bridget threw these into a second basket by the side of her. During the morning, she disposed of trousers, coats, dresses and skirts; by lunchtime, her basket was half full.

She had refrained from going to the lavatory all morning but by now was fit to burst. Knowing she would have to accept the pain, she got up and limped across the shed and into the yard where there was a small outbuilding. It was a miniature version of the shed she worked in, with its whitewashed walls and wooden slatted roof. With an effort, Bridget leaned against the toilet wall and pulled up her skirts, moving aside her pants at the crotch. As she sat down, she began to feel dizzy with the pain and quietly started weeping. But hearing women's voices in the yard, she quickly finished what she was doing. After straightened her clothes, she limped back down the yard, passing the women on their way to the toilet. As she passed, unsurprisingly no-one asked her why she was having trouble walking. Knowing of her life, Bridget guessed they assumed she had been kicked again by Nicholas.

Back in the clipping shed, the young labourer was already making mugs of tea for the women and was clearing space on an upturned basket to lay them on when Bridget hobbled back into the shed. Picking up her mug she took a quick gulp of the warm sweet liquid, noticing as she did so the smell of filth on her hands from the morning's work. She didn't wash her hands as there wasn't a sink in the toilet area. Clean hands would have to wait until she got home, and even then it would only be a quick wash with carbolic soap under the cold-water tap.

After a short break the women returned to their tasks as they were only paid for the number of baskets of 'clean' cloth they submitted. Each 'clipper' had her own card and the number of baskets she filled each day was added to the card by the foreman. The full baskets were collected and weighed by the labourer who then dragged them over to the door to the shed. Every now and again, he would add his ha'pence worth of drivel to the conversation, but he never stopped working.

Having collected the filled baskets of 'second-hand' cloth the women had worked on, the labourer needed to fill a bale with this clean material. He started by pushing the material into an empty bale positioned underneath a small crane above the opening of the large door. When he couldn't reach in to add cloth anymore, he climbed into the bale and stomped down the material until it was compacted. He continued adding more cloth until it was completely full, after which he picked up a very large needle and stitched the top of the bale closed. Setting the crane in motion he jumped down and watched as two very large grippers picked up the bale and swung it over to the stack of bales already awaiting collection. The lorry would pick up the bales periodically taking them to the various woollen mills for processing.

The work continued all afternoon. Occasionally, Bridget would stealthily put an article of clothing - a jumper, a dress or a blouse, into her bag to take home, knowing she would be fired on the spot if she was caught doing this by the foreman. Nonetheless, everyone did it!

At five o'clock, the women began preparing to leave for home, helping each other clear the area beside their workspace, and leaving their shears on top of the partly full baskets of 'already prepared' cloth, thereby making it easy the following morning to continue their work.

The labourer cleared away any rubbish that had been lying in front of the large doors before pulling them closed, leaving one of the doors partly ajar so the women could pass through. The foreman, whose job it was to make sure the building was secure, waited until the last person had left, then went to the doors and slid the huge padlock into position, using some of his strength to click the arm into place.

Calling out goodnight to each other the workers went their separate ways, but Bridget had dawdled, making sure she was the last one out of the door. When she was sure she was alone in the yard, she searched amongst the debris for a stout piece of wood to use as a crutch or walking stick. It was quite dark now and she caused herself more pain by constantly stepping on sharp pieces of wood and broken glass in her search. Eventually finding what she was looking for, Bridget slowly made her way back to the tram stop, joining the queue.

Unfortunately, there wasn't an empty seat on the tram that night, which made the return journey even more uncomfortable. At the terminus, Bridget had to suffer the long and painful walk back through the streets of the town and home.

She was exhausted when she arrived back at the cobblestones which had been her downfall in the morning and could only walk slowly back up the hill towards the house, her mind pondering what Nicholas would have to say to her. Her heart jumped when she saw him leaning over the gate, watching people coming up The Hill. But she wasn't in the mood for what was to come.

As predicted, he started shouting abuse at her long before she reached the house. 'Where've ye been? Ye should 'av been back an hour ago; ye've been wi yer tally man, 'aven't ye?' he accused, spittle dripping out of the side of his mouth. He took a swipe at her as she slowly moved past him, catching her on her shoulder.

Winnie had already collected the two children from Clara, and Bridget could see all four of them cowering. She tried not to make a sound as she didn't want to frighten them anymore than they were already. Tally man, indeed, Bridget thought. If all men were like him, she would gladly live in a world without men.

There was a chill in the house which wasn't just because she felt ill. She noticed the fire hadn't been lit; the meal would be late tonight. Without looking back at Nicholas, Bridget took off her coat and, dropping it on the chair, hobbled over to the fireplace, surreptitiously rubbing her shoulder as she went. He loved seeing her in pain, but she wouldn't give him the pleasure.

They ate their meal in silence, and the children were glad when it was over and time for bed. From their bedroom, they listened with fear as their father downstairs wound himself up into a rage; that night Winnie, Mary, and the two younger children slept fitfully in the room next to their parents.

The following morning, Bridget looked so unwell she frightened Winnie, who quietly expressed fear for her mother, asking if she should speak with the parish priest about their problems. But Winnie probably already knew the answer; that her mother would never wash her dirty linen in public. After all, half the women in the town were no doubt living with the same problem, so what did Winnie think the priest could do? After all, there was no Eleventh Commandment that declared 'Thou shalt not beat thy wife, thus creating untold fear in thy children.' The priest could only preach about the goodness of God, and that we should all try to live in His image. But what good would that do?

Forcing herself to believe she felt better, Bridget took one of the older patched sheets and cut it into wide strips, which she wrapped tightly around her ankle, tucking the end in underneath. In time, the ankle healed of course.

Bridget's work ethic and honesty were important to her, and she made every effort to pass these principles on to her children. Yes, of course she needed the money, but it would have to be something more painful than a twisted ankle to stop her from going to work. Winnie tried her hardest to be her helper, with even the neighbours expressing surprise that such a young girl could seem so grown up.

NICHOLAS HAS HAD ENOUGH

On the afternoon of Monday, 3rd August 1914, the first Monday in August which was traditionally a Bank Holiday in the UK, Germany declared war on France just days after its declaration of war on Russia. It was a beautiful day and was to be the last Bank Holiday Monday to be enjoyed in Great Britain for the next four years. The following day, 4th August, Prime Minister Herbert Asquith declared that, despite the talks which had come to nothing, Britain was at war with Germany.

> *Owing to the summary rejection by the German Government of the request made by His Majesty's Government for assurances that the neutrality of Belgium would be respected, His Majesty's Ambassador in Berlin has received his passport, and His Majesty's Government has declared to the German Government that a state of war exists between Great Britain and Germany as from 11 p.m. on August 4th.*

All public transport was commandeered for the deployment of troops, and Richmond Camp in North Yorkshire (renamed Catterick Camp in 1915), being a garrison town, became the base for army divisions. (Later, Richmond Camp served as a prisoner of war camp until the end of the First World War).

Hundreds of men immediately volunteered to fight but thousands more were needed, and the Lord Mayor of Leeds appealed for 5,000 men to join Kitchener's army, which target was vastly surpassed within weeks. So many men were mobilised that the harvest was late that year. Horses were needed for the war effort and officers searched the countryside, seizing any healthy horses they found. Temporary hospitals had to be set up anywhere there was space, usually in public houses, schools, offices and mansions. As the first group of wounded arrived back in Yorkshire after the Battle of the Marne in September 1914, thousands of people watched in silence as they were brought into Leeds City Station.

When the war started that bright warm summer, no-one could ever have imagined what was to follow. The streets, busy during the day with men milling around army recruitment offices, were places of apprehension at night. The only light was from the moon, as no artificial light of any kind was allowed. This affected stations, hospitals, houses, churches and shops, as well as streetlights and, when the moon was hidden, the streets became terrifying places. The street lighting had only just come back on for the dark winter months, as very few areas had lighting all year round.

The streets around The Hill normally had lighting from 1st September to 30th April, but there had been a problem with the gaslights on The Hill during the previous winter as vandals had broken some of the lamps, causing some of the fittings to be removed at the end of the season, only to be replaced the previous month. Now, all the streets were in darkness once again.

But even without light to show them their way Graf Zeppelins, which carried bombs managed to find places like Hull, sometimes also inadvertently dropping their charge onto surrounding villages.

The outbreak of war should have prompted a change of attitude towards food security, yet the government seemed to be confident in the Navy's ability to keep the shipping lanes open. However, Britain had been dependent on Germany, Austria and Hungary for most of its supply of sugar beet for years, and from 7th August 1916, trading with those countries ceased, making England rely heavily on the East and West Indies for all her sugar supplies. Within a short space of time, food, particularly anything containing sugar or wheat, became scarce. To make matters worse, the harvest that year was poor due to severe weather conditions and a lack of manpower to harvest the crops.

On Easter Monday, 24th April 1916, a group of Irish protestors in Dublin revolted against British rule in Ireland summoning around two thousand volunteers to take over some of the major buildings, proclaiming an Irish Republic. The souls held out for several days but were eventually overcome by the British army, and the fifteen or so leading rebels were put on trial and eventually executed for treason.

On hearing this news, Nicholas was inflamed.

Having returned to Yorkshire from Lancashire, Nicholas had once again got a job locally as a tram driver. Having done the job before, he found it easy. He also managed to hang on to it for longer than usual because he didn't get drunk very often, which helped. Oh, without doubt, he liked his drink, but the government had scuppered that, bringing out new laws which even made it illegal to buy drinks for other people, preventing him from taking advantage of his friends. Even the newspapers got in on the pronouncement, declaring that 'filthy drink' caused drunkenness which hampered war production. The 'evil government' even lowered the strength of alcohol, which meant that, even when he could get the drink, by the time he was feeling inebriated, he was usually holed up in the men's toilet getting rid of excess water.

What with the irritation at the lost chance of Irish independence, and boredom due to the lack of booze, he was becoming increasingly restless!

Then he saw the poster prominently displayed on the board outside the shop.

Single Men!: Will You March Too
OR
WILL YOU WAIT TILL MARCH 2?

Prior to 2nd March 1916, the government had relied on voluntary enlistment. However, during the previous months, recruitment had fallen, so in January 1916, Prime Minister Asquith had passed the Military Service Act 1916, a bill that conscripted men aged between eighteen and forty-one years old into the army, unless they were married, widowed with children, serving in the Royal Navy, a minister of religion or working in a reserved occupation. A second act in May 1916 extended liability for military service to married men, and a third act in 1918 extended the upper age limit to fifty-one.

He was immediately interested! Of course, he wasn't a single man as the poster recommended but, to be honest, he was weary of family life now needing a distraction, and the thought of joining the near quarter of a million fellow Irishmen and signing up would certainly take his mind off his family problems. But from birth, Nicholas had been a Loyalist through and through, and he most certainly wouldn't be fighting for England; he would be fighting for the freedom of Ireland from England. Sure, he was more than willing to take the king's shilling, and the thought of being trained for the war, which would give him the opportunity to learn how to fire a gun, excited him even more. The training would come in very useful if he ever got chance to join 'the cause'.

Spinning a story to Bridget about 'doing his bit for the country', and knowing he would find more Irishmen in Manchester, Nicholas travelled back over the Pennines and joined the Lancashire Regiment.

The barracks, as such, were just makeshift camps on various school playing fields and recreation grounds, which didn't fill Nicholas with much motivation. The officers had a hard time trying to instil discipline into the men; however, some of the Irishmen, in particular those who had only joined for a lark, spent most of their time brawling. But they hadn't considered the tough army sergeants with their years of rigorous training, who had more authority than the wayward men in both strength and the power given them by the government. The rowdiness was soon stilled.

Nevertheless, Nicholas and a few of his comrades obstinately remained inherently civilian, not wishing to become 'proper soldiers'; they were merely kinsmen answering the call for fighting men for, what they hoped, was to be a very short period of their lives. Naturally, they had no problem fighting; it was just that they saw no point in the parade ground discipline beforehand.

Over a few weeks, the army did manage to knock into shape some of the new recruits who were constantly bombarded with the message that they had now taken the King's shilling and were the property of the British Army, and that they would only be released at the end of the conflict either intact or in a coffin.

But by now Nicholas was getting tired of being 'knocked into shape' and was having second thoughts, wondering why on earth he had even contemplated fighting for the English? What had they ever done for the Irish other than take their land from them? He now had fire in my belly and was determined not to allow these English bastards to bully him anymore.

There were plenty of horror stories going around the camp from the returning injured soldiers, often with graphic descriptions of the fighting in the trenches, and from this Nicholas knew what to expect. There was also talk of men who, being so traumatised by combat, had shot off a big toe, taking away their balance, so of course making it impossible to continue fighting at the Front. After a short time in barracks jail, these men had gladly accepted an ignominious discharge. Well, none of this was going to happen to him. He wasn't going to stay around to do the dirty work of the English.

One night he didn't return to the camp after his day's leave spent drinking in the nearby town. With no papers, and still in uniform, he had to use his Irish guile to avoid being picked up by the Military Police who seemed to be everywhere. Eventually arriving back in Yorkshire, he sought out some friends and went on a much-needed 'bender' spending the next three days drinking.

When Nicholas eventually turned up at his home in the early hours one morning Bridget, rather than being glad to see him, was angry, even having the temerity to ask him where on earth he'd been? Where did she think he'd been? She went on and on about having had two terrifying visits from the Military Police who had told her that Nicholas had deserted. She said the men had put the fear of God into her and the children, by threatening them with everything from being thrown into jail to being sent back to Ireland. Well, lucky them! Apparently, if Nicholas turned up, she was told she had to contact the police.

'Oh woman, will ye just shut up! I'm sick to death o' hearin' ye moanin' and groanin'. Just shut up and stop yer nagging. All ye ever think about is yerself. Have ye any idea what it's been like these past few months?'

Bridget was shocked to hear what her husband was saying: 'But Nicholas, ye've never even left the country to do any fightin'. D' ye know what it's been like here whilst ye've been away? They've stopped me army money, an' all I have in the world is me bit of wages. God on earth, what's the matter wi' ye?'

Not liking being crossed, particularly by a woman, he said, 'Another word out of ye an' I'll wipe the floor wi ye. D' ye think I'm goin ter get meself killed fer a country fer which I've no love? I've seen too many wounded men in the town ter put meself' in that position. At least I didn't shoot me big toe off, like Jimmy Briggs just so that he'd be discharged. D' ye think I'm stupid, woman?'

After listening to her whining for long enough Nicholas decided he'd had enough and needed to get out, telling Bridget he would be leaving soon so that their neighbours wouldn't be aware he was back, though they probably already knew he was back as he thought Bridget's voice was like a foghorn. He needed to leave before the bairns got up so there would be no need to explain anything to them. Telling her he was hungry and wanted to eat before he left, Bridget quickly put some left-over soup into a pan, placing it onto the fire to heat up.

As he ate, Nicholas couldn't take his eyes off Bridget, wondering what she was thinking. Perhaps it was to the good he didn't know.

Without him asking, she opened her purse and gave him what she said was the last of her money. But it was nothing, just a few pence. 'Ugh, this woman! Is that all she thinks I'm worth? Giving me a pittance after me killing meself for her all these years.' He thought. Anyway, he was going to have the last laugh. She didn't know it, but he had his own stash of money, just so long as it was still there. Walking over to the large oak chest of drawers beside the fireplace he pulled it away from the wall locating a tin which he had secreted on the floor behind the unit. Bringing it out he opened the box in front of her, watching her face as he did so.

'I haven't spent all these years watching you waste me wages and not kept some back. An' I'll keep what you just gave me too as it's God's judgement that you should have to work to make up for what you owe me.'

Nicholas took a stiff drink of whiskey from the bottle he had brought with him and left the house for the last time without a backward glance. He'd had enough!'

Bridget had no idea where Nicholas was going which was probably to the good as, before the day was out, the Military Police had arrived at her door once more asking of his whereabouts. She took their threats in her stride. They couldn't hurt her any more than Nicholas had done.

After getting no information from her, the Military Police visited her neighbours' houses, but on receiving the same short shrift, they returned to Bridget giving her a final warning that, should they return and find Nicholas there, she and he would both suffer the consequences. What consequences? Nothing could be worse than what had just happened.

Nicholas was classed as an absconder, a turncoat, a traitor, and some of Bridget's neighbours, knowing what their own men were going through, initially ignored her, but not for long as they knew enough about Nicholas to know she would have had absolutely no say in what he had done; she was probably suffering more than they were.

LIFE GOES ON

As time went on, the family couldn't believe the peace they felt being free of the man. Bridget had to pinch herself sometimes.

Nothing more was heard from Nicholas, or of his whereabouts, until some ten months later when, out of the blue, a telegram arrived. It was something Bridget had never seen before and she didn't quite know what to make of it. Winifred took the telegram from her mother and hesitantly read the contents: 'NICHOLAS DEAD. MONEY REQUIRED FOR FUNERAL. CONTACT PATSY, COUSIN OF NICHOLAS' with an address in New York. Bridget almost fainted on the spot.

It was only later, after receiving a letter from Patsy, who she'd never heard of before, that Bridget learned that Nicholas, having left her and the children, had sailed to New York and found a cousin he vaguely knew, persuading her to take him in by giving her some cock and bull story about fighting for his beloved Ireland. Whilst in New York, he had become ill with appendicitis and had died on the operating table whilst having his appendix removed. His new American Irish family had now written to Bridget requesting money to cover his hospitalisation costs and funeral expenses. She was penniless.

Out of respect, the children were put into mourning, much to the amusement of Bridget's cousin, Kathleen, and her friends and neighbours. Winifred tried to argue with her mother, saying she was ashamed to have to pretend to be sorry about her father's death. In fact, she said, she wanted to jump for joy each time it dawned on her that he was no longer coming home.

. . .

The country was still in the throes of war. From the start, everyone had been instructed to put thick curtains on their windows and the curtains must be closed every time the room was lit. Bridget knew her old thin cotton curtains wouldn't do, so she searched amongst the rags at work and found two dark blankets, which she hid, taking them home in her bag over a couple of days. With Winnie's help she cut them in half, and hand-sewed the frayed edges making suitable curtains for both sets of windows. She then nailed the blankets up to the window frames and used large safety pins to hold the corners back when they needed daylight. There were signs everywhere saying the enemy should not be able to have any idea of the geography of the land, and the Kelly household obeyed the instruction to a T.

Of course, the bugs in the house thrived in the almost complete darkness, usually only vanishing when the gas light was lit, or if someone made enough noise on entering the room to put the fear of God into them, in which case they would scatter to the nearest crevice and disappear.

The children were old enough now to take over some of the household duties from their mother as she was at that time doing two jobs, trying to keep their heads above water. The younger of the children had small tasks to complete, but Winnie, who was now nearly twelve, had the dreaded chore of getting up early each morning and bringing the fire back to life before the rest of the family came downstairs. Even in summer the fire was necessary, as it was their only means of boiling water.

Winnie hated getting up early in the dark mornings always fearing she would stand on the bugs in her bare feet, and at times, from her bed, Bridget would hear Winnie stomping on the stone floor as she reached the bottom of the stairs giving the bugs notice that she was there.

After stirring-up the fire, which was always carefully banked up the night before, Winnie would put a pan of water directly onto the flames and potter around, waiting for the water to boil. She made sure that there was a mug of tea ready for her mother when she came downstairs, and the remainder of the hot water was usually then used by the family to have a quick morning wash.

From time to time, the black clock beetles would somehow manage to make their way up into the bedroom so, as a precaution, the family were in the habit of checking the bedding nightly before they climbed into bed. With only one room to sleep in, the three younger children slept toe-to-toe in one bed, and Winnie and her mother slept in another. To make sure the beetles stayed out of the beds as much as possible, Bridget put each of the bed feet into old tin cans which contained an inch or so of tar. But the smell of tar was very strong in the bedroom and, at first, they all felt sick, though over time they got used to it.

The beetles fascinated Cormac who would watch, transfixed, as they climbed up the outside of the tin can to the top, but with nowhere to go, they would then plop down into the tar. Once in the sticky substance, the bugs would make a frenzied attempt to climb back up the inside of the can, but their effort was always in vain and they would slowly sink into the gunge. The good boy that he was, Cormac was always ready to help, and there was never any argument when the tins needed emptying.

Bridget was finding it hard to earn enough money to feed and clothe her family who were growing up fast, and prayed that time would pass quickly to Winnie's next birthday as, in December that year, she would be eligible to work part-time in the mill; then the following year, at age thirteen, she could leave school permanently and begin working full time. The nuns at the convent were very good to her knowing her circumstances, and sometimes even the bare necessities of life were gifts from these kind people.

But one Saturday morning, as Bridget was cleaning the convent steps, Mother Mary Martin, the headmistress at school, came by to ask if she could have a quiet word with her. Wiping her wet hands on her apron Bridget followed the nun into a side room, whereupon she was given some very bad news. Apparently, the Education Department had advised the heads of all schools that an Act was in the process of going through Parliament which, if voted in, would make it unlawful for children to leave school until the age of fourteen. This would, of course, affect Winnie.

Bridget was crestfallen; she was in dire need of the extra money and had been relying on Winnie's bit to help with the bills. She was nearly in tears as she resumed her cleaning but, on arriving home, didn't mention the bad news to her eldest daughter.

The Fisher Act of 1918 was being devised to commit children to compulsory education from the ages of four to fourteen. However, to Bridget's relief, the act was not implemented until a further act of 1921 was passed.

At last, 10th December 1918 came, and Winnie was so happy she could hardly wait to get to school to tell the girls that it was her twelfth birthday. Under normal circumstances, it would be just another day and, unless her best friend reminded her, she would usually have forgotten about it. But not this day. This day she would remember forever.

Part Two

1918-1942s

Winnie's Story

WINNIE LEFT SCHOOL AT LAST

Before school broke up for Christmas that year Winnie, and two friends who had also recently celebrated their 12th birthdays, arranged to meet up and go to the local mill together to ask about part-time work. They knew they would need to be on their best behaviour when they met the Over-looker in charge of the relevant department, as there were plenty of other children from the various schools in the area seeking part-time work, and the mill would have its pick of the bunch.

The girls screamed with joy when the boss in charge of the spinning department told the group they would be taken on, although he did stress that they couldn't expect much pay for the first few weeks as they would be learning the work. It didn't matter. They all had jobs!

Winnie was probably happier than most. She had never really liked school, and only felt able to cope with another year until her 13th birthday so long as schooling only took up her afternoons. Even thinking about working in the mill set her pulse racing she was so happy. Just one more year, and then she would be free of education altogether for all the use it had been to her.

. . .

Monday, 6th January 1919, two months after the World War One ceasefire agreement was signed, and five months before the official end to hostilities with the signing of the Treaty of Versailles on 28th June 1919, was the day Winnie started working half days, aged twelve years and one month. The blackout was still in effect, but no-one seemed to notice now.

On that first day of work, all the girls from school met in town and proceeded along the route to the mill in small groups, picking up more friends from other schools as they went along. Work began at 6.30 a.m., which was hard on some of the girls as they had already walked a couple of miles before they met up.

Even before they reached the bottom of the very long road leading to the mill, they had already settled into best-friend pairings, and now walked up the road arm in arm. The excitement was infectious, and if one of them giggled the ripple of emotion instantly spread to the other girls. The nearer they got to the mill the more high-spirited they felt.

The bustle around the mill yard was hypnotic. Women were running and jostling with the men, shocking the girls with their rude banter as they fought for supremacy on the iron steps leading to the various entrances to the mill housings. The noises coming out from the mill levels was so loud that, even from outside, everyone had to shout to be heard.

Once inside, the machines were delivering their own rhythmic commands... *hurry up now, hurry up now, I've waited too long, I've waited too long... I'm waiting for you, I'm waiting for you, rat-a-tat-tat, rat-a-tat-tat* ... and on and on they went.

To begin with, the work the part-timers were given was very easy. They picked off the bobbins of wool from the long machines as they became full, replacing the spindles with empty bobbins. The people doing this work were called 'Doffers'.

But as the weeks went by and they grew more competent, the girls progressed to the work of the Pieceners – the spinning section – where they were taught to mend broken threads on the spindles which often broke as they were stretched, twisted and spun. The broken ends had to be instantly repaired, which was done by twisting the thread to make a flat knot. This required nimble fingers, and woe betide anyone who didn't do it the correct way as the knot must not show on the woven woollen piece. A poorly repaired knot was called a 'slub'. However, if the knot wasn't caught in time on inspection by the Over-looker, all would not be lost completely, as then it was the job of the Mender to repair the slub. This was a specialised job for which the Mender was paid more than the Spinner.

As part-timers, the girls didn't have their own machines of course; they helped the other pieceners when they had too many broken threads.

After a while, Winnie began to not notice the din of the machines, quickly settling into the work and enjoying listening to the banter between the women.

Her nearest friend at school was Annie and one day Winnie shouted to her over the din: 'Rather than going to school this afternoon, don't you wish you could stay here and do this all the time?'

'No, I damn well don't,' Annie replied, 'and if my mother thinks I'm going to work here for the rest of my life, she has another think coming. I happen to believe I'm not as thick as the rest of you, so I have my eye on another kind of work.'

Winnie smiled to herself. Poor Annie, she lived in another world. Her family was as poor as the rest of them, and the small amount of money she got for working part-time would be needed in her household just as badly as Winnie's home. Oh, such airs and graces. She often wondered if Annie had been born into the wrong family; perhaps the King of England was missing a daughter!

Each day when the noon siren sounded - the signal for the part-timers to stop working - the girls would collect their belongings before making the long return journey out of the mill gates, and back to their various schools to begin their useless lessons. The only day they didn't rush out of the mill gates, fearful of being late for school, was on Fridays as that was the day they collected their wage of one shilling.

A few weeks into that year Bridget received a note from Mother Mary Martin to say that, although the Act she had mentioned a few months previously had been voted through Parliament, there was going to be a delay of a year, or possibly two, before it was enacted. Hopefully this would allow Winnie to creep towards her thirteenth birthday before the act was finally implemented. Bridget breathed a sigh of relief at the news; for once in her life everything appeared to be falling into place.

The small amount of money Winnie was bringing home went on food, the cost of which seemed to be rising daily. During the war, to obtain food, each member of the household was issued with a card which was registered with the local butcher and grocer. But often, Bridget didn't have enough money to claim the food allowance on the ration cards.

The Pathé News at the cinema said the idea of rationing food was to guarantee supplies but was not expected to reduce consumption, and this seemed to be successful, as official figures showed the calorie intake hardly changed from pre-war levels. Though in the Kelly household the calorie intake had always been low.

Sugar had been first to be rationed, followed by butcher's meat, butter and cheese; eventually, margarine was added to the list. However, butter and margarine remained rationed until 1920.

In December 1919, Winnie was elated to reach the age of thirteen and now able to leave school forever. That year Christmas went by in a haze.

Bridget was also happy that Christmas. In her mind, she was already spending the extra money Winnie would soon be bringing into the house, even allowing herself to daydream that the extra shillings would enable the family to move from their present small hovel to one of the larger hovels just around the corner.

In 18 months, Cormac would hopefully start half-time work in the mill too alongside his sister, unless of course the dreaded Fisher Education Act of 1918 came into force before then. Likewise, Winnie's other siblings were growing up fast: Alice, the youngest, was almost six and Mary nearly eight. Cormac was growing into a strong, handsome boy, and Bridget marvelled at his stoicism as, despite the treatment he had received from their father, he thrived.

After Sunday Mass one day, as Bridget and Winnie were leaving church, they were approached by the nun who taught Cormac in class and she began singing his praises. 'Oh, he's such a bright boy, Bridget. He could easily pass his eleven-plus examination you know. Have you thought about sending him to grammar school?'

Turning to look at her mother, wondering what she was going to say, Winnie saw the pained expression on her face which usually meant she felt she was either being put upon, or being pushed into doing something she either didn't want to do or couldn't afford to do.

'Now, Sister, from where on earth d' yer think I could get money to send him to grammar school? Sure, it's difficult enough gettin' the money together to buy me children Sunday clothes, never mind school uniform for Cormac. Oh, it's a nice thought, but ye have to put it out of yee'r mind I'm afraid, sister.'

Yes, Winnie thought it was a great pity too, and sad for her brother; but when the time came the household was going to need his wages just as much as hers and Mary's. Hopefully the nuns wouldn't mention anything about this to Cormac at school.

But the church didn't give up so easily, and Bridget was waylaid by one of the priests the following weekend, who again brought up the subject.

'Ye're bein' a stubborn lady, ye know, Bridget,' said Father O'Dea, who was a lovely man with a twinkle in his eyes. 'Now, not too many people know this, but the church has a small stipend from the bishop to be used in cases like Cormac's, which would take care of the school uniform if ye could see ye'r way. to making any other payment that might come along.'

For once, Bridget was struck dumb for a few seconds; however, gathering her thoughts together, she again tried to explain. 'But, Father, it's not just the uniform. Ye know that I have little money comin' into the house other than the bit I'm paid and the wee bit of money that Winnie, and eventually Cormac, will bring in. And when Mary and Alice are old enough, sure, I'll be needin' their money too to help keep our heads above water. I know ye mean well, but it's 'no' and it will always be 'no'. Please, Father, can we say that's the end of it?

'No, it can't be time to get up!' Winnie looked around the bedroom, noticing that her siblings were still sleeping. She could hear her Mother pottering about downstairs and imagined she was probably getting ready to leave for Mass. Even on Sunday there's no rest for the wicked, she thought.

Climbing out of bed, trying not to waken her siblings, she dressed quickly and crept downstairs.

'Mam?' she whispered.

Bridget appeared at the opening wearing her only decent coat, a headscarf pulled tightly around her head making her look old for her thirty-nine years. Winnie suddenly felt a pang of sadness.

'I was just about ter call ye. I'm off to church now so ye get yerself off to the Fox and Hounds an' start the cleanin' an' I'll take over after Mass.'

As she opened the door, Bridget turned to glance at her daughter. Winnie smiled at her, but her mother didn't return the smile. Watching her pass through the door, Winnie's sadness intensified. Her mother looked pale and drawn; her teeth must be playing up again, she thought.

The hot tea was always welcome first thing in the morning, but sometimes the shock of the heat would exacerbate Bridget's toothache, at times making the pain almost too much to bear. Although she went to great lengths to keep this to herself, careful not to inflict further worries on her already tired daughter, Winnie wasn't blind and could see for herself the ageing effect the pain had on her mother's face. Oh, Mother, what's going to happen to you?

Going over to the long cupboard near the sink Winnie took out a packet of salt putting it on the shelf above the fire. Hopefully Bridget would notice it when she came back. There were no onions in the house so her mother would have to make do with a salt-and-hot-water mouth swill for now. Chewing a small piece of onion seemed to take away the toothache for a longer time and Winnie made a mental note to buy one the following day. It was time her mother went down to the hospital to have more teeth removed, but she understood why she resisted doing so, knowing how stressful the experience was.

Drinking the remnants of her mother's cold tea, and wishing she had time to eat a small piece of bread remembering that the smell of stale beer always made her 'gip', she quickly reached for her coat and hat. 'It's my own fault for not getting up earlier,' she said to herself.

Quietly closing the door behind her, she set off on her regular Sunday journey to the public house, to do a job she loathed although she could never make this feeling known to her mother. It was a long walk, and her shoes were badly in need of repair. The cardboard she had put into them a few weeks earlier to cover the holes in the soles had begun to disintegrate from sweat, and tiny bits of paper had formed into balls, which now hurt her feet as she walked along. Thank goodness it wasn't raining. Arriving at the first field, Winnie was sorely tempted to remove her shoes and walk barefoot, but that would mean removing her stockings as well. Then what? To put everything back on again when she reached the road, and then remove shoes and stockings on reaching the next field? She didn't think so. It was best to push on and, anyway, there would surely be a nice piece of cardboard somewhere in the cellar at the Fox and Hounds.

With great relief, the inn finally came into view, encouraging her to walk faster and she was almost out of breath by the time she reached the building. Knowing the front main door was always locked, it only being opened at noon for customers, Winnie walked along the side of the building and round to the back. There, the door was unlocked, and she entered; her senses were immediately attacked by the strong odour of ale and the fog from the smoke that hadn't had time to dissipate from the previous night. The two intermingling smells now caused her eyes and nose sting.

Taking off her 'Sunday' coat and hat she reluctantly hung them on one of the hooks on the wall inside the door hoping the smell wouldn't linger on the cloth. Then removing her shoes and stockings, she surveyed the damage to the underside of the shoes surprised at how large the holes had become.

'I wonder if I should look for a piece of cardboard now before I begin workin'', she said to no-one in particular.

But the smell was really getting to her this morning so the sooner she worked the quicker she could leave.

Putting the shoes on the floor underneath her coat the decision had been made; the cardboard would have to wait until she had finished her cleaning and before she started the trek back over the fields to her Sunday Mass.

Bending, Bridget picked up the hem of her skirt putting some of the cloth to her mouth and nose. Then, taking a deep breath she proceeded bare foot along the corridor to the Tap Room, unlatching the door to a scene that made her heart sink.

For once, there hadn't been a fight the previous evening, so the furniture was intact, but she could see a heap of burnt sawdust where someone had accidentally dropped a still-lit Wild Woodbine cigarette butt onto it. Smiling to herself, she could imagine the panic when the wood caught alight, as there was plenty of sawdust on the stone floor that morning.

Carefully tiptoeing across the room, she reached the far side without any hitches and opened the cellar door. On a small shelf on the wall inside the door there was a candle in a holder and a small box of matches. Lighting the candle, Winnie curled her hand around the flame and began the descent into the bowels of the building, stepping carefully in her bare feet, hoping to avoid any sleeping insects. At the bottom of the steps, she stood to gather her thoughts. First things first!

Putting the candlestick on top of a beer barrel beside the steps, she picked up a cloth bag that was always kept behind the barrel and gave it a good shake. Oh good, there were no spiders today!

The bag contained an old dress large enough to wear over her Sunday clothes protecting them from any dirt. There was also a very old pair of her mother's shoes which she wore when kneeling down washing floors; the constant scraping along the stone floor as she moved around caused havoc to the toes of her decent shoes. As Winnie was putting the shoes on, she glanced at the soles reflecting that they actually looked in remarkably better condition than her own, although the tops were reminiscent of her brother's shoes after he had kicked a ball around for a few hours!

Collecting the cleaning bucket, Winnie checked that it contained the scrubbing brush and block of carbolic soap necessary to wash the floors. Her other cleaning equipment – sweeping brush, dustpan, Brasso and cleaning cloths – were all at the top of the steps near the door.

The bucket was awkward to carry alongside the lighted candlestick, but she managed it with care not wanting to find herself in the dark when only halfway up the stairs. Reaching the top of the steps, she blew out the candle and put the candlestick back on the shelf in readiness for her mother to use.

Taking another deep breath, Winnie re-entered the Tap Room. Surprisingly it didn't smell nearly as bad the second time around and she was even able to hum her favourite tunes as she swept the sawdust into small piles before picking up the heaps with a shovel. As she worked the humming soon turned into a low tuneful whistle.

There wasn't a lot of time to spare and, once the debris had been cleared away, she attacked the floor with water noticing that by now the water she had boiled in the back kitchen was only lukewarm. Ah well, with a bit of elbow grease, it would be good enough to clean up the horrible spittle in front of the bar. The flagstones bordering the walls and the bar itself were a burnt orange colour from the soft stone burnish she put on them each week after she had finished scrubbing. After many years of doing this the stone had taken on a hue that, no doubt, would be impossible to remove.

By now drenched with sweat she hurriedly finished cleaning the floor, occasionally wiping her forehead on her work dress. There was a lot still to do before going off to Mass.

The mirrors behind the bar were yet again spattered with dead flies and would need cleaning. Blowing out her frustration, Winnie thought it was a pity the bar staff didn't realise, when using the insects for target practice, that insect blood hardens and, between the weekly clean, it was a hell of a job to remove it. Perhaps the smell of ale and whiskey attracted the insects to the mirrored glass in the first place, but cleaning it was a thankless task.

After cleaning the mirrors, there wasn't time left to clean the outside toilets so, sadly, this distasteful job would have to be left for her mother.

Donning her shoes and stockings once more, Winnie took down her coat and gave it a good shake before putting it on. She hung the old work dress where her coat had been in readiness for her mother's arrival. Ah, she suddenly remembered – a piece of cardboard for her shoes! She had forgotten to look for some when down in the cellar earlier. But it had taken longer than usual to do her cleaning this day and if she dawdled, she would be late for Mass. The shoes would have to wait.

Passing out through the back door the cold air enveloped her. Standing for a few seconds to allow the sweat on her body to evaporate, she took in the surroundings aware it would be impossible not to find the outside toilets even if she was blind, the stench was overpowering.

Sighing, Winnie closed the door behind her and headed for the fields and church.

Walking along the path, she accidentally trod on an empty Wild Woodbine cigarette packet and stooped to pick it up. Flexing it slightly it felt strong enough to replace the shredded inner soles of her shoes. Making the sign of the cross, she said, 'Oh, there is a God after all!' It was perfect. Laughing she balanced, one foot at a time, as she took off each shoe to remove the old pieces of cardboard. Quickly sliding off the sleeve of the cigarette packet and using the old card as a template, she tore the card into the shape of the left shoe. Repeating the exercise with the remaining cardboard from the packet on the other shoe, Winnie seemed quite pleased at her handiwork. But before putting the old cardboard with its new friend back into the shoes, she once more emptied them of all the tiny rolled-up balls that had rubbed off the old cardboard.

Realising how much time she had spent on this, she began to hurry, hoping she would get to Mass before the priest mounted the pulpit. Meeting her mother before reaching the church she didn't have time to stop and chat. But no doubt Bridget would know the toilets at the inn needed cleaning without the need for her daughter to say anything.

Once Mass was over, Winnie headed straight for home. Whilst her mother finished cleaning at the public house, her job was to prepare the Sunday meal for the family.

Getting back after the hard work at the inn and the long walk afterwards, she was exhausted and really wasn't in the mood for silly pranks. 'If the kids aren't up and ready for church, there'll be hell to pay,' she muttered to herself as she walked through the doorway. Cormac and Mary were up but, as usual, Alice was missing. Feeling too weary to run upstairs to drag the bedclothes off her little sister, Winnie stood at the bottom of the steps and, using her newly found 'mill voice', raised the roof, shouting, 'For God's sake, get up, Alice.' Alice was no doubt hiding under the bedclothes, using the cat as a hot water bottle. 'You'd better not still be in bed when me mother gets back,' was her last comment as she walked back into the scullery.

Cormac, now the man of the house, was always eager to help, particularly if it meant annoying his younger sister, and he swiftly disappeared upstairs. Shortly afterwards, there were shouts from Alice telling him not to pull the bedclothes off her, culminating in an audible argument. Eventually, Cormac scurried back downstairs, followed by the cat, after which Alice was heard stamping on the floor as she got out of bed.

'I can't imagine what she'll be like once she starts slogging at work like mother and me, having to get up at five-thirty in the mornings,' Winnie found herself muttering. She was doing a lot of that these days.

Busying herself assembling the ingredients for the Yorkshire pudding, which she normally prepared in advance of the rest of the meal, Winnie hadn't noticed at first that the fire wasn't burning very strongly. Now, becoming aware of it she silently fumed. Glancing at Cormac she thought 'someone in this household isn't doing their job properly'.

Without anyone noticing, Alice had dressed, had come downstairs, and was now standing beside Mary, holding onto her coat and hopping from one leg to the other.

'Alice, what's the matter? Have you've got St Vitus's dance?' Mary was getting agitated. Shaking Alice's hand off she walked to the door.

'Ooh Mary, that hurt! Anyway, I need to wee!'

'Alice! You do choose your moments. Go on then, but don't be long.'

Unfortunately, she ran outside just as the toilet began the process of flushing, and Winnie's stomach did a jump to coincide with the noise she heard. The toilet only flushed when water from the low kitchen sink had fed enough water-waste onto the paddle to move it, and the paddle was now turning over like a water wheel. Alice got frightened if the water wheel turned over whilst she was sitting on their high toilet with its big wooden seat, as she said she was fearful it might suck her down. Winnie was tempted to ask Mary to see to her, but hesitated, as Alice was forever being told she was a baby, and that by now, aged six, she should have outgrown some of her fears.

'Alice! Where are ye?' Mother was back home from her cleaning job.

Fortunately, Alice had already used the toilet and was out in the yard, and about to re-enter the house as Mary and Cormac were leaving. Without a word, they each took one of Alice's arms, turned her around, and marched her out of the gate and onto the cobbled street.

'Wait, wait, wait! She hasn't got her hat on.' Bridget had noticed as they passed the window that Alice was bare headed. Rushing out to the yard she handed the hat to her over the wall.

Bridget was tired to the point of exhaustion and would have loved to have rested for a few minutes, but she knew that her eldest daughter was also tired yet was busying herself preparing the meal. Whilst Winnie attended to the meal, Bridget began to occupy herself with the fire, poking the cinders into an orange flame onto which she put a small amount of coal slack. The fire picked up nicely and was soon ready to be shoved into the fissure underneath the oven itself.

Sunday afternoon was the only leisure time Winnie got, though as usual some of that time would be spent ironing, and she had earlier placed two flat irons on the fire ready for the task to come.

By Monday morning Winnie was completely worn out, and the thought of another week's work in the mill was not appealing. It was Harry, the passing mechanic, who cheered her up that day, saying, 'By gum lass, tha' must've 'ad a rare owd weekend; tha' looks as tho tha's spent most of it I' bed.' Winnie roared with laughter at the thought of spending most of the weekend lounging in bed; not in the Kelly household. It made her guffaw each time she remembered the comment. Oh, if only he knew!

Cecil, the spinning department Over-looker, was as hard as nails, and he watched the girls like a hawk. Because of the noise of the machines, they had learned to lip read, which meant telling their stories with exaggerated mouth movements. Winnie was busy walking up and down the line past her spinning bobbins when she noticed Nora from another machine waiving frantically at her to get her attention. 'I'm going to t'toilet,' she mouthed slowly. Nodding assent, Winnie watched as Nora walked away, cigarettes and matches half-hidden in her hand. She didn't care that people thought she was low life for smoking; it was becoming fashionable to smoke, and anyway, she enjoyed her cigarettes.

Nora had not noticed that Cecil was down at the far side of the room watching her. However, Winnie had spotted him, and caught him glancing at his wristwatch. After about five minutes, when Nora hadn't returned, Cecil came up to her just as she was frantically trying to re-tie the broken yarns from Nora's long machine, at the same time keeping an eye on her own.

'Who told 'er she could go off like that?' He was a big man with a voice to match.

The girls had realised long ago that their boss didn't have a sense of humour, and it was no use saying anything cheeky, so Winnie merely said. 'She was desperate.'

'No, she wa'nt! She wer' carryin' summat, probably her cigs an' a box of matches. Ah saw her.'

Winnie was now tempted to say something smart like, 'Well, doesn't it depend on what she wanted to do in the toilet, as to how long it takes?' But thinking better of it, she merely turned back to Nora's machine and tried to catch another yarn that had broken.

'Seethee lass. Tha'd better keep 't bobbins full, or I'll have thy guts fer garters. An' go an' tell Nora that if she ain't out o' there i' two minutes, then she'd better collect 'er cards from t' office.' The remarks had caught the ear of Peggy, who was working on an opposite machine, and she waved Winnie on towards the toilet. Somehow, Peggy would look after two extra machines in her absence.

Running into the toilet, she found Nora leaning against the wall smoking, deep in conversation with another girl. Inwardly seething at Nora's lack of consideration for anyone other than herself, Winnie had to gulp twice before speaking.

'Bloody come on, will yer; stop filly fartin' about and get back to yer machine. Cecil says that if yer not back in one minute, yer can go an collect yer cards.'

She felt she had already used up one of the Over-looker's minutes running to the toilet although, surely, he didn't really expect her to be responsible for someone else's inertia. It irritated her so much that whilst she was trying to keep her own job and working herself into the ground, someone else didn't care and seemed to assume her workmates would put themselves out to protect her, despite probably getting a bad reputation themselves for doing so.

Hastily following Winnie out of the toilet, Nora ran to her machine. She couldn't see the Over-looker but knew that, in all probability, he could see her.

When the 5.30 p.m. buzzer sounded, Winnie was so glad, though, like the rest of the hands, she had to wait until the night-shift worker arrived to take over the machine, which was in motion twenty-four hours a day and sometimes seven days a week.

Tom, the night Over-looker, was talking to Cecil, and she wondered what was being discussed.

Bending down, pretending to fasten her shoelace, she surreptitiously glanced underneath her machine. The half-full bobbin she had thrown under earlier could just about be seen. The threads had broken too many times to be allowed through to the next process, so Winnie had 'wanged' it as far as she could, hoping it would lay there until the next shutdown when all the machines were cleaned. But if she could see it, then perhaps others could see it as well. Watching Tom walk towards her, she felt butterflies in her stomach.

'Who's been a naughty girl, then?' he grinned. Oh goodness, her heart sank. But Tom continued, 'Ahve bin 'earin' things about thee an' Nora from t'overlooker. Tha should be careful lass. He's not one t' be messed wi tha' knows.'

With that, he strode off along the line of bobbins, picking up a broken thread and twisting it into a moving yarn again before moving on. Winnie breathed a sigh of relief.

Heading for home, walking through the empty fairground and past the houses at the bottom of the field, she felt the cold of winter for the first time, and her immediate thoughts went to the bugs and her dread of them. Apart from their smell, which seemed to permeate the house, very few had been seen during the summer. Of course, they preferred the dark and, anyway, they would be using the summertime to multiply. Oh goodness, how she hated living on The Hill. Where was the dashing prince on his charger? Unfortunately, she was a Plain Jane; therefore, he would probably charge straight past her without a backward glance. None of the men at work, married or otherwise, gave her a second look, yet she knew from conversations overheard in the toilets that some of the girls were having affairs on a regular basis. That would never happen to her. Ah well, she could but hope!

Sauntering past the Co-op store, she glanced at the main window and saw that the new spring clothes were being displayed. Stopping to take a better look, her gaze immediately rested on the small display of last-season's clothes at the side of the window which had been greatly marked down in price, and she noticed a green dress that looked about her size. It was beautiful and she didn't think it would be too outrageously expensive for her mother to buy.

Taking a few deep breaths to give herself courage, Winnie pushed open the heavy glass door and entered the shop. Although she had walked past the Co-op hundreds of times, it was the first time she had ever been inside. The enormity of the room amazed her. There were mahogany counters all along the left-hand side of the room, and the right-hand side was filled with an array of small dressing rooms between displays of mannequins dressed in the new season's clothes.

An assistant approached her, asking politely if she could be of assistance, and Winnie put on her best Sunday voice to ask to see the green dress in the side window.

Taking the dress from the salesgirl, Winnie went over to one of the small cubicles used for ladies' try-ons and began to undress, glancing furtively in the full-length mirror affixed to the back of the door. There wasn't a full-length mirror at home, so it was a strange reflection that came back to her. Did she really look like her mother as people had now and then reflected; straight and thin with no bust? Yes, she did.

The dress was made of pretty, green woollen material, which matched the colour of her green Irish eyes. There was embroidery around the collar and cuffs, and a pleat at the outside of each shoulder neatly cascading into small gathers across the waist, giving the top a blouson look. Oh, she loved everything about the dress and thought it actually gave her a figure.

Yes, she had to have it! Though now the worry was that she wouldn't be able to get her mother to agree to buy it. In her head, she began justifying to her mother why she should have the dress. Reminding her that, as Mary and Cormac were bringing a little money into the household, they didn't seem quite so poor anymore, and anyway, she would point out that she hadn't had a new 'bought' dress for a long, long time.

Hanging the garment back on its coat hanger, Winnie put it on the hook behind the door and began to dress. Once dressed, she purposefully walked out of the dressing room with the garment over her arm, and towards the counter. The assistant was talking to a colleague nearby but, on seeing her leave the cubicle, proceeded to walk over to the counter, prepared to take the dress away and put it back in the window.

Handing the dress to the assistant, Winnie said: 'Would you be able to put this dress aside for me for a day as I need to speak with me mother about it?' She made her face a picture of innocence, continuing, 'I know she'll like it, but she might want to come in to see me tryin' it on once more.'

The assistant was somewhat taken aback by the request. 'Oh! I'll have to ask my supervisor; that's not a usual request,' she said before rushing over to the office behind the counter. Winnie could see into the room through the open door, and the assistant seemed to be speaking enthusiastically with the supervisor, who kept glancing out at Winnie.

When the assistant came back over to her, she looked miserable. 'I'm really sorry, but my supervisor has told me that we can't put away sale items. If you don't want to buy it now, I'll have to place it back in the window.'

Winnie was so disappointed she was almost in tears and could only utter a soundless 'thanks' as she walked back to the door. But as she was about to pull the large brass handle to open it, the assistant rushed over and, putting a hand over hers, said, 'If you can promise to come back by this time tomorrow, I'll put the dress behind something else in the window and, hopefully, no-one will see it. But of course, I can't promise anything – you will understand, won't you?'

Thanking her quietly, Winnie left the shop with a spring in her step. The next obstacle was her mother. How would she react about the prospective purchase?

Once home, she set about raking the cinders from the fireplace and re-setting the fire with small pieces of wood, which she then lit. Once satisfied the fire was burning well, she took off her work coat and began preparing the vegetables for the meal. Mary was already cutting up the leftover meat from the previous day, setting the table and putting the plates on top of the oven to warm. Everything was ready by the time their mother and the rest of the family were gathered an hour later.

All the time she was preparing the food Winnie had been pondering how she was going to broach the subject of the dress. Realising there was no good or bad way to ask, in the end, during a quiet moment as they were eating their meal, she just blurted out: 'Mam, I've seen a lovely dress on sale in the Co-op window. On the way home from work I noticed it, so I went inside and tried it on. It fits me perfectly. They've put it aside for a day so that I can ask you if I can have it.' What's a little fib, she thought!

Preparing herself for an argument, she had begun to formulate a counter argument in defence, but was taken aback when her mother just said, 'All right, Winnie, just so long as it's not too much an' I can pay weekly. It'll also need t' be big enough t' last a few years, bearin' in mind ye'll be growin' a bit more I've no doubt. But I'll need t' see it for meself to make sure it's the right dress. If ye like, we can meet up tomorrow after work. Now get on wi yer meal, there's plenty of work t' do before bed. Have ye put a pan of water on the fire for the washing up yet?'

Just as suddenly the conversation changed, and the dress was forgotten for a time, but Winnie's memory was good enough to remind her mother again when she was lying in bed, fatigued from the day, but happy.

She got the dress the following evening but not until she had had an argument with her mother, who thought it wasn't big enough to take any expansion she might have in the coming two or three years.

Having won the argument, the dress was bought and worn, and was eventually passed down to Mary who, after she had worn it for a time, passed it down to Alice, who finally wore it out.

THE SURPRISE RELATIVE

This was the year their daily routine was to be sorely tested. Just as the Kelly family thought they had turned the corner, having finally moved to a house with two bedrooms in the same vicinity on The Hill, and they were beginning to have a little money spare for the occasional treat, out of the blue came a letter with a County Kildare, Eire, postmark. Bridget was puzzled. She didn't know anyone in Kildare. Opening the letter, she slowly read the contents:

The Little Sisters of the Soul of Mercy
Kildare
Eire

24th October 1924

Dear Mrs Kelly,

We have been advised that you are the only living relative of Miss Nellie Kelly who, at the age of sixteen, is now obliged to leave the convent and make her own way in the world. We would be grateful, therefore, if you could reply to this letter advising if you will be able to take Nellie into the bosom of your home.

Nellie is capable of working, providing she has some supervision and we, the Sisters, believe she will be better off in a family rather than continuing her life in another institution.

An early reply would be appreciated.

Yours faithfully,

Sister Mother Mary

It took a few seconds for Bridget to understand what she had just read. The nuns seemed to be saying they were expecting her to take on the care of a girl she had never even heard of. How can they expect her to do that? And what did they mean 'to take her into the bosom of your home'?

Seeing her mother's expression Winnie took the letter from her and, after reading it, gave her mother an irritated look.

'Mam, yer don't have to answer this. You don't know these people and they don't know you, though goodness knows how they got our name and address. You don't think the convent here had anything to do with it d' yer?'

Putting the letter down, she walked away in disgust. 'Just imagine; did the nuns really think we'll take in a stranger just because we've got the same name? There must be thousands of Kelly's in Ireland, what makes 'em think we're related to this Kelly? They can't just foist somebody onto us by making us feel guilty about her bein' in a home, and just when we're getting on our feet. Where in heaven's name would she sleep? My God! The cheek of it.'

But it was slowly dawning on Bridget that the girl was probably related to Nicholas somehow, though she could never remember him mentioning her. Brightening up, she said, 'Look, Winnie, I'm just thinkin' this, so hear me out. If we took Nellie in, things in the house wouldn't be too different from the way they are now. We've a house with two bedrooms with plenty of beds in them, and Cormac could sleep downstairs on the large drop-arm settee. If things worked out, we could even start lookin' fer a better house. It mightn't be too bad. The girl's old enough to work in the mill so would be bringin' extra money in. Can't ye see? There's always light at the end of the tunnel. The children would soon get used to muckin' in and I know they would accept it if they could see an advantage to themselves. What d' yer think?'

Winnie was seething and walked away, refusing to reply to her mother. Noticing this, Bridget knew better than to push the matter just then, so she changed the subject and the letter was duly put into a drawer and quietly forgotten; or so Winnie thought. But a few weeks later, Bridget found a reason to bring the matter up again.

'Ye know, Winnie, it's a bad thing we're doin' here, leavin' that poor girl in the orphanage. She must be yer father's relative after all and if he was here, sure he would be insistin' that we take her in. She's ye're own flesh an' blood. The poor girl has lived all her life in an orphanage without any love from a mother and father. Ye don't appreciate how lucky ye are.'

As her mother spoke, Winnie glanced at her judging her expression. 'My God', she thought, 'I'm in awe of this woman; how could she make such a statement with a straight face? Didn't she realise the irony of what she had just said? "The love of a mother and father." What was all that about?'

She nearly laughed, but instead replied in the same vein: 'I know, Mam, and it must've been hard for her not havin' a lovin' home like ours. But I still don't think we should just take the nuns at their word and accept the girl, without first doin' some checkin'.'

However, unbeknown to the children, Bridget had already been doing some checking as, shortly after receiving the letter, and the next time she was at the presbytery doing her weekly cleaning, she had shown the letter to Father O'Dea, who said he would give the orphanage a call and then let her know what he found out. But, in the meantime, he suggested she do nothing about it. So, quietly, their mother let them think the letter had been unimportant. Nevertheless, the news the priest gleaned from the nuns was that Nellie was in fact related to Nicholas, and the girl was going to be put out of the orphanage in the next few months whether she wanted to leave or not. There was no work nearby and at sixteen, almost seventeen, the sisters thought she was now capable of looking after herself. They told Father O'Dea that they would prefer to place her with family, or friends of family.

Bridget had accordingly given Father O'Dea her reply to pass on to the orphanage.

Having accepted it would take more persuasion to get Winnie, in particular, to agree to have Nellie live with them, the discussion with Father O'Dea hadn't at first been mentioned at home. However, the time had now come to say something as the priest warned Bridget that the girl was on the point of being removed from the orphanage and sent to her Yorkshire family. Whatever the outcome, it seems Nellie would not be allowed to return to the convent. The deed was done so far as Bridget was concerned.

One evening, whilst the family were sitting having a meal, Bridget began to explain the situation to them, laying it on thick about the poor girl being thrown out of the convent with only the clothes on her back, and comparing the poor girl to them. Looking at her eldest daughter, Bridget expected another explosion. But what could Winnie say!

'Mother, I know that we have to accept Nellie now, but I'm not happy about it, particularly as she's nearly my own age. It's bad enough having two women in the house with conflicting ideas about how things should be done without having a third person interfering. I know you've already said yes mam so, as far as I can see, the die is cast!'

Of course, Mary and Cormac, hearing about Nellie for the first time, were excited at the thought of another 'sister', whilst Alice was happy because her big sister and brother were happy.

Arrangements were made and eventually Nellie was on her way to England for the first time. Without a photograph of their new relative the family could only speculate about her appearance, but it was a shock when they actually saw her in the flesh. Her face had a vacant look and her speech and movements were laboured. Someone had cut her hair, but Winnie speculated later that they must have used a kitchen knife. All in all, Nellie was not at all as they had imagined, and Winnie realised immediately that she had no competition.

Picking up the small canvas bag her new relation had been carrying, Winnie looked over at her mother and shook her head. What in God's name were they doing?

Nellie seemed younger than her sixteen years and Bridget soon realised too that there was something not quite right with the girl; she was slow to answer when spoken to, and always turned her face away, appearing incapable of looking into anyone's eyes. Nor could she take part in normal conversations; whenever she was forced into a discussion, she would stutter and stammer and sometimes just walk away. Only Mary was able to relate to her. They giggled when together in bed and seemed to have their own private jokes. If Nellie was asked to do something around the house, Mary invariably helped her, but no-one interfered, in the hope that soon Nellie would get into the routine.

After a few weeks, by which time Bridget felt Nellie would have had time to settle in, she took Winnie to one side and asked her: 'What do ye think of Nellie's chances of workin' with ye in the mill? Would she be able to do the job d'ye think?'

Winnie's heart sank. 'Mam, how can she work wi' me in the mill? It took me long enough to learn the ropes, so I don't know how Nellie could do it. And I'd die of embarrassment if the Over-looker eventually had to fire 'er from the job in front of all me friends. Oh Mam, can't you take 'er wi' you ? Or why can't Mary take her wi' 'er?'

But Bridget was already walking away, muttering under her breath: 'No, I can't take her wi' me, Winnie, an' if ye don't want her then...' leaving the final phrase unsaid. Suddenly feeling ashamed of herself, Winnie was aware that Nellie was probably within hearing of their conversation, although, to be honest, she could never quite tell what Nellie understood as she appeared to live in a world of her own. Accepting there would be no way of avoiding a confrontation if she continued to complain, Winnie began rehearsing what she would say to the Over-looker at work.

The following morning, having already explained to Nellie what was going to happen, Mary got up bright and early and helped her new best friend to get ready for the interview at the mill. As usual, Mary was talkative, making jokes about everything and trying to cheer Nellie up. But Nellie and Winnie were both in pensive moods, not reacting to Mary's jokes. Winnie knew how she felt but didn't know how Nellie felt! And what about her mother? Was Bridget hiding out of sight waiting until the three of them had left. Well, maybe sometimes the only way to fix something is to break it yourself, she thought.

Her reflective quietness continued as they walked along the road to the mill and by the time the large red building came into view Winnie's heart was pounding. Briefly acknowledging her work colleagues and saying goodbye to Mary, Winnie led Nellie across the dirt yard and to the iron steps which led up the side of the building to her work area. As usual, Cecil was standing just inside the door at the top of the stairs ready to catch any late mongers out but noticing Winnie with another young lady he hadn't seen before seemed to confuse him a little.

'Na then lass, what's goin' on?'

Having rehearsed for so long what she was going to say, she now found all the words had disappeared and in their place was a stuttering, stammering, explanation about Nellie and her needs.

Cecil trusted Winnie. She was one of his good workers who didn't slack like some of them, and after just a few basic questions about Nellie, together with an assurance that Nellie would do her best and that Winnie wouldn't get too mulish if she wasn't suitable, he accepted to give the girl a trial run the next morning.

That evening, taking Mary to one side, Winnie explained that Nellie was going to be given a trial workday at the mill the following day and asked if she would explain this to Nellie, telling her also that she would need to be up early again.

There was a lot of whispering in bed that night but no frets.

Waking very early the following morning, wanting to be sure that Nellie was awake in good time, Winnie noticed that Nellie's side of the bed in which she and Mary slept was empty, which sent shockwaves through her body. What if, after all, she had been so traumatised at the thought of millwork that she had run away? Dashing downstairs, she nearly tripped over Nellie waiting patiently near the door, already dressed in her outdoor clothes. With relief, she rushed back upstairs ready to usher Mary out of bed, but she too was up now.

After a quick rinse of faces and a quick bite to eat, the three of them set off on the long walk to the mill.

That day, they again walked along the road in awkward silence, and it was a relief to catch up with some of Winnie's work colleagues who asked who their companion was. After briefly introducing Nellie, Winnie picked up the pace of her work friends, now walking along with them and chatting about the last film they had seen.

Occasionally glancing back to make sure Mary and Nellie were keeping up with their long strikes, she saw that Nellie was already in her own little world, her eyes fixed on the ground as she quietly counted the cracks between the pavement squares. Mary too had observed this and, having hooked her arm through Nellie's, was copying her.

Arriving at the mill, it was difficult not to fall into step with the mass of workers as they thronged through the huge mill gates, like a herd of sheep being corralled into a yard by an invisible dog. Once through the gates, everyone began dispersing to their various locations.

Mary, seeing her friends in the distance, unhooked herself from Nellie's arm and pushed her way towards the group but, shortly before disappearing into the throng, she turned and waved to Nellie and her sister, leaving Winnie feeling awkward and solitary in the mass of people.

Taking Nellie by the arm as Mary had done, Winnie guided her towards a group of workers who were climbing the iron steps to the room that had now become a second home to her. Once inside, the talk quietened somewhat, as the heavy machines demanded attention, drowning out the chatter.

Removing Nellie's coat and hanging it next to hers on an empty nail on the wall leading to the ladies' toilet, she took a deep breath, and walked back along the line of machines, seeking out the Over-looker once more. She found him standing at the top of the stairs they had just climbed, timepiece in hand, recording the last of the girls to arrive before he closed the inner heavy wooden door. Luckily, she and Nellie had been early, showing good intent.

Seeing them walking towards him, he gave Nellie a cursory glance. ''ow do, again. She's wi' thee lass, so ah'll leave thee to it to show 'er t' ropes.'

Then, presumably satisfied all his girls were present, he put his watch back in his pocket and strode away.

As Winnie and Nellie moved back along the lines of spinning frames, their thousands of spindles noisily rotating, Nellie put her hands up to her ears to try to drown out the din. Rattle, bang, clatter went the machines. Down the rows of machines, the girls were busy, dodging the long mules spinning the fibres into yarn, as they picked up the broken yarn threads and skilfully reunited them, each piece having required three or four rubs between fingers and thumb. They were doing this so fast they made it seem easy, but Winnie knew differently.

The nightman was still at work at her spinning mule when she arrived with Nellie. Explaining about her companion, she asked if he would stay and work extra for five minutes whilst she showed Nellie how the machine worked and what was required. He talked as he walked along the mule, deftly piecing together the yarns, agreeing to stay on condition that Winnie could arrive the following day five minutes earlier to make up for it.

As he worked, Winnie began to explain to Nellie how the machine functioned and what the nightman was doing. To her surprise, after only going over it a few times, Nellie declared she wanted to 'try for herself'. Standing back, they watched as she twisted the two broken yarns together, exactly as she had been shown, taking both yarns (north and south), catching them between her fingers, and skilfully twisting them together by using her index finger, second finger and thumb. The spinning-machine was moving so fast that she missed a few initially and Winnie helped her with the excess broken yarns, but after only a short time, she decided to leave Nellie to it and just get on with her own work.

The girls took their lunchbreaks at the same time, and as soon as she could catch the eye of Cecil, Winnie waved him over.

'Nellie has learned the job quickly an' I can leave her to it now. If the machine she's workin' on is spare can she use it? I'll keep an eye on 'er for a while. And what about givin' 'er the job, then?'

'Well, ah'll 'ave ter take a look tha' knows. Leave it ter me an' I'll cum back ter thee lass.'

Pleased that Cecil was going to take a look at Nellie's work and hopefully give her a job, Winnie was happy, and actually felt inclined to have a proper conversation with Nellie. It was strange talking to someone you have always thought of as 'not quite right', but her smile was contagious.

'Our Mam will be happy if yer get a job; it's hard tryin' to keep the household going with only two and a half wages comin' in, an' I'm sure you'll feel better too as you'll be paying yer way like the rest of us.'

Catching the sight of the Over-looker out of the corner of her eye, Winnie noticed him talking to his boss, and from time to time they looked her way. She held her breath as she saw him leave his boss and walk back over to them with a smile on his face.

Looking at Nellie, he said: 'Ah've looked at what tha've done, lass, an' they're as reight as a bobbin; tha's got t'job.'

As he was leaving, he winked at Winnie, and she watched in fascination as he moved across the room, his slight limp reminding her of a sailor in a storm. As he was walking, he took a packet of cigarettes out of his pocket and headed for the men's toilet.

Over the next few months, Nellie seemed to be losing some of her nervousness and mostly gave the impression she was happily fitting in with the family. But there were also times when she looked painfully sad, particularly if she thought no-one was watching her. Winnie mentioned this to her mother, but she didn't show a great deal of empathy. Bridget had her own problems; usually it was not knowing how she was going to pay the next household bill. She didn't have the time, or the energy left in her to agonise over someone else's mindset.

Cormac and Alice loved Nellie being in the house, treating her like another big sister; if there was a change in her, then they were too young to notice.

Nellie stayed with the family for eighteen months, during which time her melancholy became so obvious that even her own colleagues at work asked why she always looked so sad and miserable. Winnie wondered if she had been institutionalised for far too long; maybe she missed the group of girls she had grown up with. It had become obvious that Nellie's speech was getting more and more difficult to understand but, unfortunately, neither Winnie nor Bridget had the experience or patience to deal with her.

'A'ta'te, are we going to church tomorrow?' Nellie asked one Saturday evening as Winnie was kneeling on the floor beside the bath, rubbing clothes on the rubbing board, sweat pouring down her face.

'Bloody hell, Nellie, yer know we're going to church tomorrow. It's Sunday for God's sake, isn't it? What the hell's matter wi' yer?'

'A'ta'te, bbbut I was only asking, a'ta'te because I nnneed to go to confessions and that's all I was asking for.'

Going over to the settee, on which Mary was sitting wide eyed, Nellie flopped down beside her and began to cry on her shoulder.

Still muttering under her breath Winnie turned to look at Nellie and, as if noticing her for the first time, felt an unexpected surge of pity. The poor girl had been uprooted from the only home she had ever known and dumped into a family who were as alien to her as she was to them. She must have been feeling very lonely, and it didn't help that she had so many personal problems.

Getting up from the floor, she went over to Nellie and, leaning over, put her arms around her to comfort her.

'I'm really sorry, Nellie, I know I shouted at yer, but I didn't mean me voice to sound so harsh. Confessions are probably still on if yer want to have a walk down to church. Mary, why don't yer go with her? I'm sure yer've plenty of sins of yer own to confess!' Winnie tried to smile but she was dog tired and probably looked as bad as she felt.

Mary was a good girl. Instantly jumping up, she wiped the tears from Nellie's eyes with the back of her hand and, smiling, yanked her off the settee, drawing her towards the coats hanging behind the door. Locating Nellie's coat and her own, she took them both off the hook and, turning to Nellie, said, 'Come on, Nell, let's have a race. I bet I can beat yer!' And off they dashed, their coats flying as they bounced through the gate.

Bridget had been standing in the background, silently watching the scene unfold and, although she wasn't prone to showing any emotion, it was impossible not to recognise what Winnie could see with Nellie.

Sighing, Winnie resumed her washing, but with a heavy heart. 'Oh, Mam, what can we do about Nellie? She's so unhappy with us. If it wasn't for Mary, I think she would have run away long ago.'

Bridget walked over to the fire, which was flaming brightly, and stood looking down at the flames for a few seconds. 'Ye know, Winnie, after our talk the other day, a thought that has flashed through me mind a few times since then has just come back to me. Why don't I have a word with Father O'Dea? I was thinkin' Nellie might be happier with employment in service with a family rather than in the mill. I know she's settled into the job, but I think she doesn't like living here with us for some reason. I'll talk with Father tomorrow after Mass. Neither he nor the nuns should think we're not lookin' after Nellie well enough, especially as the nuns and priest knew of the predicament Nellie was in originally. Now don't ye worry, we'll solve the problem for her.'

She didn't notice the tears running down Winnie's cheeks as she bent over the bathtub. 'Oh, Mam I have to ask again - what have we done?' she whispered.

The following day, Winnie went to the early morning Mass with her mother. At the end of the service, and after the final blessing from the priest, they watched as he stepped down the altar steps, along the carpeted aisle, and out of the door into the room at the side of the altar. Bridget leant over to Winnie and whispered: 'I know he's busy, but I do believe our predicament is important and needs his attention, so here we go.'

Waiting a decent amount of time, they left the pew and followed the priest's footsteps into the vestry, expecting to find him there; instead, only the altar boys were there, milling around. Bridget asked one of the boys if Father O'Dea would be free yet, but the priest, on hearing her voice, called them into the 'undressing room' next door, where they found him opening the top drawer of a long unit standing against the wall, above which hung a crucifix. For a moment, he ignored them, silently praying whilst at the same time placing his vestments into the top drawer. He removed the chasuble, carefully folding it in half, then undid the belt that held the stole across his body. Removing the stole, he kissed the cross at the edge before placing it on top of the chasuble in the drawer. Finally, removing the Alb, the long white robe, he draped it over a coat hanger, and hung it behind the half-open door. Standing again for a few seconds, mouthing another prayer, he then closed the drawer. Turning, he gave his visitors his full attention.

Afterwards, Bridget told her daughter that, as she watched the ceremony in the sacristy, her mind had flashed back to the day she had once silently watched a similar ritual, all those long years ago, when she had gone to see the priest to discuss her marriage to her father. If only she had taken the advice the priest had given her!

'Now, what can I do for ye, Bridget and Winnie? Ye look all mithered. What is it?'

As Bridget unburdened herself to the priest, they saw his stance harden. Turning around to the long drawer he began to busy himself again, his back to them. They couldn't tell whether he was praying or quietly seething, but they waited, not daring to disturb him. Winnie noticed the back of his neck and ears slowly begin to redden and when he turned to face them again, he was alarmingly angry. Looking directly at Bridget, he said: 'Bridget, what in God's name are ye playin' at? Is it because she's too much trouble fer ye now? Why has it taken ye so long to decide ye don't need her anymore?'

It was only the second time in her life that Winnie could remember seeing her mother looking so shocked that she couldn't speak. This was the last thing she had expected from the priest.

After regaining her composure, Bridget said: 'But Father, sure, it's got nothing to do wi' what we feel; it's what Nellie feels. It's because Nellie is desperately unhappy. Even her friends are telling us this. We've problems gettin' a word out of her, and if it wasn't fer poor Mary, who looks after her most of the time, she'd be totally miserable. Father, I don't think we can give her what she needs. Ye know how hard it is fer me. I don't have time for me own children, never mind someone else's.'

Bridget looked at her daughter; if she was seeking inspiration, Winnie had none. Turning back to the priest once more, she continued: 'Is there a chance ye could get her into service or somethin', for instance, a housekeepin' job where she could live in? It would help her an' it would help us, Father.'

Father O'Dea's face was hard. 'Well, Bridget, it's the last thing I thought would happen, but if ye're sure this is the best and kindest way o' dealin' with it, then I'll have to go along wi' ye. But I'm not at all happy. I'll get back to ye, Bridget. Now good day.'

Having had his say, he quickly walked off out of the door, leaving the visitors to ponder what had just happened.

True to his word, Father O'Dea spoke with Bridget the following week. He had found a suitable live-in job for Nellie in the next town, he said, and suggested that they discuss the matter with their 'charge' as soon as possible. Nellie went along with the preparations without a murmur, almost as if she was relieved but afraid to ask any questions in case it didn't happen.

The appointment with the prospective employer was arranged for Nellie for the next Saturday, and during that week Bridget prepared Nellie as best she could.

With the address of the establishment in Bridget's best coat pocket, and carrying the small amount of clothes Nellie possessed she, Winnie, Mary and Nellie caught the tram to Bradford on the appointed day. Not very much was said during the journey, although Mary and Nellie, who were seated behind them did, from time to time, quietly giggle at something they had seen. From this, Winnie sensed Nellie was not holding a grudge at the change in situation; however, it did cross her mind that perhaps she wasn't fully aware of what was happening to her.

On alighting the tram, and carefully following the directions given by Father O'Dea, they began to wonder if he had misunderstood their request to settle Nellie into service; they appeared to be in an area of wealth and privilege. What would a simple girl from Ireland know about working in such grand splendour?

From the street, the address they were given proved to be a double-fronted, imposing Victorian mansion sitting in a beautifully stocked flower garden circling the front and sides of the property. They peered in amazement through the closed double gates.

Bridget, obviously worried, turned to Nellie, asking: 'Do ye think ye'll be alright here? It's not so far from the tram stop for the shops and ye'll be able to come and visit us every week if ye want to. But if ye aren't happy here, then ye know we'll take ye back don't ye?'

But Nellie was transfixed by the view.

Seeing a bell push on one of the pediments at the side of the gate Winnie was about to ring it when Mary and Nellie, fighting each other to be the first to place their finger on the large button, covered hands and rang it together. A young girl wearing a long apron appeared out of the side tradesman's entrance and ran down the drive to open one of the gates, silently closing it behind them after they had entered. The girl took her charges up the drive towards the side of the house where she then took her leave and disappeared.

An older lady, standing at the open door waiting for the visitors, was also dressed in work clothes. Inviting them inside she then politely asked if they would remove their street shoes.

Giggling, the two young girls kicked off their shoes, but Bridget found a chair to sit on bending with a grunt as she undid her shoelaces. As she stood once more, Winnie noticed there were dirty marks on her mother's light brown stockings and she silently pointed these out.

'Now, don't ye be drawin' attention to me feet,' she said in a loud stage whisper. 'It's not dirt, it's just newsprint from the folded paper I had to put in me shoes to cover the hole in the sole.'

Collecting her mother's shoes as well as her own and those of the girls, Winnie pushed them out of sight underneath the chair. Then she quickly caught up with her mother and the girls as they followed the maid into the hallway.

At first sight, Winnie thought they must be in the sitting room because of the space, except that it was empty apart for a half-moon mahogany table against the wall midway between the hall and the kitchen. The walls were painted a delicate grey which contrasted beautifully with the pristine white painted doors and frames. The floor, covered with polished black and white marble tiles, led from the entrance and along the hallway to a beautiful sweeping staircase, just like the ones seen in films.

Stopping to marvel at this Winnie was about to ask the maid a question, but she was obviously in a hurry as she began to steer them towards the dining room through a door on the left. The room they entered was more conventional, though the oak flooring was so highly polished Winnie was afraid her mother might slip in her stockinged feet. Taking hold of her arm to steady her, they both stepped carefully over to the chairs alongside the mahogany dining table and sat down. The maid, having done her duty, smiled shyly, excused herself, and disappeared.

Seated with their backs to the door, Bridget quietly began voicing to Winnie her concerns about Nellie. 'Don't ye think Nellie will be takin' on too much responsibility at her young age and become overwhelmed with the job, making herself ill into the bargain?'

Winnie was inclined to agree but wasn't sure she was expected to give an answer.

'Now, I'm thinkin' that we can look fer the maid who brought us in, tell her to let the lady of the house know that we've decided against the position, and then we can quickly leave. What do ye think, Winnie?'

She shuddered at the thought!

'Mam, we can't just get up and run out of the house. You'd have the priest to face if we did. Let's just wait until we've met the lady; she might be really nice.' Winnie was finding herself taking on her mother's worries, and it was upsetting her.

As they were whispering to each other, they failed to notice that the girls, who were sitting further along, had begun breathing on the table, writing their names through their breath.

'Holy Mother of God! What the hell are ye girls doin'? Get those marks cleaned off this minute.' Bridget now looked even more anxious; the lady of the house could appear at any moment.

But they sat at the now perfectly clean table for a long time, thinking that perhaps they had been forgotten.

Growing bored, Winnie got up and moved over to the window. Looking out she marvelled that even the back garden was impeccable. Picking up the edge of the curtain framing the window, she felt the cloth, but her rough hard fingers snagged the brocade, and she shook it back down. Crossing over to the ornamental marble fireplace, she then casually ran her finger along the top of the mantelpiece; no dust. How could that be? At home, they were constantly having to dust and, as they cleaned, they could usually see the dust settling back onto the furniture.

The painting above the mantelpiece was done in oils, but Winnie facetiously declared it must have been painted in the dark as it merely consisted of splotches of various colours slapped higgledy-piggledy over the canvas. Everyone laughed, even Nellie. Surely no-one in their right mind would buy such a thing. But of course, she knew they did, and that they paid more money for it than she would ever earn in a lifetime.

Oh dear, poor Nellie really was out of her depth here.

As Winnie was about to pour scorn on one of the photographs on top of the mantelpiece, she heard footsteps outside in the hallway. Shuffling her way over to the table again, she sat down just as the lady of the house, Mrs Grant, entered the room, smiling. She looked much younger than anticipated and Winnie breathed a silent sigh of relief; but she wondered what her mother was thinking.

After introductions, Mrs Grant asked if they would like to look around the rest of the house to which they all agreed, and it was suggested they separate, Mrs Grant taking Nellie and Mary with her, whilst Bridget and Winnie could look round at leisure.

They were quietly inspecting the kitchen when Bridget unexpectedly remarked: 'Ye know Winnie, I can remember what it was like when I was in service meself and think I know why I'm feelin' so upset. I remember how I would go completely ter pieces when I was asked ter do too many things at once as there was always a member of staff bein' critical; usually this was the person whose ambition it was to climb the ladder faster. And it was so easy ter get on the wrong side of people. I'd been unable to cope, even as strong-willed as I am, so how now, I wonder, can I possibly expect Nellie, with her lack of socialising skills, to cope?'

Deciding to look for Nellie and Mary, to see how they were getting along, they met them both in the hallway, deep in conversation with Mrs Grant, and were just in time to hear her telling Nellie she would like to give her a chance in the job, explaining that it would be for a one-month trial period and, if she was 'trainable', then she would offer her a permanent position.

Nellie grinned like a Cheshire cat on hearing this, obviously over the moon at the prospect of working in the big house. In fact, she could hardly hide her joy, though perhaps she was just happy at the thought of not having to travel back to The Hill with the Kelly's. They will never know.

With a heavy heart and somewhat grave misgivings, Bridget, Mary and Winnie each gave Nellie a hug, saying their goodbyes at the door, promising to see each other again the following week. They silently walked out of the house, down the long drive and headed for home.

It took a while for Mary to understand that Nellie wasn't going to be around to be her best friend anymore, and for a few nights she cried herself to sleep. Although Nellie did visit the next week, and the week after, and for a few more weeks and months, they soon realised she was never going to be the same Nellie they had taken to the big house. She had changed. Thankfully, she had become more confident and was now somewhat her own person.

After Nellie's departure, the family quickly picked up the pieces of their lives and, shamefully, Winnie was relieved that their family life had returned to its previous equilibrium. She did think about Nellie occasionally and envied her ability to disappear into a structured world where she didn't need to rationalise or to think too much about; one Winnie could never imagine. Over the next few months, the periods between visits stretched, until eventually Nellie severed her connection with the Kelly family, and in time, her name was forgotten by everyone, except Mary.

THE FLEAS

'Where the hell have yer been? Ye'll cop it when Winnie and me mam see yer!' Mary was furious with Alice and was backing away from her.

'Take yer bloody clothes off – NOW – and get them fleas, and YOU, out of the house, or there'll be trouble!'

Alice looked crestfallen. She thought Mary would have a bit more sympathy, especially as the bites had now turned into red raw stripes which must have been obvious to her sister.

'Where HAVE yer been? I went out an hour ago looking fer yer. I looked everywhere, in all yer usual haunts, but you were nowhere to be seen.'

Alice looked down at the green woollen dress she was wearing that had been passed down through Winnie and Mary, and for the first time noticed fleas dotted around the cloth.

Trying to sound brave, she said 'Well, Mary, if I'm goin' to take me clothes off in the yard, in front of all the neighbours, you'll have ter bring me summat to wear. I can't stand in the yard half naked.'

Muttering to herself, Mary went back into the house and came out carrying a canvas sack, but no clothes.

'What did yer say, Mary? I didn't catch that,' asked Alice, although the look on her sister's face was enough to warn her off saying too much. Even though she hadn't quite heard what had been said, she knew exactly what it would be.

'Well I wasn't with any boys and I don't know why yer always think that. I went fer a walk with Agnes and Maureen.'

'Don't talk rot! Yer know bloody well that's a lie. Ye've been lyin' in the mucky rags doing God knows what. One of these days, you'll get yerself into trouble, lady, and you'll have only yerself to blame.'

Mary threw the canvas sack she was holding towards Alice, telling her to put her clothes inside. Then she waited near the toilet door for the sack to be handed back. When the door opened again and Alice reappeared, she was wearing only her knickers and bra, and wasn't quite prepared for the sudden indignity she met as she was pulled out of the doorway and back into the middle of the yard, whereupon Mary started picking the fleas off her underclothes. By now, the original small red welts had begun to merge into large lumps on her skin and looked quite sore.

Out in the open, the fleas also seemed attracted to the brightness of Mary's white blouse and they began to jump onto her. 'Oh my God,' she cried as she batted her own clothes down with her hands, 'I'll swing fer yer one of these days, lady. It's alright getting yerself into a mess, but why should I always be the one to have to get yer out of it?'

Mary and Alice didn't notice their older sister leaning over the gate, unloosening the bolt.

Now what! Winnie thought, as she was confronted by the image of her two sisters running about the yard, slapping themselves.

'What in God's name are you two doing? I can hear yer both screaming and shouting at the bottom of The Hill. What's the matter wi' yer both?'

They each gave her their version of the argument but, to be honest, she wasn't all that interested. She had jobs to do before her mother came back from her work.

Pushing past her two sisters, Winnie walked into the house. She'd had a long, hard day, and a long walk home afterwards, and wasn't in the mood for nonsense. Taking off her coat, she was about to hang it on a hook behind the door when it occurred to her that Alice had probably already entered the house before Mary realised the mess she was in and, if so, there would be fleas everywhere.

Swearing, she picked up her coat and took it into the back kitchen, dropping it onto the old sewing machine table. After drinking a cup of cold water from the kitchen tap, she went over to the fireplace and leant her head against the cool mantelpiece for a few seconds. Looking down, her heart sank. She had black-leaded the oven and hearth two nights previously and had left it gleaming, but now the whole stove was covered in grey dust. It was a losing battle trying to make this old house look neat and tidy, especially as there were four other people to mess it up again, and they probably did so without a second thought for her hard work.

The noise she was making as she raked out the cold cinders from the previous night's fire didn't cover the noise emanating from outside, which made her mad. As she was collecting the cinders from the hearth, she slammed the half-closed oven door shut with her elbow.

Having emptied the grate of cinders and picking out some of the larger pieces to use again, she went outside and put the dirt left on the shovel into the bin, ignoring the racket still going on between her sisters. She then laid the fire, putting the coals and wood in the correct order, intermingling these with her paper 'plaits' (sheets of paper rolled into long fingers, folded in the middle and plaited down to the ends). Soon, the fire was blazing nicely, and she pushed some of the hot coals into the space underneath the oven so that it would be hot by the time she finished preparing the evening meal.

Eventually the arguing outside died down. Alice came in and went into the back kitchen to wash herself with cold water, whilst Winnie continued preparing the potatoes and carrots for adding to the leftover meat from the previous day. She liked to have the meal nearly ready in time for their mother getting home from work, although this night things were delayed.

Alice took her time with her ablutions as usual, hoping she wouldn't be asked to help with the preparation of the evening meal. When she felt she couldn't stay in the back kitchen any longer, she decided that now would be a good time to do some piano practice. Having started taking piano lessons a number of years earlier, Mary and Winnie had noticed that her usual habit, whenever being asked to help around the house, was to sit down at the piano and start practicing. They had both stopped asking her for any assistance as they were tired of the arguments that always ensued.

Mary was helping in the background, as usual, ladling pans of cold water into the water pot at the far side of the oven and, when the coals were hot enough, she would push some of the embers underneath the water pot to heat water for the dishes after their meal. If there was time, she might heat up some water a second time for a warm bath in front of the fire, if anyone wanted one.

Suddenly, Alice stopped playing. 'What's that screaming noise? Can you hear it?' They all listened. The noise seemed to be coming from the fireplace.

Winnie's heart jumped, and she ran over to the oven, pulling open the door. To her horror, she could see the cat inside. He was crying in pain and hopping about on the hot oven plate. Pulling him out of the oven she put him onto the hearth rug. Her sisters looked on in horror. The cat couldn't stand because his paws were burnt, and he was yowling like they had never heard before.

'What can we do, what can we do?' Alice was panicking.

Mary looked sick. 'Bloody shut up, will yer, shut up!' With that, she ran over to the sink in the corner of the room and began vomiting.

Winnie was crying tears of dismay, her heart breaking at the knowledge that she had locked the cat in the oven. She knew damn well that the old deaf cat sometimes slept there, and it had been her habit to look into the oven before closing the door and lighting the fire. She couldn't blame her tiredness for her lack of concentration; she always arrived home from work tired. No, it was the bloody shouting and screaming she had encountered on arriving home that had caused her to forget her routine, and this was the result.

Picking up the cat she ran out into the street, looking for help from anyone who happened to be within earshot. Through her tears, she could see her mother walking slowly up the hill.

'Mam, please help me,' she shouted.

'What's wrong wi' ye?' Bridget looked dismayed on seeing her anguish.

'It's the cat,' she wailed. 'I shut him in the oven and lit it.'

His feet were bleeding badly now, and his cries had subsided into a faint whimper as he sank further into shock.

'Oh, me Jesus, show me here.' Realising that she needed to do something quickly, Bridget took the cat out of her daughter's arms and, hurrying into the house, carefully placed him on the settee, telling Winnie to bring a bucket of cold water. While she did so, Bridget went into the back kitchen and brought back the round wooden lid used for covering the washing tub. When the bucket was nearly full, she helped Winnie to lift it out of the sink, putting it onto the linoleum-covered floor.

Going back to the settee, Bridget gently picked up the cat, giving it a final stroke, knowing it was the end of the road for the poor animal. Then, taking a deep breath, she pushed the cat under the water in the bucket and swiftly lay the piece of wood over the top. Then she sat down on top of the piece of wood and waited.

The strength of the sick cat surprised Bridget who held onto the edge of the kitchen table to give herself leverage; yet still he managed to lift both herself and the piece of heavy wood an inch or so off the bucket rim. With two hands, she forced the lid back down and waited for the next surge of strength. Again, the lid was forced up as she hung on grimly, saying afterwards that she regretted not filling the bucket up to the very top, realising too late that the cat was probably taking breaths in the space between the water and the lid. But there was nothing she could do about it now. She daren't remove the lid.

In the background, Mary and Alice were screaming in horror, fearful their mother would lose control, which was unsettling even to her. Bridget was hard, but she wasn't heartless. Having done this before, but only with new-born kittens, she remembered how even they had fought for their lives.

Eventually, the pushing stopped, but Bridget waited a few more minutes before removing the lid, saying she would surely lose her nerve if she had to look into the cat's terrified eyes. Taking the dripping dead cat out of the bucket, she put it into the low sink to drain off some of the water. Then picking it up, she took it outside and laid it in the dustbin on top of the ashes.

As soon as Cormac stepped through the door an hour later, his ears were met with a cacophony of voices vying to be heard, each telling him their story about what had happened earlier. But Winnie's account was the loudest, and it quietened everyone for a while, each left with their own thoughts about the poor cat.

The next day was a Holy Day of Obligation at church and, as they got ready to attend Mass, the family was pensive, their minds still on the horrific events of the previous evening.

Incredibly the sermon of the day at Mass was Thou Shalt Not Kill. Listening intently to the priest, Winnie's heart felt heavy with grief and sadness, her memory of the event still in her thoughts. Was it her imagination or was the priest's gaze lingering too long on her face?

Glancing sideways, she saw that her mother's eyes were closed, seemingly deep in prayer, her lips moving very slightly to emphasise emotion.

The wave of compassion that Winnie felt for her at that moment nearly overwhelmed her, causing tears to well up in her eyes. Raising her eyes to the altar, she silently prayed, 'God bless my mother and give me the strength she possesses to bear my own torments in life.'

GROWING UP FAST

Having left school at thirteen, Cormac had initially begun working at the mill with his sister, but he didn't take to the work and eventually moved on. He was by this time working for a company manufacturing asbestos belting and was bringing in a decent wage. Although the danger of working with asbestos had been implied since the early 1900s, it certainly wasn't apparent to the Kelly household.

As with many of his friends, by the time he reached his late teens, Cormac's favourite pastimes were drinking and smoking thus most of his evenings were spent at the Irish Nash, a Catholic club.

'Are yer going out tonight, Cormac?' Winnie had walked over to the fireplace carrying a large pan full of cold water.

Looking up from the book he was reading he laughed. 'Well, if you're having a bath, I'm sure I'll be going out. Ah, but on condition that you wash my work clothes in the water when you've finished. I'll go for a pint or two so will be out of here in a second.'

Sighing, Winnie knew he wouldn't be the only one asking her to do some washing this night.

Marking a page in his book, Cormac got up from the chair leaving to go upstairs to collect his dirty washing. He was back in no time and, as he headed for the door, he dropped his soiled clothes on top of Winnie's pile already on the floor. She smiled. It was a pleasant surprise to see that he didn't have much to wash this time, and at least he was leaving her to enjoy her evening.

Mary would be going out soon too as she was courting John, a tall, handsome, moustachioed Irishman who seemed to make her very happy. Winnie had been somewhat surprised at how pliable their mother had been when Mary told her she had met a young Catholic man; after all, she was only 20. Perhaps it was the prospect of getting one of her children off her hands and into a Catholic family that tempered her thinking.

John arrived, and he and Mary disappeared, leaving Alice in the house with Winnie and their mother. Now, how could Winnie entice her sister out of the house so that she could have her bath in peace? The tin bath was normally set up for bathing in the small back kitchen, but there was no fire in there this night and the room was cold. To add to the discomfort, the bathwater was never very hot once cold water had been added to make up the volume, the capacity of water from the boiler not being quite enough for a hot bath. If the house was going to be quiet – Bridget would be reading and so didn't interfere with the arrangement – then Winnie could set the tub in front of the fire in the scullery.

'Are you going out as well?'

Alice looked over at her sister obviously trying to gauge why she was being asked.

'No, I'm not going out tonight, Winnie. I need to practice my piano piece before my next lesson. I haven't had time to practice until tonight.' Winnie noticed the self-satisfied smile on her face.

'You bugger, you've been out almost every night this week, gallivanting around the streets. The one night I want you to go out – and you know it, lady – you decide this is the one night you can't go out.'

'Mam, can she talk to me like that? For one thing, I haven't been out every night. I didn't go out on Tuesday. And anyway, it's not your business what I do. I want to practice my piano piece, so bugger to you, too.'

'Hey now ye, stop that language now.' Bridget had been busy reading and had only just tuned into the conversation. 'What in God's name has come into this household when ye'll swear like that an' not bat an eyelid? If ye had had the hand of yer' father, ye probably would not be using that language now.'

Winnie scoffed. 'For God's sake, Mother, shut up! I couldn't stand me father and you couldn't stand me father either. Don't even bring his name into a conversation in this house. I loathed and detested him. I know he wouldn't be living here with us now if he'd survived that operation and come back to this country. After what he did to us and what we saw him do to you, we'd have driven him out of the house and out of our lives. He was a no-good bully, and it amazes me that yer still have feelings fer him. He was the scum of the earth and good riddance.' She was seething by the end of the sentence and all thoughts of a relaxing bath had left her mind.

Reaching for her coat, Winnie stormed out of the house, but it took more than a short walk around the block to calm her. Eventually finding she had indirectly arrived in the high street within a stones-throw from the Irish Nash, where Cormac was probably enjoying his pint, she wondered if it would be alright to go in and beg a drink off him? She hadn't brought any money with her, having just grabbed her coat, but she would be doing his washing eventually so it would be tit-for-tat.

Climbing the stairs leading to the bar, her ears encountered an ear-splitting din. An Irish baritone, singing songs of the homeland, was striving to be heard above the customers' loud conversations who, in turn, were competing with the constant ping of the till.

Cormac was standing at the bar talking to a friend, and Winnie pushed her way through the throng to reach him. As she neared him, her attention was drawn to the difference between the two men. Cormac was thin and gaunt but his married friend, who he had known since they sat beside each other in junior class, had a healthy glow and was quite thick around the waist, although no-one could have described him as fat or even heavy. Poor Cormac. His life must be hell living with four women. Winnie had been worried about him for a long time; he seemed to prefer the drink rather than the food she and Bridget prepared. She had often thought the apple doesn't fall far from the tree. Their father must be laughing all the way to hell, his influence still dominating the Kelly household!

She pulled his hair lightly when she was at his side and he turned suddenly, an angry expression on his face. But seeing his sister, his face broke into a smile.

'What on earth are you doing here, I thought you were having a bath tonight.' He caught her bitter look. 'Oh, oh, what's happened now?'

Winnie looked down, wondering what to say, not wishing to be a taleteller. 'Oh, the usual. It'll sort itself out. I just fancied a drink and remembered that you'd be here.'

Cormac ordered a bottle of stout and a clean glass for her and, picking up his own glass of beer, he excused himself from his friend, and carried them over to an empty table. The room was noisy with talk and not many people were listening to the singing man. A few men – strangers to her – were passing between the tables, proffering wicker baskets to the seated people. The men seemed to loiter until hands had gone into pockets and money had been dropped into the vessels before moving on to the next table.

'What are the men doing with the baskets, Cormac? They seem to be collecting for something.'

Cormac shrugged and with a smile said, 'You don't want to know.'

But she did want to know and when one of the men finally arrived at their table shaking the basket, Winnie asked him what it was he was collecting for.

'We're collecting for the Irish Republicans* back home. We're fighting for our independence from this hellhole and need all the money we can get.' He was now holding the basket underneath her nose, much to her annoyance.

'Well, I'm English, not Irish, and I don't agree with what yer doing, so yer get nothing from me I'm afraid.' Her anger of an hour ago had returned and she looked across at Cormac, who was just about to put some money into the basket.

'Ye Gods, why on earth d' yer keep coming in here, Cormac? There has to be an alternative place to drink in besides this one!'

Watching the man leave to move over to another table, Cormac took a mouthful of beer. Then shaking his head, he smiled again.

'Surely, you're not so naïve, Winnie. For God's sake, it's an Irish club catering for Irish people. What on earth did you expect?'

THE NEXT TEN YEARS TOOK ON A STRANGE NORMALITY FOR the family.

Mary married John, and eventually their first baby, a son they named Stephen, was born. Cormac lived his existence as he had always done – working by day and drinking by night, and Alice's life continued as it always had; she didn't have a single care in the world.

At long last, life was good in the Kelly household. Bridget was surrounded by her remaining two girls and her son, and she seemed happy.

For Winnie, life too carried on as before. She cooked, she cleaned, she worked and, surprisingly, she dreamed... she dreamed that one day she would meet someone who would show her a better life although, at nearly thirty-one years of age, the dream was beginning to dim.

*The *IRISH Republicans (IRA) was created in 1919 with the sole purpose of using armed force to render British rule in Ireland ineffective and thus end British rule in Northern Ireland.*

WINNIE MEETS HER MAN AFTER ALL

She saw him for the first time one lunchtime as she was queueing for food in the mill works canteen. He was seated with other men, at a table near the kitchen, and they accidentally caught each other's eye. Winnie could have killed herself as she actually blushed. Getting over that, she managed to smile but, although he was still looking at her, the smile wasn't returned; he appeared to look straight through her. Well, sod him, she thought, that's what I call rude. But the man kept looking.

Balancing her plate on the tray, she purposefully walked near the man's table, her eyes skimming his face as she did so. 'Hiya!' She spoke to one of the other men she knew by sight.

Continuing her walk, squeezing between tables packed tightly together, she began to lose control of the tray which started to wobble. Damn, she thought, I'm making a bloody idiot of myself and I thought I was being clever. Next time, I'll just walk back to the table on the same route everyone else takes!

Glancing at her colleagues as she sat down, she noticed them quietly sniggering and snorting, presumably having seen what she had just done, which made her feel even more stupid. 'Oh, shut up, you lot. I was showing that bloke at the end of the table what a 'real' woman looks like. Mind yer, he doesn't look all that bad himself.' They now began to bellow with laughter, Winnie joining in, covering her mouth with her hand as she did so.

Eventually, the joviality ceased, and the conversation moved on to the latest film being shown at the local cinema. But Winnie was intrigued by the quiet man. At a glance, he reminded her of her brother.

'Does anyone know who he is?'

Maureen looked up from her plate. 'Who d'yer mean? The leading man in the new Margaret Lockwood film.' They all began laughing again.

'No, you dolts. I'm talking about the chap with the wavy hair, the one I nearly poured me gravy over.'

Standing up quickly from the table, her colleague Jean, a girl from the weaving department, said, 'If you like, I'll go and ask,' and before Winnie could say anything, Jean strode over to the table and said something quietly to the man, who appeared to nod. Smiling, she returned to the table.

By now, everyone was silent and in shock.

Finally finding her voice, Winnie asked: 'What in God's name did yer say to him? I can't believe yer'd do something like that. I'm doubly embarrassed now; I'll never be able ter look him in the face again – not that I've done that yet, anyway.'

Jean sat down and, taking a bottle of HP sauce from inside her sleeve, she placed it on the table. 'What's embarrassing about asking if I could have the HP after he's finished with it?'

The laughter was even louder this time, but when Winnie looked over to the table again, the man had gone.

For a few days, she looked out for 'the quiet man' in the canteen but he never returned and, as the days passed, she had almost freed her mind of him, getting on with her usual mundane life. But then one evening, she noticed him in the 'clocking-out queue' almost directly in front of her and, like her, he was waiting to use the machine.

As people moved along the line, Winnie dodged between their heads, trying to get a better look at the man. She thought he had a good face, and she particularly liked his brown eyes – were they really brown? His hair was a nice shade of brown too, and wavy. But she needed to have another look at his eyes, as they would be his trump card so far as she was concerned, having been brought up with mostly Irish people, whose eyes generally seemed to be either blue or green.

Nearing the *clocking-in/out* machine, she took a slow, deep breath and, reaching between the few people in front of her, touched his shoulder. 'Hiya, I haven't seen yer fer ages; have yer been off work?' Winnie had decided that she would have to take the initiative as he seemed too shy.

Turning, he was obviously surprised to see her. 'Oh, oh, hullo. No, I haven't been around for a bit; I've just today started the day-shift again as I've been on night's for the past few weeks, since the last time I saw you.'

Ah, she thought, then you did notice me before. Though, on second thoughts, she knew he could hardly have avoided doing so.

As they continued to stare at each other the silence between them seemed ear-splitting but, as there was apparently nothing more to say, the quiet man turned to his colleague and continued their conversation.

When his turn came, the quiet man stamped his card in the clocking-out machine then, putting the card back into the rack beside the machine, he followed his colleague to the outer door, picking up his jacket from the hook on the way.

Retrieving her own coat, Winnie dashed outside after him, but to her disappointment, the quiet man was nowhere to be seen. She had hoped he would be waiting for her.

After spending the night thinking about him, the following morning at work Winnie excitedly recounted the events of the previous evening to her colleagues, who each expressed their delight for her. However, she was to later hear that some of the girls had called her foolish saying she had probably misinterpreted the quiet man's signals, reasoning that by his actions he couldn't be particularly interested in her. But thankfully they kept their thoughts only between themselves.

Her spinning machine had been operating continuously since the previous evening when she had bidden goodnight to the night worker who had taken over its running. Now, back to work, she temporarily again forgot about the man until, sometime mid-morning, she was taken out of her hectic routine by the sound of her name being shouted over the noise of the machinery. Looking up to where the sound was coming from, she saw her colleague, Annie, whose machine was sited near the heavy oak fire door, waving at her.

'What the....! Is there a fire?' Winnie looked around, but her co-workers were still at their machines, concentrating on their own work.

Puzzled at what Annie wanted, she shouted a couple of times to the colleague nearest her to get her attention, pointing to Annie, enunciating that she needed to see her. Getting a nod confirming her machine would be taken care of, she walked swiftly towards the door. By now, Annie was frantic, waving her arms and mouthing, 'Hurry up, silly sod! Somebody downstairs wants to talk to you.'

Before leaving the work floor, Winnie glanced back. If the Overlooker was watching, he would start his stopwatch, but he was nowhere in sight. Crumbs, she thought, he must have cloth ears if he hasn't heard all this racket.

Still puzzled as to why she was being summoned, Winnie hurried towards the stairs leading to the ground floor. Moving down the stairs, she was met with raucous laughter and assumed that Joe, the loom tuner, must be around. Joe was responsible for setting up the looms and repairs, and he got a huge kick out of banter with the women. The noise from the looms was losing the battle as they tried to compete with the hilarity.

Crikey, he's really the butt of the joke today, Winnie thought, preparing herself to become part of the enjoyment. But reaching the bottom of the steps she was shocked to see 'the quiet man' standing against the wall half-way down the room. He was looking mortified, being only too well aware that most of the lewd comments were aimed at him. Her heart began pounding ten to the dozen. Poor man. She felt a pang of respect for him and whatever he wanted to speak with her about had taken courage, knowing he would come face to face with women who could be so unkind when gathered into a group.

Walking firmly over to him, trying to smile without opening her mouth too much, Winnie said, 'Hiya, did yer want to see me?'

Gently taking her by the elbow, he guided her back over to the entrance to the stairs. Then leaning towards her, he raised his voice above the racket: 'Erm, well..., I wanted to ask you something – but you probably won't want to, but if you did, would you like to meet tomorrow after work? Maybe we could go for a drink together?' The stuttering and stammering caused his face to go red.

Wow, could this really be happening to her? It was just what she had hoped for – well, not quite like this.

'Oh, erm, could we talk tonight after work? I'd love to go for a drink with yer, but I have a slight problem. D' yer mind meeting me outside at five-thirty so I can explain?'

He was smiling too now but without opening his lips also, and the thought crossed Winnie's mind that perhaps his teeth weren't too good either!

Returning to her machine, Winnie was up in the clouds and hardly able to control her grin. What a good feeling she had about the quiet man, whose name she discovered was Reg. She couldn't believe her luck. He was only the second man she had dated in her whole life; how lucky was she!

But, throughout the day, her mother's voice intermittently leached into her brain, causing her heart to flip.

Oh, I know me mother won't be happy about this, she decided, but that's her problem, not mine.

As arranged at 5.30 p.m., Reg was waiting at the mill gates. She could see him as she stood at the top of the stairs leading down into the mill yard; he was leaning nonchalantly against one of the stone pillars.

Dashing down the steps two at a time, she landed at the bottom and, taking a couple of deep breaths, set off walking towards him. He wasn't actually looking her way which gave her the chance to properly inspect him properly. Gosh, she hadn't noticed before, but he looked a bit like Clark Gable; he was even smoking a cigarette just like Clark did in the films, narrowing his eyes as he put the cigarette to his lips to inhale the smoke. She was so impressed.

. . .

Reg blinked hard. Oh, cripes, where is she? My eyes are stinging like heck, and I can hardly see. She'll think I'm a dimwit and that I'm crying if she sees me like this. Why in hell did I light this damn cigarette? It isn't as though I need to calm my nerves. And these blasted people rushing past aren't helping, wafting smoke into my eyes making them sting all the more. If she isn't here in a minute, I'll have to go, I can't stand this much longer.

Gosh, Winnie thought as she now stood in front of him, he must have an allergy, His eyes are so red, although through his tears she could see that they were actually brownish-green. Why does he smoke cigarettes if he has an allergy, she wondered? When she knew him better, she would have to ask him. His chin is nice, with a dimple again just like Clark, although the dimple is spoiled a little by the wart alongside. But his eyebrows are strong, and he has good lips. Yes, he really is more than she could have hoped for.

'Would you like one?' He held out a packet of Capstan Full Strength cigarettes towards her.

Winnie shook her head. 'Oh, no, thank you.' I'd love one, she thought, but I don't have time to stand around smoking as the family will be home soon and they will wonder where I am.

'I'm sorry, Reg, but I really can't stay long. It's a bit difficult to explain but you see, I need to get home before the rest of the family get back from their jobs as I normally start preparing the evening meal for us all. It's a routine now and I don't know what would happen if I didn't get back before the others.' She tried to laugh, realising what she was saying sounded feeble and that he was probably thinking it was just a lame excuse.

He listened, nodding. 'Can't your sisters and brothers help?'

Not expecting him to ask questions, Winnie was taken off guard. 'Well, yes, I could ask them but, but, everybody's tired when they get back from work. I try to get as much of the meal ready as possible before me mother arrives back, after which she helps with the remainder of the meal. I know it sounds daft, and I'm really sorry, Reg, but I can't make it tonight. What about tomorrow after work? I'm fairly sure I can arrange that if you want.'

Docking his cigarette out against the wall, Reg took her by the arm and, in silence, walked her towards the bus stop. By now, she was feeling worried. He hadn't replied to her suggestion and she wondered if perhaps he was thinking she was going to be too much bother. As they waited at the bus stop in silence, Winnie desperately tried to think of something to say, perhaps something witty. But her mind was a blank.

The bus arrived too soon for her but, as she was about to get on, he finally said, 'Well, if you can arrange it, yes, I'd like to see you tomorrow.'

Beaming with pleasure, she ignored the strange looks on the faces of the passengers as she walked down the aisle of the busy bus towards the back, seeking an empty seat as she went. Swaying with the movement of the bus, she did her best to avoid the elbows of the seated passengers in the aisle seats, eventually reaching an empty seat beside a sleeping man.

The journey back was slow and busy, with more passengers trying to cram onto the already full bus. The ticket collector, a dour-faced man, stood on the platform ordering people off the bus when he thought he had enough customers, taking no abuse from anyone, neither King nor subjects.

During the ride home, Winnie tried hard to think of an excuse for not going straight home after work the next evening and, rather than have an argument, she finally decided she would tell Bridget she was going to the pictures with a girlfriend. White lies were much better than black rows.

She threw her coat onto the chair as soon as she arrived home and began rushing about preparing the evening meal. Having been delayed, and getting a later bus back, she needed to put a spurt on if she was going to catch up before everyone came in.

AMAZINGLY, BRIDGET ACCEPTED HER DAUGHTER'S EXCUSE for not intending to be home the following evening, and Winnie went upstairs to bed feeling happy. However, once settled in bed, she lay there restless, thinking about Reg, wondering why he had asked her out and not one of the other girls. 'After all, I'm not the most glamorous woman in the mill.'

Pull yourself together, girl, she said to herself, you need your sleep. Drawing the bed covers over her head, she began to count backwards from one hundred, imagining the numbers flickering in front of her eyes; before she reached nought, she had fallen into a deep asleep.

The glorious day dawned and, before she could say Yorkshire pudding, Winnie had finished her day's work, rinsed her face in the sink in the ladies toilet at work, and Reg and she were walking down the steep hill towards town. It was a lovely bright summer evening and the still warmish sun calmed her nerves.

In the glass cases on the wall outside the local cinema were the photographs of the film for the week, which this week was Modern Times a silent film with Charlie Chaplin and Paulette Goddard. Beside the photos were extracts of some of the dialogue.

'Isn't it awful when you have to sit next to somebody who can't read?' Winnie said, reading the introduction to the film, and they both laughed as she related the story of the woman she once sat alongside who requested from her, 'Will tha read ter me?' as the words were being displayed along the bottom of the screen.

This was often the occurrence when people were unable to read, but the noise of constant talking was aggravating to the point of distraction, and eventually someone would snap, shouting at the top of their voice: 'For goodness sake, will tha shut up!'

Whenever she got chance Winnie surreptitiously scanned Reg's face, trying to judge if he was the handsome Prince she had imagined she would meet one day, and from time to time, she caught him glancing at her too. Maybe he had expectations too!

When he asked her out a second time, she was thrilled. But without money, they couldn't go far; even at a shilling, cinema tickets were only just within their reach and only for specific weekend occasions. But it didn't matter as they were mostly happy just walking in the parks, and around the streets looking in shop windows.

Winnie had decided early on that it would be better not to immediately tell her mother about the relationship, so instead had invented a different story each time they went out. It was a fact that, in her mother's eyes, it would be bad enough she was seeing a man, but that he was an Englishman would be, in her mind, a cause for excommunication from the Catholic Church! So, quiet it had to be; and in any case, she had no illusions as to her charms and this quiet man could disappear as quickly as he had appeared.

Six or seven months into the relationship, Reg asked if she would like to go with him at the next works holiday to visit some family members in Worcestershire, and she was thrilled initially at the thought of getting away for a few days. It sounded like a good idea, but the more she thought about it, the more she realised it would be very difficult to arrange.

'Oh, Reg, it sounds a really good idea, but I wouldn't know what to tell me Mother. Also, I don't have any money put by. Like everybody else, I've saved just enough to pay fer the week I'll be off work, so I'll be able to pay me mother fer me board and lodging, but there'll be nothing to spare. Would yer mind if I think about it and let yer know in a few days?'

However, she didn't get a chance to think for very long as, to her horror, Winnie found she was pregnant. What shocked her most was that, at the age of thirty-two, she was more concerned about her mother's reaction, than that she was expecting a baby out of wedlock, which was a disgrace in itself.

Reg's family visit was to take place during the August 'Wakes Week' holiday; this was the only holiday week allowed at that time and was the traditional week in the northern mill towns of England whereby factories and mills shut down to enable annual maintenance of the machinery. Each northern county would take their holiday at a different time during the summer, but unfortunately, August, for the Kelly week's holiday, did not always produce good weather.

At this time no-one was paid to take any holiday from their work; instead, everyone saved a small amount of money each week to cover any discrepancy in their wages whilst away from their jobs. The week's holiday was precious.

In the past, Winnie had always looked forward to spending a few days in Blackpool with her work mates, but things had changed now;

she had met a man and, whether fortunate or unfortunate, was soon to become a mother.

Deciding to kill two birds with one stone, she chose the works holiday week to tell her mother of the impending trip with her secret man-friend, and at the same time to tell her of the predicament she was in. Having already revealed her pregnancy to Reg and discerning, by his reaction, that he was more than happy at the revelation, Winnie was pleased that one hurdle had been overcome. However, she knew it was going to be more difficult to face her mother; consequently, she felt she was going to need the support of Reg when she broke the news.

Over the months he had known Winnie, he had heard a lot about Bridget, not much of it good unfortunately, and he expressed reluctance to meet her for the first time, particularly under these circumstances. But in the end, he agreed on the visit one Saturday afternoon, when Winnie knew her mother would be alone.

It was unfortunate that the couple had not discussed exactly how it was going to be done but, whilst Reg fully understood her urgency to get the problem off her chest, rightly or wrongly he expected Winnie to wait a while before broaching the subject of the baby, or to at least wait until he had a chance to get the feel of her mother. However, Winnie was so nervous about the whole encounter that, after the introductions had been made, and Reg had been invited to sit down, she just blurted out the news of her pregnancy.

Her words took a few seconds to sink in and, at first, Bridget didn't appear to grasp the implications of what she had just been told. But when the words finally did hit her, the transformation from mildly affable to utmost outrage was the scariest sight Reg had ever witnessed in his life.

Bridget got up from the chair on which she had been seated and, walking over to him, her face set in anger, she stood over him and with a jabbing finger, ranted and raved, every remark punctuated with a jab. Catching him at a disadvantage, being seated, Reg was trapped and unable to get out of her way. Her final comment, after telling him he would have to marry Winnie, was, 'An' I'll see ye in hell for what ye've done to me daughter.'

Moving away from him, Bridget at last gave Reg the chance to get to his feet. The look on his face was sheer horror and, without a word to

Winnie, he turned and walked out of the house, leaving Winnie staring after him feeling totally ashamed. What had her mother just done?

With her emotions flipping this way and that, and her hormones kicking in, she felt panicky. The thought that she was about to lose this kind, quiet man, the one man who would take her away from this oppressive woman, terrified her.

With dread in her heart, she hurried after Reg, hoping to reach him before he got on the bus that would take him back to his lodgings in the next town. Catching up with him, she tried to talk, but he wouldn't let her speak; his face was set in anger. Silently, she walked beside him until they reached the bus stop, where she once more tried to reason with him. But Reg told her to go home; that there was nothing to say. He needed time to think.

Feeling sick with worry, Winnie slowly walked back home. She didn't know whether her apprehension was from the dread of seeing her mother again after the row, or from the fear that Reg might change his mind about marrying her.

Bridget was already in bed when she arrived back to The Hill. But Cormac, now home from his night out, was still downstairs. From the banging and crashing on the floor above, it was obvious that something bad had happened in the intervening hours and, seeing his sister in tears as she walked in the door, he gave her one of his oh, don't tell me! faces, before asking what was wrong.

Between sobs, Winnie began to unload the events that had occurred earlier. He listened quietly, making no comment until she had finished her story. Getting up from the chair he was sitting on, he went over to the door leading upstairs to the bedrooms and, closing it, sat back down.

'Oh Winnie, I'm really worried about you. I can see black clouds overhead and not just because you have no money to start married life, but because I know how much you are tied to our mother's apron strings and won't be able to cut those strings so easily, no matter who else comes into your life'.

Winnie was shaken that this man, who was so quiet and unassuming, could have understood her heart so easily.

She spent a restless night. Her whole world had just collapsed, and she feared that perhaps she would now be destined to remain a spinster, forever taking orders from her mother.

Leaving for work earlier than usual the next morning, Winnie hoped to catch Reg before the workpeople in his section arrived. Finding him standing beside his machine, obviously waiting for her, she wondered what to say. 'Sorry' was not going to be enough, but it was all she had.

'Please, Reg, I don't know what to say to yer about last night. I'm really sorry. Now yer know what I've had to put up with all these years, and we both know why me mother reacted like that, and she knows too.' He was very quiet. 'What're yer thinking, Reg? Have yer changed yer mind? I really wouldn't blame yer if yer did.'

'I can't change my mind now, can I?' he said. 'It's too late, the deed's done! But your mother has so much hatred for the world. Strangely I feel sorry for her. My family would think she was from another planet. What can I tell them about her? She's going to be the mother-in-law of Hades.'

Unexpectedly, the tension evaporated, and they both began to laugh.

Afterwards, he said that never in his life had he seen such anger. After all, as he pointed out to Winnie, she was a woman in her thirties, not a young girl, and it wasn't as though he had raped her. The poor man, he had been the recipient of an unprovoked attack and, although it had been a verbal attack, nonetheless, he said it was as strong as being physically punched in the face.

That evening, they walked around the town, sharing a bag of fish and chips.

It was an almost perfect evening; except Winnie couldn't prevent her mind from wondering what was happening at home. She knew her Mother would still be under the illusion that everyone's world revolved around her and the house, as it had always done. She would anticipate her eldest daughter being home that evening when she arrived back from work. Even if the world was coming to an end, Winnie knew she would still be expected to be in the house, preparing the family meal. It gave her quite a jolt to realise that she was challenging her mother, something she had never done before as, always after a quarrel, they had continued as though nothing had happened.

Now, after the previous evening's debacle, she was not looking forward to seeing her mother again after she left Reg to catch his bus back to his digs. Her heart was pounding as she opened the door, waiting for the onslaught. But the only sound from the room came from Alice practicing her weekly piano exercise. Bridget was sitting on a fireside chair reading, and Cormac was nowhere to be seen, presumably out drinking.

The fire was blazing up the back of the hearth and Winnie could see clean plates stacked up beside the kitchen sink. No-one said a word as she stepped inside the room and closed the door. Pausing, she surveyed the scene; all was peaceful. Going over to the sink, she picked up a clean cup. The room was still quiet except for the piano music. Moving to the fireplace where the old black kettle seemed to be constantly on the boil, she took down the tea caddy and said to no-one in particular: 'Does anybody else want a cup of tea?'

Alice interrupted her playing and glanced over her shoulder at her sister. 'Yes, I'll have one if yer making a full teapot.' Then turning back, she resumed her piano piece.

Bridget looked up from her paper and nodded her assent, and with that, the room reclaimed its normality, as though it had been spinning out of control for twenty-four hours and the rotation had suddenly returned to order.

The world went into a recession after the Wall Street Crash of October 1929, and this particularly affected the British economy, which had not yet recovered financially from World War One. There was a gradual recovery in the 1930s, but by mid-1938, Britain was once again in decline.

A rumour had been circulating at the mill since early summer 1938 that there would be redundancies in some of the departments and, although Reg and Winnie were worried, they were determined to take their holiday before the bell rang and they were counted out.

The June 1938 'Wakes Week' holiday eventually arrived, arrangements were made, and Reg and Winnie looked forward to their first few days together in Worcestershire with Reg's sister and family.

The journey by bus to the Midlands took longer than had been anticipated but it gave the couple a chance to talk about their future together. The old landlady at Reg's lodgings treated him like the son she was never able to have, but she had strict rules where visitors were concerned: 'No ladies allowed at any time.' Reg had always respected this rule as, after all, it was his landlady's home too, but it meant they had to use someone else's space to be together which, of course, meant they were never totally alone for very long. The holiday was going to be completely new to them, and Winnie was as excited as a little girl.

Once at their destination, they had a wonderful time. Winnie could only marvel how different the landscape was, and she easily found herself being seduced away from the thrill of the Big Dipper of Blackpool to the clean air of the Worcester countryside. Constantly taking deep breaths to fill her lungs, she hoped the soot and dirt of the mill would be quickly blown away. The weather was beautiful, and it felt so right to be walking in the sunshine with the man who was soon to be her husband. They quickly fell into a daily routine, each morning taking a walk down the very long garden behind the house. It was laid out in rows of vegetables, fruit and flowers and as they walked, they collected anything ripe, hoping to outperform the snails and worms in their mission to eat everything before them. In the quietness, the couple sometimes sat on the bench at the end of the garden beside an old windmill and talked about putting the world to rights.

Of course, the looming prospect of becoming unemployed and their lack of finances, together with the imminent arrival of their baby, were their biggest concerns at the time, though the future of our country would have lain heavy on their shoulders if they had known what was to come.

During 1938, in cinemas throughout Britain, Pathe News was showing film documenting Adolf Hitler's march into Austria and, during the months following, he made himself crusader of the three million or more ethnic Germans living in the Sudetenland, a region of Western Czechoslovakia, now threatening war with Europe unless the Sudetenland was allowed to be annexed to Germany. To avoid a war, Neville Chamberlain met with Hitler, who confirmed that he only wanted those parts of the Sudetenland which spoke German. Chamberlain believed this was a reasonable demand and, alongside the French, he submitted a draft agreement to the Czechoslovakians, which was immediately rejected by them. However, Czechoslovakia was informed that it could either resist Nazi Germany alone or submit to the pre-agreed annexations.

Realising the hopelessness of fighting the Nazis alone, on 30th September 1938, Czechoslovakia yielded, agreeing to abide by the pact. The settlement had given Germany the Sudetenland and, by implication, full control over the rest of Czechoslovakia.

On his return to Britain, Chamberlain delivered his controversial "peace for our time" speech to crowds in London.

Like all good things, the holiday swiftly came to an end, the couple returning to their monotonous jobs in the dark, depressing town. Of course, Winnie felt the gloom more than Reg; after all, she was also going back to her mother and The Hill.

The downturn began to bite hard in the north. The gradual recovery of the early 1930s had not been evenly spread; in the south east of England, a housing boom created jobs and security, whereas areas such as Wales and the north of England, centres of industry, were crippled with unemployment. This had spawned hunger marches on the government, including the Jarrow March of 1936. At the time, there was scant protection for the unemployed and, with no government assistance, many people were destitute.

The recession had taken on a disturbing reality at the mill. Although redundancies had been slow initially, as the orders began to dry up men, chosen from the various departments, were gradually laid off. Reg had known it was coming, but when he was finally given his cards in early December, it was a blow.

As Winnie prepared for her wedding, she tried hard to feel excited, but the dark winter nights and the knowledge that Reg and she were penniless made everything feel depressing.

The wedding took place on Monday, 26th December 1938 (Boxing Day). Reg had taken 'instruction' from the new parish priest, Father O'Hara, on the previous six Tuesdays, and afterwards had signed the record book held by the church. Thus, he had made a commitment that any children from the marriage would be sent to the Catholic church and school.

The ceremony was short as there was no Mass, and after the wedding Winnie and Reg had no choice but to go back to The Hill. With only her meagre wage coming in, where else could they live?

Of course, Bridget was in her element; she could now criticise this man to her heart's content knowing he didn't have a leg to stand on. How strange it was that she, in her late fifties, had no problem finding work, yet this man her daughter had married was unemployed.

REGINALD

Going back to The Hill after their wedding was troubling to Reg, as the realisation of what he had undertaken was almost too much to shoulder.

The day after Boxing Day he went down to the Unemployment Office to register for some benefits as was his entitlement, but he knew that whatever money he was given, it was never going to be enough to make a decent contribution to the household.

After registering at the Unemployment Office, he walked the streets, trying to rid his mind of the depression he was feeling, knowing he would have to face facts eventually. Retracing his steps of earlier that day, he wondered what the next few hours had in store for him.

Walking slowly back up The Hill, he pondered: 'if I continue walking, will the journey take me to a happier place? It must.' But he had to face facts; he was unemployed, his wife was five months pregnant and still working in the mill, and they were living with his mother-in-law who hated him with a vengeance, though the feeling was mutual. He was desperate to get them both out of the situation but with no job and no prospect of getting a job, what could he do?

Reaching the gate, he opened it and entered the yard, walking lethargically. Taking a deep breath, he paused in front of the old brown door and counted the cracks running up the main section. Were there more now than yesterday? Maybe the constant door slamming had loosened the wood joints. Taking the key out of his pocket, he looked once more at the door, and the useless thought went through his mind that the house must be south-west facing, something he hadn't thought about before. The cement was crumbling away from the York stone pediments on either side, which was another indication that the house faced south-west and received too much sun. He gave a quiet chuckle. Did it really matter? Was he just staving off the inevitable? He would have to open the door sometime. Glancing to his right, his eyes rested on the small patch of garden that had once contained vegetables, but which was now overgrown with weeds. Bridget had already told him that, as he had all the time in the world, he should dig the patch up and replant it with vegetables, adding that she had no intention of supplementing Winnie's small income to keep the two of them food.

Turning the key in the lock, Reg stood in front of the closed door for a moment to gain his composure before entering the house, bracing himself for the onslaught that must surely come. It crossed his mind that perhaps Bridget was standing behind the door, waiting for his return, and had spent the long hours he had been out winding herself up. But of course, he knew she wouldn't be waiting. One of the many things she threw out at him was that she, an old woman, was managing to find work, so why not him?

He hated the sight of her; the thin grey hair scraped back into a knot, the green unsmiling eyes, and the deep voice. What was that song about green eyes? Oh yes. When Irish eyes are smiling. Whoever wrote that song had never met Bridget! She had never once smiled at her son-in-law. She was thin and tough, and her strong, rasping voice could put fear into many a man, particularly him. In a moment of madness – and it had been only one moment – his life had changed forever. His own mother, as he remembered her, was a gentle, kind, quiet lady with a benign smile. How he would have loved to have been able to ask for her help until he found a job. She would, without doubt, have said yes, and would have prepared the best bedroom and put on the best bedcovers, and been delighted to have been given the opportunity. Oh God, what had he done? He remembered being inconsolable when his mother had died of cancer just before his twenty-first birthday, and he wondered what she would have made now of the grown man? He knew for certain she would have treated him better than Bridget treated her eldest daughter. Ah well. Turning the latch on the door he walked in.

'Well, then, did ye find something?' It was Bridget mimicking the voice of a quiet, reserved lady, sweetly asking a question of her lover, but her green eyes were full of anger.

His heart nearly stopped at the shock of seeing her there. She must have heard him coming in the gate and so had, after all, been waiting behind the door.

Reg didn't answer. Brushing past her, he dashed upstairs to the safety of the bedroom. Unfortunately, it wasn't so much a bedroom as an open landing, giving Bridget air to vent her fury at him from the bottom of the stairs. He lay down on the bed, burying his head deeply in the pillow and sobbed for all he was worth. He had lost all his pride, all his determination, all his strength. Bridget could call him a lazy good-for-nothing all she liked; nothing could hurt him anymore. He was at rock bottom.

Reg lay on the bed staring at the cracks in the ceiling, waiting until he heard the sound of the outside door opening and the voice of Winnie asking her mother if he was in. He didn't hear the reply but there was a sudden silence, then the sound of Winnie running up the stairs, swearing under her breath. Coming over to the bed, she put her arms around Reg and held him tight. 'What have I done to yer, Reg? When we first met, you were a happy man going about yer daily life without a care in the world, and now, look at yer.'

Realising they were gazing at each other, the sadness evaporated and they both began to laugh quietly. Winnie leaned away from him and said, 'Don't worry, luv, we're out of here as soon as we can, and I promise we won't set foot in this house again, ever, of that I'm sure.'

All through the night they talked about their future, even fleetingly discussing if they should go their separate ways, the thought of which terrified Winnie. They knew full well why Bridget was angry with Reg; it was because the household was about to lose its skivvy and he was an easy target for her venom. Winnie had known all along that her mother had never expected her to leave; she had been too useful all these years. It made Reg's blood boil to think how his wife had been taken for granted while the rest of her siblings did whatever they wanted, always knowing that good old reliable Winnie would make things comfortable for them.

Very little changed over the next three days, particularly their resolve to move out of the house that Winnie had always called home, but which now had become her jail. Like Reg, she hated the sight of the four-bedroom walls. Their saving grace came when Reg had the idea that perhaps his brother-in-law, Tom, who lived with his sister Rose and family four miles away, might be able to find him a job. With no telephone, and with letters taking too long, it was decided that it would be best to speak with him face to face.

Getting up very early the next Saturday morning, Reg and Winnie hoped they would be out of the house before anyone else arose. The house was cold, and Winnie had been tempted to lay and light the fire for the family, but one look from Reg had stopped her in her tracks. After sharing a mug of cold milk and a slice of bread and butter, they were ready to leave the house. Quietly turning the key in the lock to secure the door after leaving, they tiptoed the few steps across the yard towards the bolted closed gate.

'Oh God, how many times have I intended greasing the bolt and hinges,' Reg whispered. 'We're going to wake everybody in the street.' Winnie began slowly shifting the rusty bolt along, a quarter of an inch at a time, using her saliva to ease the movement.

As he stood waiting for Winnie to open the gate, without warning the hairs at the back of his neck began to bristle. Looking upward towards Bridget's bedroom window, Reg saw her standing there, smiling down at him. He was furious.

Moving Winnie aside, he grabbed the bolt, ramming it back, causing the gate to fly open almost knocking her off her feet.

'For goodness sake, Reg,' Winnie whispered loudly. 'Don't you have any patience? You're goin' to raise the dead.'

As she moved through the gate, Reg saw Winnie look up to Bridget's bedroom window, probably to see if her mother had been awakened by the noise. The curtain was still moving slightly, although Bridget wasn't now visible having already stepped back into the room. Not knowing what had just happened, Winnie was furious at Reg, muttering that she had wasted so much time trying to move the bolt quietly whilst in the end he had merely used brute force and ignorance and probably just woken her mother. Aware of an atmosphere now, Reg followed Winnie out of the gate, bolting it behind him, moving on without an upward glance. Winnie was still furious with him as they hurried down the hill.

He had to admit that his explanation of what had occurred between her mother and him didn't much make sense, and when he tried to explain it, Winnie said that perhaps he was beginning to imagine things. Yes, she agreed she had seen the curtain moving, but suggested the noise he'd made had probably wakened her mother so, of course, she was going to get up and look out through the window.

Realising there was no point in arguing he didn't respond. They continued walking in silence.

Winter dawn broke, followed by a brilliant blue sky. Streetlamps were being turned off, curtains were being drawn open, and people were busying themselves preparing breakfast, or whatever things other people do on a lazy Saturday morning.

On their route, they couldn't avoid passing the mill where they had both met and worked and fallen in love. Reg stopped at the open gates, glancing through into the yard. His heart sank. 'Did I really work there just a few short weeks ago? Oh God, how far have I fallen!'

Sensing his misery, Winnie asked him, 'What's the matter, Reg? Yer haven't changed yer mind, surely? I can't bear this. What the hell do yer want to do?'

He really didn't know what he wanted to do. How could he explain that to her? He didn't have all the answers, not immediately, anyway.

'Look, Winnie, I know we're married now and have a family coming. I don't want to change that. But I feel that I'll only be happy when we've left The Hill; I just can't take any more. If you want, I can ask Tom and Rose if they would let me sleep on their settee for a few weeks, and you could go back home. In the meantime, we could look for something for ourselves before the baby's born.' It was an idea that had surprisingly just come into his mind.

Winnie looked crestfallen. 'Reg, please don't suggest that. I don't want to be there any more than you do. I just feel so confused; all this stress is addling me brain. Please don't leave me.'

He had no intention of leaving her. Taking her arm, he said, 'Come on. We've got things to do.'

Yes, they did have things to do, and before the end of the day, their lives would change forever; they had been given the promise of a small, rented cottage in the nearby village, and Tom said he would be happy to make enquiries about work for Reg.

'Oh, bliss,' said Winnie looking up to heaven. 'Maybe my Maker isn't so unhappy with me after all.'

The next few days were bearable only because there was light at the end of the tunnel. Winnie went to work as usual on the Monday morning, and Reg waited upstairs until everyone else had left, then he began to set things in motion.

The kettle was only lukewarm, but he made himself a quick cup of tea; it wasn't very drinkable as the loose tealeaves floated on top of the cool water. After a few sips he emptied the contents of the cup into the sink, washing the cup and putting it to dry on the drying board.

Hurrying back upstairs, he collected some of their clothes, bunching them into as many implements of transportation he could find, together with any other bits and pieces that belonged to them. When he was ready with the first batch, he set off on his journey back to his sister Rose and to what he hoped would be the beginning of a new life. After drinking a hot and very welcome cup of tea with her, he returned to The Hill with haste to collect more of their possessions.

Reg spent the following four days repeating this process, and on the afternoon of the fourth day, upon arrival at his sister's house, he was given the good news that the vacant cottage would be theirs! Having taken a chance by removing all their belongings from Bridget's house, it was a happy man that returned to The Hill late that afternoon to await Winnie's arrival from work. It did occur to him that Bridget might return home first, so he was on tenterhooks, waiting nervously in the bedroom for the sound of Winnie's key in the lock. Hearing her familiar footsteps in the yard, he dashed downstairs to give her the good news. She was ecstatic. 'At last,' she said, 'we'll have our own home and soon have our own baby.' Putting her arms around him and looking into his face, she told Reg that for the first time since he had been obliged to move into Bridget's house, all his tension had gone, and she was right. But now he was no longer prepared to scuttle back upstairs to avoid being in the same room as Bridget when she returned from work.

‘Please let me tell me Mother about our moving out, Reg. I don’t want any more trouble than is necessary. Please let me tell her.’

Oh no, he thought. This is my play and I’ve done all the rehearsals. I’ll tell her! But he left Winnie’s statement in the air. Having spent much of the afternoon running through what he was going to say to Bridget when he saw her, he certainly wasn’t going to miss the chance of letting her know how he felt, although she knew that anyway.

Bridget was surprised to see Reg downstairs with Winnie as she entered, but her instincts promptly came to the fore, sarcastically remarking, ‘What’s the matter? Ye look happy for once. Ye haven’t by any chance found work after all, have ye?’

Smiling at her, he gave her the good news of their imminent departure, hitting her metaphorically between the eyes. Of course, in retaliation, he expected her to get the better of him verbally, and she did, calling him all the bad names under the sun. She criticised him for, as she put it, impregnating her daughter and causing her to live in sin, for making her daughter work whilst he lazed about in bed all day, and even scoffing at his supposed masculinity (she had probably heard him weeping), even accusing him of lying about his prospects, though he had never discussed his life with her. She wasn’t the type of woman a man could sit down and speak with. She had such a hatred of all men.

When she eventually stopped shouting, Reg had his turn, telling her what he thought of her for using his wife as a skivvy despite now being heavily pregnant, adding that Winnie’s siblings were no better. Because Winnie had always done the work, they assumed it would continue. Oh my God, no. This was the end and he told her this would be the last time his wife would ever kneel in front of their fire to clean out their grate, or cook their meals, or clean their house. Good riddance and goodbye.

The tension in the room was unbearable. He thought he’d said enough, but maybe he’d said too much? Glancing at Winnie, who was now staring at her mother, Reg turned on his heels and hurried back upstairs to their bedroom; he was shaking so much he thought his bones would collide.

Resting on the side of the bed, it was a relief when Winnie eventually appeared and sat beside him. Holding his hand, she assured him he had done the right thing, and that he had said ‘it’ better than she could ever have done. A short time later Alice arrived home having spent the previous night with a friend. As soon as she walked through the door she could feel the unhappiness in the air. True to form, Winnie had already prepared the evening meal for everyone, and as she and Reg were eating theirs upstairs, they listened to the events taking place downstairs.

'What's the matter, Mother? Has something happened?' Alice asked. Bridget had stopped crying now and her feelings had been replaced with anger. 'Ye'd better ask that man living with ye'r sister. Sure, he's poisoned her mind against us all and is movin' her out as far away from us as possible. She's me eldest daughter and has been here for the last thirty-two years, but now she's goin' with him.' From upstairs they heard the cellar door open; Alice was probably hanging her coat up on the hook. Then the sound of her footsteps could be heard as she ran up the stairs to speak with Winnie and Reg, presumably hoping she would be able to get more sense out of them, knowing of course that they had been listening to the dialogue.

Winnie got in first. 'We've had a terrible row, and I imagine you know what it was about. Anyway, we're leavin' tomorrow. Reg has already taken what little we had to his sister's house. We've had enough, Alice. I can't take any more from me mother, who seems to think that Reg is scum. He's from a better family than ours, I can tell you. His family are lovely, gentle people and it makes me wonder about religion sometimes. Here we are, going to Mass every Sunday, listening to the sermon about 'love thy neighbour' and 'do unto others as you would have them do unto you', and all that malarkey, yet we're just a bunch of hypocrites, as we don't believe a word of it. We certainly don't act on it. On the other hand, Reg's family are just ordinary people who probably never actually think of God, yet they live their lives as if they were brought up in monasteries and convents. I've never heard any one of them so much as utter a wrong word about anyone.'

By the end of the dialogue, Winnie was furious, and she walked off into Cormac's empty bedroom, leaving Alice looking at Reg and wondering what to say.

It was with sadness that Winnie walked away from The Hill the next day, carrying any remaining packages she could actually call her personal possessions. She was leaving her family home and the security it gave and, even though she had said many times that her present life had been hell, it was the only life she knew and felt safe in. Glancing at Reg, Winnie was aware he had a spring in his step which gave her stomach a jolt. Unexpectedly, a terrible loneliness had come upon her, as if she was alone inside a cage looking out at happy people smiling back at her. Inwardly shaking herself free of the image, she soundlessly sighed. Ah well, as her mother had angrily told her many times, she had made her bed and now she must lie on it.

Maybe she should be feeling irritated rather than sad! After all, what was Reg giving up for her? Yet she was giving up everything for him, particularly her home and family. But then she remembered; how many times had she asked herself why in heaven's name had she brought this quiet, kind man into such a conflict-riven household as her mother's? Her mind was in turmoil.

The following few weeks sped by in a whirl of activity. Reg got a job but not with his brother-in-law Tom; instead, he began working in a local mill, doing work similar to his old job, which was more acceptable to him. Winnie only worked a few more weeks before having to stop as she was finding her weight gain troublesome.

Being housebound didn't worry her initially as there was enough work to do in the home. Reg's family had put together a small collection of odd pieces of furniture which they were happy to loan out, and some used curtains were given by her sister-in-law, Rose. But it didn't take long for Winnie to realise being at home all day was dreary. There were only so many times she could dust the furniture.

Feeling quite lonely she longed for her old life back. Thus, and regrettably, she only managed to stay away from her family for a few weeks. Having retained the key to The Hill, it seemed justifiable to continue with the routine she had followed all her life, rationalising that she could walk to The Hill, do what was needed, take the tram back returning home in time to prepare the evening meal before Reg returned from work, and no-one would be any the wiser. However, what she didn't know was that, at the time, being worried that his wife would be lonely after the hubbub of work, Reg had asked his sister to keep an eye on her.

Unfortunately, Rose had been keeping more than just an eye on

Winnie. Although she apologised to her afterwards, she said she had felt it incumbent to disclose to Reg the miserable secret she had been hiding for a little while. Each day, seeing her brother leave for work, she noted that Winnie had left immediately afterwards. Of course, it wasn't her business to ask Winnie why she was rushing out of the door as soon as Reg had gone, but she thought she knew. Having already been told about Bridget, Rose suspected Winnie was visiting The Hill each day.

Reg was seething when he heard about this and couldn't wait to confront his wife. 'Winnie, what the hell's going on? I thought we'd agreed that you wouldn't be used by your family anymore. I know in the end there's nothing I can do about it, but I had hoped you would be settled into a new routine once the baby was about to be born, and that you wouldn't have any spare time to look after the other house; that's what you said you would do, that you would try to forget them for a while.'

'Will you keep yer voice down Reg! For once can we not entertain the neighbours with our arguing. There isn't much I can say to you other than that I'm at my wits end looking at these four walls every day. I feel like a prisoner in the house. After all, the baby hasn't arrived yet.'

WINNIE WENT INTO LABOUR EARLY EVENING OF 12TH MAY 1939 (which was also Reg's thirty-second birthday,) and gave birth to a healthy son the afternoon of the following day. The baby, who they named Michael Walter (the latter name after his paternal grandfather), was beautiful, typical of a new-born with no hair, but from the start he demonstrated as a child with a strong personality.

There was no spare money to buy a cot, not even a second-hand one, and baby Michael slept in the bottom drawer of their chest of drawers. It was a cosy bed which safely sat on two chairs wedged against the wall.

Over the next few weeks, things did settle into a routine of sorts though, unfortunately, the house was small, the walls were thin, the baby cried, and the neighbours complained! Being out at work all day, Reg didn't get enmeshed in these verbal remonstrations with the neighbours, though the arguments usually left Winnie either seething or upset. To escape the unfriendly neighbours, she now openly continued to visit The Hill. Reg hated that Winnie still felt the need to do this, though he should have known from the start it was always going to be part of her life. After many arguments and after a long discussion, they came to a compromise. Winnie promised she would visit only once or twice a week, and in return, he would try to stop complaining. However, he wasn't expecting to receive the news he was about to receive on his return from work one night, the night he felt his world was coming to an end, in more ways than one.

AGONISING HOW SHE WAS GOING TO MAKE HER ADMISSION, Winnie was very quiet during the meal one evening, and this was unusual for her. Reg, although sensing there was something she needed to tell him, being a peaceful man, no doubt felt he shouldn't disturb the calm in case the storm was too alarming. But, being unable to harness her apprehension for long, Winnie finally blurted out, 'I've looked at a lovely house to rent back in town, not too near The Hill, about 10 minutes' walk away, and I've told the landlord we'll have it. I'm sorry I didn't tell you before, Reg, but I had put out a few feelers a while ago in case anyone knew of any houses going to rent, and I met a friend today who put me in touch with a landlord. It's a nice house in a nice street. It has a big downstairs room and a big bedroom. There's also a tiny landing that might do for the cot. You know how I don't like it here, Reg. It's all right for you, you're out all day, but the neighbours are driving me crazy.'

Reg thought he was going to be sick and put his hands over his face trying to cover the embarrassment. Noticing his hands shaking Winnie wondered if he was going to faint. But why? She wasn't asking him to do anything for her mother. It concerned her to see him so overcome with anxiety, but it didn't make much sense to her.

When he recovered, Reg stated that he could not, under any circumstances, move back to that dreadful place, and he tried hard to meet his wife half-way. But there was nothing he could suggest that was remotely like a compromise for her and, of course, she was streets ahead of him as she'd had time to think of all his objections beforehand; she had an answer for each one.

. . .

The move back near Bridget did prove to be traumatic initially, but events overtook the situation. On 1st September 1939, when Michael was nearly four months old, Germany invaded Poland, and on 3rd September 1939, England and France declared war on Germany. This was to be the start of a change in all their lives. Winnie continued her routine of looking after the two households. But she desperately needed to get back to work as Reg wasn't earning nearly enough to keep the three of them.

NORTH TERRACE

Once the war firmly took a hold, people began noticing the lack of necessities, and in January 1940, some food became rationed. Butter, sugar and bacon were only obtained once a week by submitting a coupon, and meat, tea, biscuits and dairy rationing followed shortly afterwards. There was an ample supply of fruit and vegetables, but the variety was very limited.

Number 55, the house Winnie had found to rent near The Hill, backed onto another house, each house consisting of a bedroom and a living room. There was a passage running beside both houses leading to steps down into a small backyard. Underneath the living rooms of these two houses was a further two-roomed accommodation occupied by a couple in their eighties. For younger people, this cottage below would have been perfect; the rooms were accessed from either the front or the back. But the disadvantage for these old people was, whichever way access was gained, they had to climb up and down steps and because the accommodation was below pavement level at the front, underneath Winnie's living room, their only view was a high stone wall making the room very dark, though this probably worked okay as the couple slept in this front room. Their scullery was the room at the back, underneath Winnie's neighbour and, of course, this was much brighter as it looked out onto the small open yard. They were also nearer the shared outside toilet.

There had originally been an electricity supply to No. 55, but this was disconnected as they couldn't afford the electricity charges. Gas was already installed which was much cheaper. The light in the living room was from a gas mantle hanging from the centre of the ceiling. There was a connection for gas upstairs, but this was merely a bent pipe sticking out of the wall with no mantle fitted or protection of any kind. On the rare occasions that this gas pipe was lit, the bare flame, moving in the draughty bedroom, would produce black smoke which surged out from the top of the flame, discolouring the ceiling.

The living room was small, yet it was the heart of their life and every inch enveloped them. There was a table to eat from and a coal fire to warm them, to cook their food on, and to heat water for washing dishes and themselves. There was a gas washing machine, a wireless, and a settee and armchairs to provide comfort after a long tiring day, as well as a small sideboard for any precious possessions, of which there were few. Without electricity, the wireless was powered by a two-volt lead acid battery which had to be recharged weekly. The container was a heavy glass box with connecting sockets arranged in rows sitting in sulphuric acid. An employee from the local garage collected and replaced this accumulator each week for a cost of five pence.

Access to the living room was by a door from the tiny square hallway. A further door at the opposite side of the living room opened up onto stone steps that ran down into a cold, dark coal cellar but, again, there was no light in this area and a lighted candle was the only illumination.Bags of coal were emptied through a small square metal grate situated in the front yard of No. 55, and the coal remained where it landed, in a pile, on the floor of the cellar below, ready to be used. The cellar was draughty as wind blew through the gaps in the badly fitted grate in the yard that, over many years, had been kicked and thrown and dropped so many times it was buckled and bent, and now didn't sit properly over the hole. A draught could blow the candle out, leaving only the dim light from a tiny window at the bottom of the steps to show the way back upstairs.

At some point, the stone walls of the cellar had been whitewashed, but the coal dust in the air drifted onto the uneven stone surface giving it a three-dimensional effect, which only added to the mysterious shadows emanating through the candlelight.

Outside, in one corner of the yard at the back of the houses, was a single toilet used by all three families. Beside this was an air-raid shelter. Both buildings were built of bricks. In the event of an air raid, three families would use this shelter but, as it was above ground, it's difficult to know how useful it would have actually been. The toilet walls were whitewashed, giving it a clean perspective, though the corners of the small room were filled with spiders' webs. The outside of the toilet pan was of brown glaze, and the inside was a cream glaze, badly cracked. The oak toilet seat had lost its patina; dry, rippling grains were now evident from the constant scrubbing with bleach, making it uncomfortable to sit on. To the left side of the wall, beside the toilet, was a large nail on which hung squares of newspaper for hygienic use. It was a very cold and draughty place to sit for long and only used when complete necessity warranted. In winter, to prevent frost seizing up the pipes, a small paraffin heater was put just inside the door. As the toilet served the three families who used it, it was well cared for.

The strain was beginning to show on Winnie as she still worried about the household budget. Reg wasn't bringing in nearly enough money for three but there was little chance of her getting a job with Michael still so young. Sometimes, she felt she was being pulled two ways, trying to keep the peace with Reg while continuing to help at The Hill.

ON 18TH JUBE 1941, THE LONG-DREADED BROWN ENVELOPE arrived for Cormac. He was needed in the service of his country.

The letter arrived a few days after his thirty-first birthday, and about a month before, on a hot Sunday morning in July, Winnie's second child Anne was born.

With no dependents other than his mother Bridget, Cormac was assigned to the Middle East Force (MEF), and after just one short leave in England, he left for North Africa, his mother being advised of this in a greatly redacted telegram.

The redacted telegram was the last communication Bridget mother was to receive from Cormac for more than two years. She prayed nightly for his safe return nearly going out of her mind with worry, and only work and the thought that she had her three daughters around her kept her sane. Then, out of the blue, a communication arrived from The War Office telling her that Cormac was in hospital in North Africa. That is all she was told. No indication as to where in Africa he was recuperating, or the extent of his injuries or illness. But it didn't matter. His eventual return home was all Bridget wanted.

But Reg was not to get away scot-free either. He received his Form N.S.12A Enlistment Notice on 24th February 1942 and was enlisted on 5th March 1942 at the age of thirty-five to the Pioneer Corps of the British Army, with the Army Service Number 13114417.

Because of his age and dependants, he was in the latter group of men to be conscripted. His Territorial Army training was mostly carried out in Scotland where he was trained in, among other things, the use of mustard gas, the popular consensus being that gas would be used by the enemy.

With Reg away, Winnie now desperately needed to find work and, although it was only on a part-time basis, she was given her old job back in the mill. Her daughter, Anne, was placed in the local nursery, which only had a vacancy in the mornings, necessitating Winnie needing to rush back from the mill at the end of her shift to collect her and then, in the afternoons, to collect her son, Michael, who was now at school.

Bridget had completely put out of her mind any consideration that Winnie, her eldest daughter, might be 'running her blood to water' to earn a few extra pounds, when she herself should, or could, have been looking after her grandchildren. But no, she wasn't in the least bit concerned, her belief being that, if you had children, you looked after them yourself exactly the way she had had to do, otherwise you shouldn't have children.Mary was living in Bradford with her husband John and son Stephen. She was lucky to be working full-time at her local mill, enabling her to earn good money. They were further fortunate as John, who was from farming stock which was considered to be a useful profession during the war, would not be called up.

The north of England seemed to be booming, much of the war effort taking place there. The woollen and cotton mills were working full out, and some of the factories were even making Spitfire gears and midget submarines. Many of the factories expanded four-fold to accommodate the war work and, of course, the largest number of the new workforce was women.

By the summer of 1944, with Michael at school and Anne old enough to go to the local nursery full time, Winnie took on a few extra hours work in the mill. But she so looked forward to the weekend, if only to catch up on her housework.

'QUICK, QUICK, GET YERSELF DOWN TO THE SHOPS, WINNIE, the grocer has some biscuits.' It was her neighbour knocking on her open door, calling out to her. At the time, Winnie was kneeling on the floor, cleaning out cinders from the fire grate, her hands filthy. Michael, bless him, was trying to help but he was mostly in the way.

'Winnie, Winnie. Are you there?'

Jumping up when her neighbour's words finally sank into her brain, Winnie ran to the door. 'What did yer say? Biscuits at the grocers? Which grocers?'

'Oh, for goodness sake, you won't need to know which grocer, you'll see the long queue before you reach the shop. Go on, get down now. I'd offer ter look after the kids for half an hour, but it'll probably take longer than that and I'm going out soon.'With food rationing continuing to bite, the arrival of anything extra in a shop caused great excitement in the town and, knowing that once the supply of biscuits was gone there would probably be no more for months, Winnie knew she must hurry. Giving her hands a cursory wash under the cold tap, she donned coats on the children, although Michael's coat was put on under duress as he much preferred playing in the cinders. After a tussle with him and finally putting Anne into her pushchair, Winnie took hold of Michael's hand and rushed down the short terrace as fast as his small legs would go.

It was a shock to see how long the queue really was. The neighbour was right; it was obvious which grocer had the goodies. Snaking along the line, looking for the end of the queue, Winnie was determined to stand it out however long the wait, though she hadn't expected to still be waiting two hours later. Nearing the doorway, she could see that people were leaving the shop with small paper bags clutched tightly in their hands; so, there was still hope of some biscuits for tea.And then, she was finally there.

Parking the pushchair containing her baby under the shop window and setting the brake, still holding Michael's hand she entered the shop. This wasn't her usual grocer as Winnie normally shopped at the Co-operative Society around the corner where she found the annual dividend useful. Consequently, she was feeling a little pang of anxiety as she faced Mr Allen, the shopkeeper. However, having resolved long ago that the only thing to do in such circumstances was to face it out, she decided to suck up to him!

Beaming at him she said, 'Lovely day, isn't it? I'm really glad it wasn't raining, although I would still have waited in the queue, even to the point of getting wet through, as everyone says you have the best bargains in town. Oh, by the way, how's your wife?'

As she talked, she was keenly aware that Mr Allen was reaching beneath the counter, presumably picking up some 'seconds' biscuits, rather than handing over one of the now dwindling packs on display on top of the counter. Well, she would just have to accept that she's not one of his favourite customers and take what she could get. But much to her disappointment, he brought out a very small, neatly wrapped packet, much smaller than the ones on show, and handed it over to her. Feeling quite let down after all the time she had queued, she still tried her best not to show it and thanked him, handing over the coupons and money.

Leaving the shop with a heavy heart Winnie put the biscuits under the cover behind her daughter's head. Then lifting Michael onto the pushchair, hoping he would have a nap, she walked back towards the tail of the snaking line of people. Several women called out from the queue to ask what she'd been given and, at first, Winnie was reluctant to retrieve the bag to look inside as the contents felt so meagre. But her eyes nearly popped out of her head when she saw there were eight beautiful milk chocolate biscuits snuggling in a corner of the paper bag. Her mouth immediately began to salivate. Like the rest of the population, Winnie hadn't had a chocolate biscuit since the beginning of the war.

Back home in the yard, Michael hopped off the pushchair and ran up the two steps ahead of her, waiting on tenterhooks for the door to open. Now fully energised after his nap, once inside he began a chasing game around the settee, a solitary game as he was the only player. The child was up and ready to go, and Winnie wondered if perhaps he should be out playing with his little friends, getting rid of some of his energy.

Giving him a small cup of milk to drink to distract him, Winnie went outside to her still sleeping daughter and, with great care, manoeuvred the pushchair up the two steps, through the door, and into the living room. Leaving Anne in the carriage, she recovered the small paper bag from the pushchair, putting it on the table whilst she covered up her daughter again. Of course, Michael noticed the bag and he was about to look inside when he was stopped.

'No, no, no. These are special biscuits for special people,' he was told.

Gently removing the bag from his little fingers, Winnie looked around, searching for a secure place to put them out of harm's way or, as she thought at the time, hand's way! Opening the cupboard door beside the fireplace, looking inside for inspiration she saw the line of tins on the second shelf. Moving some of the tins to one side, Winnie placed the packet of chocolate biscuits safely out of sight.

The thought that the cupboard may not be the safest place flashed through her mind as it was situated next to the fireplace, although the fire wasn't yet lit so was in no danger of melting the chocolate. Leaving the packet there she hoped for the best. 'Now, why don't yer go and play outside for a bit, luv?' Gesturing to the open-door Winnie told him, 'I'm sure the little boy across the road would like to play with yer.'

Michael was only too willing and quickly disappeared through the door and out into the small yard. Smiling, his mother watched through the window as he crossed the road heading towards the house opposite, knowing he was safe - the street was a cul-de-sac, and no-one had a car. The coalman's cart was the only vehicle to ever drive up the street, but he wasn't due for a few weeks.

With Michael out of the way, Winnie set about her daily tasks, at some point in the afternoon, went outside to use the toilet in the back yard. Seeing her lower-ground-floor neighbour outside, she briefly got into conversation with her about the fairness of only one shop being given the opportunity to sell precious foodstuff like biscuits. After talking for a few minutes, Winnie remembered that she had left Anne sleeping in the pushchair so, excusing herself, she rushed back through the shady passage and out into the sunlit front yard, where she caught sight of some children in the street eating chocolate biscuits.

Surprised that a mother would queue so long for such treasures, and to then hand out the prized possessions to small children, her mind began to race.

Hurrying back into the house, Winnie saw that the cupboard door was wide open, and a chair was sitting underneath it. Dashing over to the unit, her heart beating fast, she already knew the biscuits were gone. Looking into the cupboard, she saw that the tins had been moved and there was now no small brown paper bag hiding there.

Before Winnie reached the door, she was already screaming her son's name, and continued screaming it as she ran into the road. What had he done? Oh my God, what had he done? A woman walking up the road, on seeing her anguish, hurried over to her asking if she could help.

In tears by now, Winnie blurted out that the biscuits she had stood in line for, for more than two hours, had gone, and that she could see the children in the street eating them. The stranger tried to calm her down, though it didn't help when she said that she had noticed children eating chocolate biscuits but had just thought that somewhere in the street was a very kind mother!

It really didn't help at all.

I'll kill him, she thought. I'll kill him!

Part Three

1941-1959

Alice's Story

ALICE MEETS THE LOVE OF HER LIFE

'Oh, hell, I've caught me other finger on the metal now. That'll be all four fingers in sticking plaster. It's a good job I'm not a concert pianist!'

Turning, she flipped the blood off her finger onto the floor. The girls around her laughed, but they knew what she meant as the work could be lethal.

Like all single females aged eighteen to thirty, in 1941 Alice had been drafted into the war effort and had chosen to work in industry rather than joining one of the Women's Auxiliary Services. Having taken a job in a munition's factory, she was now earning as much as the men.

On her way home from work that night, she stopped off to visit her sister, Winnie, knowing she would be at home with the children. 'We have such a laugh at work, even though it's sometimes dangerous,' Alice was showing Winnie her four plastered fingers. 'You ought to be there sometimes when the lads are making comments. Talk about cheeky.' Alice noticed her sister was only half listening as she talked, but she had thought Winnie would be interested to hear how they laughed and joked at work. Admittedly she knew her sister was a bit envious of her good fortune as she had often said she wondered how high she would need to jump before she didn't land squarely on her two feet! Nonetheless, Alice was stunned when her sister said, 'Oh, Alice, stop going on about your blasted job, you're so bloody lucky. I'd give anything to get employment with you. I'm earning a pittance in the mill. The 2s. 6d a day I get from the army and my meagre earnings don't go anywhere near paying off the bills and I'm always in debt. With a bit of extra money, I could maybe get the electricity reinstalled and surprise Reg when he came back on a home leave. You never offer to help; you could at least enquire if they need any part-time workers where you are?' Alice's face began to go red, which didn't go unnoticed by Winnie. Doing her best to cover up her mortification, Alice managed to say, 'Goodness, Winnie, there are plenty of jobs in the munition's factory, I've told you that before. But when I've mentioned this in the past, you've always said you can't work shifts and can't work too many hours as you need to look after the kids. I don't think there are any short-time jobs around, but I'll speak to the manager, if you want.' During the conversation, Alice had tried to busy herself doing something with her coat as she knew she was still blushing. Oh dear, now her sister's suspicions would be aroused.

Looking over at her sister, Alice could see that she was smiling to herself. Had Winnie already realised she was seeing the married Works Manager she talked about now and then, although, she doubted her sister would care less what she did in her spare time if it meant she could get some extra work and money. The teapot was in its usual place on the shelf above the oven. Taking it down, Winnie glanced inside but didn't put any more tea in the pot; presumably, there were still leaves there from the previous brew. Returning the teapot back to the shelf to warm, she no doubt thought it didn't matter about using old leaves, after all, she wasn't entertaining the queen was she!

They both sat on the settee in silence, watching the flames creeping up the sides of the kettle on the fire. In the semi-darkness, the flickering flames were mesmeric. The kettle began to hiss, quietly at first, then reaching a crescendo, shaking them out of their stupor. Getting up from the settee, Winnie picked up two clean mugs from the drainer at the side of the sink and put them on the table. The kettle, now boiled, was ready for the teapot.

Whistling quietly to herself, she went to the shelf at the top of the cellar steps and picked up a bottle of milk from the half-filled bowl of cold water she always kept there. Lifting the foil lid, she sniffed the milk: 'Oh no, I don't believe it, it's going off. This is the second time this week it's happened. For goodness sake, I can't do anything about it. I've already left for work before the milkman comes in the morning, so the bottles of milk sit on the doorstep in the sun, waiting for me to come home in the afternoon. Oh crumbs, I don't know what I'll give the kids if the other pints are the same. I've tried boiling the milk when it's on the turn, but it doesn't taste the same.

Blowing out air in exasperation, she came back over to the table, glancing at her sister as she passed her. But she didn't say anything. Alice waited patiently for the onslaught she felt would come eventually.

Making two cups of tea, and placing them on the floor near the hearth, Winnie sat down beside her sister. Glancing at her as she did so, she noticed how nicely cut and waved her sister's hair was and remembered that she could even afford a gold tooth at the front of her dentures. Finally, it got too much, and she said, 'I wish I'd been more like you, Alice, able to take the world as it comes rather than always worrying about life's necessities. I'll be honest with you; I've always envied you your disposition. Goodness knows who you take after as neither Bridget nor 'him' had your temperament. Someone somewhere in the past must have collected all the happy genes and waited for you to be born. Between the two of you, you and Mary seem to get all the breaks in life. Thinking of what we talked about before, there isn't any point in asking about a job for me, Alice. Let's face it, I can't even manage part-time work. I get so fed up... what with the milk and....,' she trailed off.

Alice felt sorry for her sister recognising she really was in a pickle. And yes, she did know how fortunate she was but, she thought, 'most of us are fighting a battle other people know nothing about', so although Winnie was envious of her, she didn't know the problems she might have. Maybe it was time Winnie tried once more to persuade Bridget to stay home and take care of her grandchildren although, remembering the last time Winnie mentioned the matter to their mother, she had left the house with a flea in her ear. From day one, Bridget had always let Winnie know that she had no intention of helping in any way if it was going to eventually benefit that man. No, her mother had probably rehearsed hundreds of times what she would say if she was ever asked to look after her grandchildren on a daily basis. It was never going to happen. She wasn't interested, and they already knew it.

It was lethal working in the munition's factory, and after a couple of years, Alice was tiring of the twelve-hour shifts, which were interfering with her prospective love life. So, she applied to change her employment.

Not wanting to move far from home, she chose to follow in the footsteps of other girls who had left munitions, choosing work as a clippie (a bus conductress). Public transport work was considered an occupation as important to the war effort as farmers, miners, dock-workers and factory workers.

On the morning of her training, Alice arrived at the Town Bus Depot with time to spare. The only door ajar was one leading into a huge barn-like structure, and inside were red buses with their black tops, standing in line like guardsmen waiting for a command during a Trooping of the Colour ceremony.

Passing along the walls, Alice was attracted to the notices pinned up between the blacked-out windows, some giving general advice to staff, but others giving advice to the population in general: "Careless Talk Costs Lives" and "Be like Dad, keep Mum".

Smiling at the thought that her father had ever 'kept' her mother – in fact, from what she was told, it had been the other way around – she continued reading.

Further down the notice board, a poster advising against harmless chat whilst on leave depicted a number of people sitting on a bus and behind them were smiling caricatures of Hitler and Goering. It certainly made her think.

Looking around the depot, there didn't appear to be anyone in charge, but spying a small group of girls talking quietly in a corner, she decided to tag onto them. One of the girls seemed a little more enlightened than the rest of the bunch and, recognising that the group had grown, suggested they should look for the office and ask for directions to their training room.

'I think it's going to be dead easy,' said a girl trying to squeeze through the narrow office door at the same time as Alice. They both laughed, and the girl introduced herself as Elsie. 'I don't know about you,' she continued, 'but I'm ready to go without any so-called training. I doubt it's going to need an Einstein brain to do this job as it appears straightforward. I think we just need to make sure we have a few pencils on hand to write up the tickets, after which all we need do then is memorise the route numbers. Simple!'

Oh, to have such confidence. Alice had been so worried about the training that she had hardly slept the previous night, nor the night before that if she was being honest. However, as Elsie had predicted, the job was easily learned, yet it was going to be a little more onerous than just sharpening a few pencils.

The small door to the now familiar bus shed had been wedged open and Alice once again walked into the great waiting room of buses. Entering, she looked around and was surprised that none of the girls she had done her training with were there. Walking over to the main notice board on which she had been told her roster would appear, it crossed her mind that perhaps the inexperienced girls were being put on 'cleaning crew' and other light duties on their first day rather than being given the privilege of working on a beautiful red bus. This had always been a possibility; however, to her great surprise, Alice saw her name displayed in large type: ALICE ANN KELLY (conductress) CHARLIE DIXON (driver), and the route number displayed beside their names.

Oh well, this is a start, she thought. Now all she had to do was find Mr Charlie Dixon and then, hopefully, they would be on their way.

Little did she know then but arriving for work that first morning was to be a turning point in her life. Alice did find Charlie and, in doing so, eventually found herself in a relationship with a married man, a relationship that was to last until he died in 1959.

THE WAR ENDED. ALICE STAYED IN THE SAME OCCUPATION, still seeing her beloved Charlie, and still living with her mother, Bridget, on The Hill.

Cormac did return, as his Mother had earnestly prayed for, but he was not the same man who had left all those years earlier.

For a while, people were happy, then the euphoria wore off and reality set in. Food was still rationed, and jobs weren't easy to come by. In some parts of the country, manufacturers had been badly hit by the German bombs and it took time to rebuild these companies. Luckily, in general, the northern part of England suffered far less shelling than the south, though Hull, in particular, was said to be the most severely damaged city in Britain.

Reg was demobbed on 25th May 1946 and, upon returning home, resumed his job at the mill. There was great excitement on his return, though it took Michael and Anne a little time to get used to the unfamiliar man who had suddenly come back into their lives. Cormac also got his old job back in the engineering company, and he tried hard to forget the war refusing to ever speak about his army service.

In time, factories did start up again, and eventually there was plenty of work for everyone, but some rationing continued until 3rd July 1954. It had been really funny to sit in the cinema and watch the News, as housewives, celebrating Independence Day, had ceremonially torn up their ration books in Trafalgar Square. The government had announced the end of all rationing after fourteen years and finally the country was happy. Meat was the last item to come off the ration, and already butchers were predicting price rises. For the first time since the beginning of the war, Smithfield Market opened at midnight instead of 6 am for the delivery of meat.

As for Alice, her friendship with Charlie continued, and before very long, she was introduced to his wife and children. At first, maybe because of the age difference, they were just work colleagues, but over time they were thrown together so often that, in their mutual loneliness, they eventually became lovers. It was a strange ménage à trois as, unlikely as it may sound, Alice was accepted as part of his family; was it possible Charlie's family didn't know of her real relationship with him? That's doubtful. But Charlie's mother-in-law lived with the family, including four children, in their small, three-bedroom council house and Charlie was probably telling the truth when he said he wasn't having a 'relationship' with his wife anymore. Perhaps his wife was glad he was getting what he needed from someone she knew rather than someone she didn't know.

It seemed, Bridget was also happy as she had her son and a daughter with her, although Cormac was her main concern.

In late 1948, Charlie's wife, grown-up daughters and teenage son moved to Bridlington on the East Coast where they bought a very large house. They converted it into a bed and breakfast accommodation and settled down to another life. The move suited everyone, particularly Alice as she was now free to spend more time visiting with Charlie. As the months and years passed, the neighbours had begun calling her Mrs Dixon, assuming they had now married. However, although his first marriage to all intents and purposes was over, Charlie nonetheless remained 'unfaithfully married' until his wife's death in 1950.

Although, at the time, Alice's illicit relationship with Charlie continued unabated, Bridget seemed unaware of it. For some reason, she was under the impression her daughter was back in touch with an old schoolfriend who she now worked with and, of course, she had no wish to tell her mother any different.

'Now, don't ye use up all the butter, Alice. I've kept some potatoes back from dinner time and want to make a potato cake. Why can't ye bake things at yer friend's house? Doesn't she have an oven?' Bridget was obviously anxious about Alice using up her food.

'No, Mam, she's working the late shift and I wanted to take something cooked to pay for the night's lodging.' Alice was in the process of sifting flour which was floating all over the table.

'Sure, wouldn't it be easier to buy a simple pie rather than usin' up all me fat? And look at all the apples ye've bought! I don't understand ye. It's Sunday, supposedly a day of rest. I've got all ye're washin' hangin' around the fire takin' up all the heat and then ye're about to use five shillin's worth of gas to bake somethin' ye could have bought yesterday whilst ye were out. Ye do amaze me, Alice.'

Shaking her head, Bridget let out a huge sigh then, picking up the Catholic Times newspaper she had bought at church that morning, she sat down on the settee and began to read.

At this time, Bridget's granddaughter Anne, was sitting in the rocking chair in the corner of the room and, having had her attention drawn to the washing on the winter-edge by her gran, she noticed some odd things hanging here. There were some small squares of towelling with tapes attached to each corner and some loops of elastic tied with knots at the end. There were also some fancy shorts, like the ones she had seen boxers wearing on the screen at the cinema and which she had assumed belonged to her uncle Cormac, although she thought she had only ever seen woolly undergarments from his washing.

Very soon the pies were made – Alice had managed to make two – and the washing in front of the fire disappeared.

When she left the house to visit her 'friend', Alice was carrying a large bag.

Anne was sorry to see her aunt leave, but it was Sunday and she would soon be going home herself.

WINNIE DIDN'T CARE VERY MUCH FOR CHARLIE. HE WAS much older than her sister who had been in the prime of life when she met him, and the illicit relationship had probably prevented her sister from marrying and having children of her own. The man certainly knew the right words to keep Alice interested (except 'will you marry me?'). Like a limpet shell, he had well and truly clamped himself onto her.

Sometimes Winnie found it difficult to keep her mouth closed feeling as strongly as she did about Charlie, but one day she upset her sister badly. During a conversation, when Alice was singing his praises, Winnie had heard enough and abruptly interrupted her in mid-sentence. 'You're an idiot, Alice. Don't you see? Charlie is now living alone in the family home and his life is carefree. His wife is dead now, so he no longer has to keep her, his children are grown up and living their own lives, and he has a lady-friend at his beck and call and convenience. What more could a man want? You are stupid'.

Alice blushed. 'Charlie has always said he would marry me, but he just needs time as his wife hasn't been dead very long.'

Sighing, Winnie replied, 'But, of course, he isn't going to marry you, you silly sod. Why should he? He has everything laid out on a plate. He's been stringing you along for years, but you haven't seen it. And I have to add as well that I can't for the life of me see what you see in the man. He's a miserable toothless old sod, who's spent years sucking out every ounce of yer youth and vitality. He must have thought he'd died and gone to heaven when he met you. Oh Alice, what more can I say?' Walking away, she picked up a tea towel that had been lying on the chair and began dusting the sideboard with it.

Alice started quietly weeping. Perhaps her sister was right, and Charlie didn't intend marrying her after all. To try to make herself feel better she retaliated, 'Well you can't tell me about Charlie's shortcomings when your own husband isn't perfect.' But the words landed on deaf ears.

Watching Winnie dusting, or pretending to dust, Alice began to ponder. She was now in her mid-forties and no doubt felt to some degree past her best, having waited such a long time for 'the man of her dreams' to become available. If Charlie wasn't going to ask her, then perhaps she would ask him as he had often said to her, 'I'd marry you yesterday Alice, if I wasn't already married. If the opportunity arises in the future, wild horses won't stop me from marrying you.' Well, maybe now was the time he should be honouring that promise.

ANNE WOULD BE A BRIDESMAID

Much to Winnie's surprise, Charlie turned out to be a man of honour after all and, though she didn't see any of the qualities that her sister saw in him, she did accept that the man made her happy. The marriage was held in the Catholic Church after Charlie had dutifully taken the church's 'Course of Instruction', promising in writing that any children they had would be baptised as Catholics and brought up in the Catholic faith. But, at her age, there was little chance Alice would be bringing a child into the world.

Her niece, Anne, who was their only bridesmaid at the ceremony, was eleven years old and it was the first time she had ever been a bridesmaid; in fact, it was the first time she had ever been to a wedding. Charlie's son, Michael, who was a year younger than Anne, acted as Best Man. The day went surprisingly well; even Bridget appeared to give her approval.

The reception for just a small group of friends and family was held at Charlie's, and now officially Alice's, home. Somehow, everyone fitted into the tiny front room, which looked much larger than it actually was as someone had had the sense to move the large settee and armchairs to the back of the room, leaving the seated guests looking at the brown and cream tiled fireplace.

Anne found a pouffe wedged between the sideboard and tv and sat, listening with interest, as guests talked nonsense whilst consuming the wine and snacks prepared earlier by Charlie's eldest daughter, Maureen. She and his son, Michael, were the only members of his family to attend the wedding as his two younger daughters had declined the invitations. They were still feeling bitter that their father had been having an affair much of the time he was married to their mother and couldn't stomach pretending everything was alright now.

The room soon became foggy with cigarette smoke and, feeling the need for some fresh air, Anne got up and headed down the hallway towards the kitchen. On the way she passed her grandmother, who was standing in the doorway of the under-stair cupboard, with her back turned, holding a vacuum cleaner.

'Are you all right, Gran?' she asked. 'Are you looking for something?'

Bridget looked startled. 'Sure, I'm looking fer the toilet. I thought it was in this door, but it might be the other door. Now, run along an' I'll catch up with ye now.' She watched as her granddaughter continued on towards the kitchen. The door to the kitchen was partially open and Winnie had heard the conversation; smiling to herself, she shook her head.

Cormac was nowhere to be seen. Although he had attended the church ceremony, he was of the opinion that receptions, both weddings and funerals, were for people who had lost the will to live in both instances. Gatherings didn't interest Reg either, but he had been cajoled into attending. By nature, he was a quiet man, and so had managed to stay almost invisible during the day, leaving the reception early with the excuse that he was working that night. He did occasionally work Saturday nights, although not this Saturday.

In the evening, after the taxi had left to take Charlie's daughter and son to the railway station to catch their train back to Bridlington, and after the last of the remaining guests had departed, Anne went into the kitchen to help her mother and aunt clear away the debris. As they worked they joked that perhaps Charlie could use some help moving the furniture back to its original place, and hoping Bridget, who was in the room with him, wasn't interfering. They could hear her grating voice which, by the tone, appeared to be castigating someone. Suddenly the sisters stopped what they were doing, looking at each other in horror, realising the implications of what they were hearing,

Winnie rushed out of the kitchen, down the hallway and back into the room where, without a word, she took hold of her mother's arm, guiding her back into the kitchen. Bridget had had too much to drink!

Winnie's face was like thunder. 'What the hell are we going to do with her?' she said in a loud whisper. 'She can't stay on her own at home tonight. I wouldn't trust her not to do something stupid. She's going to have to stay here with you, I'm afraid Alice. God only knows what Charlie thinks of the family he's just married into.'

Quietly leaving the kitchen the two sisters moved down the hallway, holding onto their mother by her elbows as they steered her towards the stairs, her drunken voice rasping unintelligible comments. Ah well, the newly wedded couple wouldn't be consummating their marriage that night!

Although Anne followed them upstairs, she left the intimacy of the situation to her aunt and her mother, who between them quickly undressed Bridget and redressed her in one of Alice's old nighties. She was sound asleep and snoring long before the light was turned off, and they crept out of the spare bedroom and back downstairs breathing a sigh of relief.

It had been an interesting day, but Winnie decided it was time to call an end to it and go home. As they were gathering their coats and scarves, they thought they heard a scraping noise coming from upstairs. Stopping, they listened. But now it was quiet – they must have been mistaken. No! There it went again!

Winnie and Alice, with Anne close behind, quietly went upstairs to see what was happening and reaching the main bedroom, from where the noise seemed to be emanating, they were shocked to see Bridget searching through the bedroom drawers. Standing outside the door, they waited, curious. Bridget was looking through every drawer in turn, removing clothes to take a closer look, then bundling the items back into the drawers haphazardly. With her glasses perched on her nose, she slowly read any personal document she found, and any jewellery was examined minutely. She was so intent on what she was doing that she had no idea she was being watched.

'Mother! What are you doing?' This was Winnie using her best mill voice whisper. Bridget jumped, then turning around and only seeing her daughter, whispered, 'I'm looking ter see if 'she' has left anything in the drawers.'

'Mother, who is 'she'?' Alice had suddenly appeared from behind Winnie. But Bridget held her ground and now focused on her youngest daughter: 'Ye know who I mean – his wife... I'm only looking out for ye; he's had a wife before ye came along, an' I'm looking ter see if he's kept anything of hers. How do ye know he's going to be faithful to ye when he wasn't faithful to her?'

The two daughters were appalled. What on earth was in their mother's mind? Did she really think she was protecting her daughter or was she just prying? But whatever Alice thought, she couldn't tell Charlie about this as it would offend him too much. He had actually told Bridget, on leaving church that afternoon, that she was going to be the mother he didn't remember ever having, having lost his own when he was young. Still shocked at what they had seen, the sisters put their mother back to bed with the dire warning that she must not go anywhere near the bedroom again.

Leaving Alice and Charlie to talk about their eventful day, Winnie and Anne made their way home, Winnie muttering her misgivings at leaving her mother in a strange house, both because she couldn't be trusted, and also because, in her inebriated state, it would be so easy for her to fall down the stairs. But the deed was done.

THE FOLLOWING DAY, AT THE INSISTENCE OF HIS ELDEST daughter, Charlie and Alice were to spend their honeymoon at the family boarding house on the coast, being assured that there would be no trouble from his other children as they had been told to make themselves scarce and would be staying with friends. Anne had also been invited, and as Bridget, who was by now sober, was already with them it was agreed that she would go too. So, after collecting spare clothes for both Anne and Bridget, they all went on honeymoon with the happy couple, somehow fitting into Charlie's Standard Eight car, registration number FUG 333.

Amazingly, the honeymoon went without any disaster befalling the newlyweds.

Sadly, Alice and Charlie were only married for eight years when disaster struck. Charlie, now in his sixties, had had short periods of illness in recent years, nevertheless, it was a terrible blow when Cormac arrived at Winnie's house with the shocking news that Charlie had died. It was 29 March 1959, Easter Sunday.

They were to learn later that Charlie had been working that day, driving a coach of holidaymakers to the East Coast. He had returned home feeling tired but not complaining of anything unusual. After his evening meal with Alice, they watched television for a while. At around 10 pm, Charlie said he was feeling sleepy and was going to bed in preparation for another long day's driving the following day.

Alice loved TV and now, with the room to herself, she put her feet up on the settee and settled down to watch her favourite programme, Mantovani and his Orchestra. It was almost Midnight when it finished – would she be too late for a cuddle from her husband?

Climbing into bed beside him, Alice said his name, speaking quietly in case he was already fast asleep; but he didn't answer. Gently putting her arms around him to give him a cuddle, it occurred to her that he felt and looked different. Calling his name again, she gently shook him, but he didn't respond.

Realising something was very wrong, Alice jumped out of bed. Hurrying downstairs, she grabbed her coat from behind the door and ran outside to her nearest neighbour who had a telephone.

Medical help arrived quickly, but sadly Charlie was already dead. The diagnosis was a heart attack. The only saviour of this was that Charlie had died peacefully, in bed, and not at the wheel of a coach carrying fifty-six passengers.

His funeral took place one week later at the local crematorium, and he was buried in the graveyard overlooking the house in which he had lived for most of his married life. He hadn't travelled far!

. . .

However, no-one could have foreseen the tragedy that was to take place just seven weeks later when, on Monday 19th May, Cormac was himself taken seriously ill at Bridget's house. Unfortunately, no one near her had a telephone to alert anyone, so a neighbour travelled down to Winnie's to give her the news.

Winnie was devastated, fearing the worst, and her anxiety was compounded on arrival at The Hill to the sight of a doctor tending her dear brother. The doctor confirmed that Cormac had had a heart attack, and he was trying desperately to persuade him to be hospitalised. But Cormac was refusing; was he perhaps remembering being in hospital in North Africa during the war?

A taxi was summoned, and Winnie and Cormac took the very slow journey to Winnie's home in the next town. Even with the assistance of the taxi driver, it was difficult for Winnie and Reg to manoeuvre Cormac out of the car and into the house. He was in so much pain he could scarcely breathe and looked ashen and exhausted. With slow precision, he was half-carried, half-walked up the stair's steps and into Michael's bedroom, where he was gently placed onto the bed. Fortunately, Michael was not sleeping at home that night.

The doctor came again later that evening, and after the visit, Cormac seemed more comfortable and had a restful night. However, the following morning, he took a turn for the worse and, at the request of the doctor, an ambulance was requested to admit him into hospital.

Anne stood at the bottom of the stairs with her mother, watching the tragedy unfold; her lovely uncle was being carried down the stairs on a seat-stretcher. His eyes, open as he passed her, appeared unseeing, neither recognising scene nor sound. He looked deathly. Had he already given up the ghost?

His time of death was officially marked as the time he was in the ambulance being carried to the hospital. But the family believe he left them before he was lifted off the bed, not wishing them to be present to watch, in anguish, as he took his final breath.

Anne was heartbroken and fearful when she thought of death. For the first time in her life, she had been so close to death she could have touched it. Her uncle's eyes were open as he had passed her but was that a muscle spasm? Of course, it was. She then remembered the times she had seen the old men lying in their coffins when she was a small girl, though she now thought of them as mere illusions; she didn't know them, she only knew of them. But this was a man she had known and spoken with all her life. She was part of him, and he was part of her, and it was difficult to understand how he could no longer be here. He was only forty-nine years of age.

Amazingly, Charlie's grave had not been filled in, so Cormac's body was interred on top of him; their only connection in life and death being their wife/sister, as they had only met once, and that was at the marriage ceremony.

PART IV

1941-1956

My Story

MICHAEL AND ME

Michael and I were growing up fast. We were both at school and my brother, now aged nine, had the responsibility of taking me there and seeing me safely home. He sometimes got distracted, and at those times, I found myself tagging along with him and his friends, acting as fielder if they were playing cricket in the quarry. Most times, we arrived home without mishap.

My dad was working twelve-hour night shifts at the mill because he could earn more money that way, and my mother worked full time during the day. However, even though Dad was at home when we returned from school, he would normally still be in bed, not needing to rise for a further hour. The huge house key hung on a long piece of string nailed to the back of the door and, like thousands of other kids our age at that time, Michael and I were trusted to open the door, go into the house, and remain there quietly until Dad came downstairs to get ready for work.

North Terrace was a mixture of Victorian houses. One side of the street consisted of beautiful detached and semi-detached houses with gardens backing onto a field. Part of the field was divided into allotments; a number of these contained hens which roamed around freely in their safe little patches. The opposite side of the street was the poor side, consisting mostly of stone-built, back-to-back terraced houses, usually with a large three-bedroom house added to the end of each terrace.

We lived on the poor side next door to a retired couple, Mr and Mrs Jones. They had a grown-up son who had lost an eye in a motorcycle accident. The father, an ex-pit worker, was a tall, gregarious, grey-haired, pock-faced man, all topped off with a long beaky nose. His wife adored him, and the emotion shone in her eyes.

As a small child I was very quiet and, although I had a few friends in the street, I preferred to stay at home by my mother's side when she wasn't working, where I would play alone. However, as I grew, I became a little more outgoing and took a special interest in our next-door neighbours. Mrs Jones always greeted me with happiness, and it was only later in life I learned she had longed for a baby girl, a sister to her only son, but had miscarried, and the opportunity had never arisen again. She always seemed to know when her 'little neighbour' was visiting, as the door would often open before I even reached the path.

Mrs Jones would invite me in, and I would sit on the big settee next to Mr Jones who, after a brief conversation, would bring out a metal money box made in the shape of a man dressed in bright red trousers, white shirt, black bowtie and a blue coat. There was always a supply of pennies ready for me to put onto the upturned palm, and once the penny was placed on the hand, the tin man would jerkily put the coin into his mouth and 'eat' it. Oh, how I loved this and would laugh and laugh each time his hand went up to his mouth. After a while, a cup of milk and a biscuit would appear, and I would sit there happily in my own little world, enjoying the snack. Even after all these years I still have such fond memories of this lovely couple.

I don't know when or how it started, but Mr Jones began to ask me how many 'corns' I had, and I would take off my long grey stockings and show him my feet. If he saw anything that looked remotely like a corn, his thick stiff sausage fingers would pick it off, taking care not to hurt his 'trusting little neighbour'. However, by the time I was eight years of age, I was already travelling with my parents to the Bradford School of Chiropody where, free of charge, student chiropodists would practice their training on the feet of unsuspecting guinea pigs.

My feet were particularly bad for a child so young, presumably because, until they wore out, I wore clogs for school. These were laced, grey-leather shoes with shaped wooden soles, similar to the footwear worn by miners. Unfortunately, these ugly shoes only added to my introversion, as I usually wasn't allowed to do Physical Education in the school playground because my clogs made too much noise. I would have to stand at the side of the yard near the wall and watch the other children exercising and running about.

In the summer months, I progressed from clogs to pumps, but my feet were growing at such a pace that these soft shoes were constantly being replaced. Now and then, to make them last a little bit longer as my feet grew, my father would cut out the toepieces from the top, giving me open-topped shoes. This usually made walking painful as often my toes would peep over the end of the shoe and, as I walked along, my toes would get trapped between the end of the shoe and the hard surface of the pavement.

Mr Jones continued to 'pick' my corns until the School of Chiropody finally gave him nothing more to pick. But I still visited my lovely neighbour on every occasion possible. I seemed to have an affinity with older people and, because I was so quiet, they accepted me easily.

I WAS MOSTLY HAPPY IN THE LITTLE WORLD IN WHICH I lived; it seemed safe and certain.

One day, my mother gave me the small task of shaking the fireside rugs. In doing so, I had to climb onto the low wall near the coal grate because I needed the extra height to allow me to shake the rug without it collecting dirt from the ground. Before starting, I saw a neighbour walking slowly up the road towards me, so I waited to allow her to pass before beginning to shake the rug. As she reached me, she remarked to my mother, who was sweeping the yard, that she was fortunate to have a little helper like me and, to my surprise, my mother replied, 'Yes, she's worth her weight in gold.' I was pleased as I had never heard my mother compliment me before.

As I was pondering what had just been said, I was aware that the neighbour had walked past me, coming into our small yard, and had entered our house. I could now hear my mother and our neighbour speaking quietly about Mr Henry, the old gentleman who lived down the street who I sometimes also visited, although I hadn't done so for a while. He had been taken to hospital a few weeks earlier and I thought I heard them say that he had died.

When the neighbour left, I asked my mother about Mr Henry's death. Surprisingly I wasn't afraid. Being brought up a Catholic I had been taught about Heaven and Hell, though I had never known anyone who had actually died before. I wanted to know what a person looked like when they were dead, even what happened to them afterwards. I can now understand why my mother found it difficult to explain to me, a child, what happened after death and I believe she gave me the universal answer: 'I'll tell you when I'm not so busy.'

Maybe two or three days later, I brought up the subject once more, but this time my mother said I could go to his house down the road to see him for the last time if I wanted, as his family had brought him back from the hospital so friends could say a final goodbye. I was intrigued and thought this would be a way to get my answers about death.

Before I left, my mother explained that Mr Henry's body would be in a coffin and that I wasn't to be scared; that he would look like my father when he was asleep. She had also told me what to do on entering the house, so I was almost prepared for what I would see. The tiny room was filled to overflowing with the coffin and the three or four people already there, the coffin sitting between three chairs, one at each end and one in the middle.

As silent as I had been taught on going into church, I went over to the chairs to have a look at the old gentleman lying there. It was quite a shock to see him; he didn't really look dead, at least not the way I thought he would, and yes, he did look like my father when he was asleep just as my mother had explained.

He was wearing his grey three-piece pin-stripe suit – the one he had always worn when he went shopping, and I could still see feint stains on his waistcoat where he had spilled food. His grey hair was neatly combed, as had his thick grey moustache still tinged with brown from his pipe tobacco. Even his eyebrows were neat. But he looked much thinner than he did when he had been jauntily walking down the street.

I knelt beside the coffin and closed my eyes. Joining my hands silently in prayer, I whispered, 'Oh Angel of God, his guardian dear, to whom God's love commits him here. Ever this day, be at his side, to light and guard to rule and guide. Amen.' Making the sign of the cross, I left, and I was deep in thought as I walked the short distance up the street to home.

'Will Mr Henry be in heaven now?' I remember asking my mother.

'Well, he will if he's been a good man,' she said. 'Why do you ask?'

I was pensive for a while, then asked, 'Well, how big is heaven? Won't it be too full by the time I die?'

My mother laughed. 'Well, maybe people die again after they've been in heaven for a while, which then makes room for more people. Did you say a prayer for Mr Henry?' she asked, obviously trying to distract me.

'Yes,' I said. 'I asked his guardian angel to look after him. So, I know he'll be alright now.'

And with that, the subject was quickly forgotten.

It was only a matter of weeks later that the old gentleman's house was rented out, this time to a lady called Elsie Wild, who eventually became ill and had to be taken to the local mental hospital. I never visited her as I was always afraid of her.

Now that Mr Henry had died, I needed to look for an alternative old person to fixate on. Further up the street at No. 61 lived another old couple who were probably in their eighties. The lady was spotlessly clean, seeming to wear a clean apron every day. She always smelled of Vicks and, strangely, always had a piece of cotton wool sticking out of her left ear. But, even more bizarrely, she had thin pieces of bandage and cotton wool wrapped loosely around her two wrists. She was never seen without these trimmings and neighbours had no idea what their medical management was. She still had her own teeth though not many, and the ones she had were very large and brown and crooked. Unfortunately, this lovely lady had agoraphobia and could only walk as far as the end of the garden path leading from her house onto the street. If she needed anything from the shop, she would lean over the gate to attract attention, frantically beckoning anyone who noticed her. She always offered money for running errands, but I was told by my mother that I must never ever accept payment, which I didn't, and I would gladly run down to the bottom shop, always hoping the purchases wouldn't be too heavy.

There was a quarry at the back of the houses which, though a public right of way, was also the workshop and storage area for a local builder. All the children in the neighbourhood loved playing in the quarry, though we were constantly warned by our parents of the hazards, which included mounds of sand used for making cement which could rise to more than six feet. One of the pits was stacked with bricks from The London Brick Company, making the area doubly dangerous. In winter, the boys would make two small walls of bricks to act as goalposts for their football games, and in summer, the bricks would be piled closer together to be used for their cricket games.

At the far end of the quarry, at the edge of the path, there lived a couple in a small caravan. The lady had only one leg, the other having been lost in an accident at some time. When venturing out, she would sometimes wear an artificial leg which showed white beneath her skirt, though most times when I saw her she was using a wooden shoulder crutch to stay upright. Her husband wasn't there very often as it seems he was sometimes in trouble with the police, hence away in prison.

In the caravan, the couple kept a monkey of all things. If anyone dared go near him, he would bare his teeth and jump around the caravan in a frenzy. Because of the danger when this occurred, visiting children would be asked to leave.

I just couldn't resist visiting the lady with the monkey, particularly if I'd previously followed my brother onto the quarry only to be told that I wouldn't be allowed to play the game of cricket, or whatever game the boys were playing. Rather than go back home, I would go to the caravan and, if the door was open, ask if I could look at the monkey.

When the monkey was calm he wasn't frightening at all, so I never did tell my parents about the incidents when the monkey was ferocious, knowing I would be severely reprimanded for my foolishness at visiting the caravan in the first place.

The summer school holidays were always a problem for my parents. The break meant that we had to be left alone during the day, it not being possible for my mother to take extra time off work. Dad permanently worked the night shift at the mill, sleeping during the day, so it was hoped that, if there ever was a problem, then at least he was within reach. My brother spent every spare minute playing out on the hot summer days, but this usually left me on my own. Fortunately, these times were kept to a minimum because Aunt Alice was occasionally at home during the day when her work shifts permitted and, even though my grandmother wasn't prepared to act as a full-time child minder, she would also arrange to take at least one week's holiday during the summer school break. So, The Hill was a magnet for my visits. I loved being at my grandmother's and must have been the only person in the world she never shouted at!

Between June and September each year, the Yorkshire mills still closed for two weeks for the Wakes Week. The air would be stilled, the shutters would close, and the floors would be swept for the first time since the previous holiday. Engineers did their work on machines which wouldn't have been possible with the machines running twenty-four hours, seven days a week. During these two weeks, there would be an exodus from the Yorkshire and Lancashire towns, Lancashire people mostly taking in the air at Blackpool, and Yorkshire people either at Blackpool, Scarborough or Bridlington. The short break gave the mill workers a chance to rid their lungs of the smog and smoke from the mill chimneys and household coal fires.

One holiday, when my Aunt Alice wasn't seeing Charlie, she suggested that she and Mother take my brother and me on holiday, her favourite place at the time being Scarborough in the north-east of Yorkshire. The town is built on a rocky headland supporting the eleventh-century ruins of Scarborough Castle. There are two bays, one to the north and one to the south, and the beaches have soft golden sand, unlike most of the south of England beaches which seem to be mainly pebbled. It was a perfect place to spend a week's holiday. Mother was always happy to take a break, but we were continually short of money, and this time was no different. However, with Aunt Alice's help, and with thrifty accommodation, we set off on the 75-mile journey by charabanc for Scarborough, stopping off for a ten-minute break at York to enable people to use the toilet and avail themselves of a cup of tea.

It was exciting for us children and even though the accommodation probably wasn't to everyone's taste, it was clean, which was the main thing. The room we were allotted at the boarding house contained one double bed and two single beds. I chose the single bed which butted up against the wall and I 'reserved' this by putting my paper carrier bag containing a few clothes on top of it! The room was so small that I had to sit down on my bed to allow my brother to pass by me to reach his own bed under the window. Mother and Aunt Alice moved over to the double bed and flopped onto it. Unfortunately for my brother and me, my mother and aunt would be snoring in unison for the coming week!

I saw two notices pinned up on the back of the bedroom door and got up to read them. They were lists of instructions, and I started to reel off the first one for the family to hear.

TO ALL RESIDENTS

RESIDENTS MUST VACATE THEIR ROOMS BY 9 A.M. EACH MORNING AND ARE NOT ALLOWED TO RE-ENTER THEIR ROOMS UNTIL 5 P.M. THERE IS A SITTING ROOM ON THE GROUND FLOOR FOR RESIDENTS' USE, BUT YOU ARE REQUESTED TO PLEASE BE QUIET AS THE HOUSE IS ALSO A FAMILY HOME.

DO NOT LEAVE WET CLOTHES ON THE LANDING.

DO NOT BRING COOKED FOOD INTO THE ROOMS, I.E. FISH AND CHIPS.

PLEASE USE THE ASHTRAYS PROVIDED. DO NOT TAP CIGARETTE ASH ONTO THE FLOOR, OR LEAVE BURNING CIGARETTES ON WINDOWSILLS.

DO NOT ALLOW CHILDREN TO RUN ABOUT THE HOUSE. PLEASE KEEP NOISE TO A MINIMUM.

IF RESIDENTS WISH TO HAVE FOOD COOKED FOR AN EVENING MEAL, THEY MUST PLACE THEIR UNCOOKED FOOD IN THE LARGE CREAM FRIDGE IN THE KITCHEN BEFORE 12 NOON EACH DAY, HAVING FIRST MARKED THEIR NAME ON THE PACKAGE AND THE PROPOSED METHOD OF COOKING. THE PROPRIETOR HAS THE RIGHT TO CHANGE A RECIPE IF NEEDED.

(SIGNED) THE PROPRIETOR

The second notice, which I also read out, was short and merely gave instructions to residents in the event of the house burning down!

Reading everything on the two notices, I felt I was more afraid of the second than the first, although I got the distinct impression that the first notice was the most upsetting to Mother and Auntie, judging by their indignation.

Having arrived at the boarding house late in the afternoon, that first evening we went out to eat – fish and chips, of course! The following morning, going down to the dining room for our breakfast, we didn't know what to expect. 'Light breakfast' was included in the deal. On arrival, we found the dining room already filled with guests, but as we had been given a table number on check-in the previous afternoon, we headed for it. There was a lot of noise in the room, mostly people talking to each other, but each family seemed to be keeping to themselves.

Walking between the tables, I glanced on each one to see what they were eating. They all had the same thing – Shredded Wheat. Oh, horror of horrors – my brother only liked corn flakes. I thought it best I keep my mouth closed.

Finding our own table, we children were 'instructed' to sit down by my mother, who then proceeded to read the small notice glued to the middle of the table. Getting bored with the wait, I glanced around the room and noticed a long sideboard set against the wall. There was a queue of people slowly meandering towards it, and I surreptitiously pointed this out to Michael. With the wind behind him, he jumped to his feet, nearly upturning the table as he did so.

'Sit down. You can't be left to your own devices for two minutes without causing trouble. Sit down and wait till we're ready.' This was Aunt Alice being her 'mummy self'.

'But, but...,' Michael tried to point out the problem.

'I've told you to be quiet! I won't tell you again.' Our aunt had been in mid-conversation with my mother and had no intention of stopping talking. No matter how much he tried to interrupt her, she wouldn't give him chance to speak. I was silent, not wanting to be on the receiving end of anyone's sharp tongue, but I kept an eagle eye on the queue, and particularly the cereal table.

Eventually, the conversation began to wane and, looking around her, Mother herself noticed the queue. Jumping up, she too almost knocked the table over, but of course no-one got reprimanded this time, my aunt's only reaction being to look up to heaven as though pleading for some higher assistance. Michael and I, now close on the heels of our mother, joined the breakfast queue and as instructed, spread ourselves out, keeping a space for Aunt Alice, who lagged behind. Foot by foot, we slowly edged towards the table of cereal and were almost there before I was able to see what was on display. On seeing two tall cardboard packets, Michael exclaimed, 'But I don't like Shredded Wheat, don't they have a choice'?

'Yes, Michael,' said Aunt Alice. 'They give you two choices – Shredded Wheat or nothing, so what's your choice going to be?'

I was hungry and didn't mind what was there. So, when it was my turn, I took a large bowl, filled it with two pieces of cereal and poured so much milk into the bowl that it was slopping around near the top as I walked back to our table. Eventually, we settled quietly to eat our breakfast; even Michael seemed to enjoy his two pieces of Shredded Wheat after all, particularly after he had nearly emptied the sugar bowl onto them.

My brother and I finished our breakfast at the same time, but my mother and aunt were still only halfway through theirs, having spent time talking in-between mouthfuls. After a few seconds, Michael and I stood up in unison, our movements not being noticed initially, and we both began to head towards the door.

'Where are you going?' asked Mother. 'Have you forgotten the notice on the bedroom door, and what we talked about before coming down here?'

Yes, now we remembered...we needed to go out to buy food for the evening meal, so would be going shopping first and pleasure would have to come second. What a bore!

Having eaten a good breakfast, we left the boarding house filled with excitement. Luckily, the shops weren't too far away, and we walked together sedately for the first few minutes. Eventually, I got bored and started skipping along, trying to avoid any cracks in the pavement, but Michael had more energy to diffuse and began running with all his might along the pavement, gradually gaining speed as the road fell away.

From our vantage point, we saw the lady coming out of the grocer's shop halfway down the road, but Michael didn't notice; he was by now in his own world, and anyway, he was travelling too fast. Coming to a sudden stop as he hit the lady, he knocked the shopping out of her hands, scattering the contents over the pavement.

My mother rushed down the road, leaving my aunt muttering under her breath.

'Oh, I'm really sorry, he's so clumsy,' said Mother in her poshest voice as she reached the old dear. Then, turning to Michael, in her angriest mill voice, she said, 'Will yer bloody well stop runnin' about like a madman, and walk quietly like Anne?'

Now, bearing in mind that I had eventually become wedged between the two bodies of my mother and aunt as they walked along the road, my skipping obviously having annoyed them, I didn't really have much choice but to walk quietly.

Poor Michael, he was now hemmed in, like me, being made to walk between Mother and Aunt Alice. But he was still like a wind-up toy on the verge of unwinding.

We found the shop and purchased our meat and vegetables for the evening meal; it was going to be minced meat as this was the most economical. Then, with enforced slowness, we returned to the boarding house. Once there we trooped en masse into the kitchen, only stopping to look for the refrigerator. Michael spied it first and ran over to it, opening the door before my mother had chance to stop him. Out tumbled some of the food other residents had purchased. I heard the slap without seeing it but there was no reaction from Michael!

We hurriedly scooped up the produce from the floor, carefully stacking it on one of the near empty shelves. Then, finding a different shelf, we deposited our own food. By now, there were four pairs of eyes peering into the fridge looking to see what the other guests were going to be eating that evening. I spied a bloody packet of liver on one shelf and recognised the long carcass of a skinned rabbit on another, and I was glad we weren't having anything so gory! I knew we were having something with minced meat and hoped it would be fried meatballs, but when I asked if that would be the case, I was told to 'wait and see'.

Michael and I spent the rest of the day racing between the beach and the amusement arcade, whilst Mother and Aunt Alice sat at a table on the beachfront with their glasses of milk stout. We were constantly being scolded for getting our only pair of shoes damp from the seawater, but it was a bind to have to keep taking them off each time we stepped onto the sand. We knew we weren't allowed back to the boarding house until 5 p.m. at the earliest, so did our best to amuse ourselves.

There was a small queue waiting outside the boarding house by the time we returned at 5 p.m., and as soon as the door was opened, we rushed upstairs to our room. After a quick handwash in the sink in the room, we went back downstairs to eat our evening meal. Michael and I looked forward to eating this as we were hungry after playing on the beach all day. To my delight, we had shepherd's pie that night!

My mother guessed that the family sitting at the table next to ours were from West Yorkshire like ourselves, though their accents were slightly different from our own. Mother said she thought they were loiner's! (a loiner is a demonym, describing the citizens of Leeds). The children were noisy; more so than Michael and me. The girl was shouting at her brother, 'No, you was wrong, I didn't say vat. I said I fought vey'd gone t' shop ovver vere and not vis one!'

Mother appeared distracted and I noticed that she was leaning slightly towards the next table. Suddenly, she nodded her head, indicating that we should all lean into the table towards her. Perhaps she had been ruminating and had remembered some 'ode' from Wordsworth that she wanted to convey to us; or maybe it was some French phrase she had remembered from our visit to the Brontë Parsonage Museum in Haworth when, one Sunday afternoon, she had taken it upon herself to read each placard on every item in every room, which was written in both English, and in French of which she knew not one word!

We waited with bated breath. Then, with a straight face, she uttered the infamous words: 'D'yer know? None 'er them there kids c'n speik reight!' nodding towards the children at the table she had been observing. My mother's perception of others was awesome, she not noticing that she had, in one stroke, covered herself in both glory and censure. What a gem of information.

We laughed until we could laugh no more, and my cheeks were aching. But my mother looked serious; she wasn't laughing. What had she said that was so funny? Poor Mother.

The following day we got up early. My brother and I were keen to go down onto the sands again, but Mother once more broke the news that we would need to go shopping for provisions before we could do that.

As it happened, it was quite a while before we finally reached the sands as, after organising our evening meal, it had been decided that Michael and I both needed pumps so our only pairs of shoes wouldn't get spoiled any further. At the shop, I chose a white pair with a small T-strap across the instep which closed with a small button at the side, and Michael chose a pair of white pumps with laces. We both asked if we could keep them on, and our old shoes were put into a paper bag which my mother carried. Then off we happily went to the beach, stopping at one of the shops to buy two cheap bucket and spade sets.

It was 11.30 a.m. by this time and my aunt must have been thirsty. She suggested we children go onto the sands while she and my mother visit a cafe nearby for a drink. Michael and I both ran with glee onto the sands, but before we had chance to settle, Mother called us back, asking us to be attentive for a moment whilst a landmark was chosen. It was explained that this would be the place to always look out for if we got lost – it was a Penny Arcade with lots of small 'world flags' outside and was easily recognisable if we moved away. After making sure we were going to be all right, Mother and Aunt Alice left, waving back to us as they departed.

We ran along the sands to reach the edge of the waves lapping the dry sand, and there we began to busy ourselves – me to build a sand-castle and my brother to build his fort. Michael's pumps were getting filled with sand as he scrabbled about, so he took them off and laid them at the edge of his sand fort. It was exciting as the water was coming up from the sea and slowly filling the moat of his fort; then his pumps fell into the water, which made him mad. Without a second thought, picking up the pumps he moved a short distance from our 'architecture' and dug a hole wherein he dropped his pumps, carefully covering them up again with a thin layer of sand. Finding a small piece of wood, a remnant from a candy floss stick, he marked his buried treasure. Satisfied, he came back to his fort to play. After a while, the beach began to get busy, people coming from everywhere, either walking or playing chasing games. Families appropriated small portions of the sand, placing their towels and bags down carefully before sitting down.

All of a sudden, we heard a shout. 'Michael! Anne'! It was Aunt

Alice's voice, but it sounded far away. Scanning the road in the near distance, it was only then we realised how far we had moved from where we had been left, and where we were supposed to be playing.

'Come on, Michael,' I said. 'We'll get into trouble if we don't go now.' Collecting our buckets and spades, we headed in the direction of our aunt and mother. It was difficult trying to hurry as the soft sand was filling my shoes making them uncomfortable. My brother easily overtook me, and I wondered why he wasn't having the same problem walking. Then I noticed – he was in his stocking feet.

'Michael,' I shouted, 'you haven't got your pumps on.'

My brother stopped in his tracks, looking down at his feet as if noticing for the first time that he had protrusions at the end of his legs! His grey, knee-length stockings had turned light brown with the sand and were bunched around his ankles like seaman's waders.

'Oh heck, where are they?' he wailed, and he ran back towards the sand fort. I thought I'd better wait for him. As he ran, he searched the sand, looking for the candy floss stick he had left, but where now dozens of candy floss sticks lay – not one of them standing up.

With great apprehension, we made our way back towards my mother and aunt, and I was scared about what would happen when Michael told them what he had done. But my aunt immediately noticed that Michael was in his stocking feet.

'Where're yer pumps, Michael?' she asked.

'Over there,' was his response, which was a brave reply considering! He pointed to the beach thronging with people, to which both Mother and Aunt shouted in unison, 'Where the hell have you put them?'

After a brief explanation, the two women jumped down onto the sand and demanded to know exactly where Michael thought he had dug the hole. Well, it was somewhere on Scarborough beach, but he didn't know exactly where! After half an hour of walking and digging and fuming and asking people to move so they could examine the sand beneath their towels (such a futile expedition!), the four of us left the sands and made our way back to the shoe shop once more to purchase another pair of pumps. Walking along the pavement on leaving the shop, my mother and aunt continued to lambast my brother with the things he should and should not have done. I was getting quite nervous by it all and thought Michael must be close to tears, but when I looked over at him, he was busy kicking a stone with his new left pump, totally ignoring what was being said. Mother and Aunt Alice didn't appear to notice!

My aunt was still engaged in her verbal assault as we came to a junction in the road. On the far corner Mother spied a fish and chip café. Their feelings of hunger must have been more powerful than their anger and, probably realising that their scolding was falling on deaf ears, they herded us across the road toward the café door.

Grabbing Michael by the arm, our aunt duly escorted him up the stairs to the restaurant. It was a large room with small tables almost filled to capacity, and at each table were chairs to seat four customers. Noticing a vacant table in the middle of the room, we wound our way between the tables and chairs to reach it. My mother and my aunt sat opposite each other so that my brother and I could be monitored. I was glad to be seated and relieved that the anger of the previous hour had drained from my aunt and mother, the only mention being the financial cost of the morning so far. A waitress came to take our order but, because the café was very busy, Mother told us she didn't expect we would get our food for a while, and she was correct; after what seemed a lifetime, the food eventually arrived, though it took a little while longer for it to be distributed as I didn't want any mushy peas and only a few chips, but Michael wanted more bread and butter. After redistributing what we didn't want and receiving what we did, we eventually began eating our meal.

I noticed that Michael had been sniffling on and off ever since we sat down and, by now, the noise was obviously getting on Aunt Alice's nerves. 'Will yer get yer hankie out please and blow yer nose before yer send me into perdition. Yer driving me mad today. What the hell's matter wi' yer?'

Reacting to the reprimand, Michael searched around in his pockets, looking for the piece of old shirttail my Mother had given him to use as a hankie. Locating it in his left-hand pocket, he pulled it out. Unfortunately, he had collected half of Scarborough beach in his pockets whilst we played on the sands, and he spread sand all over the fish and chips on Aunt Alice's plate. There was such a scream from the two women that everyone in the restaurant turned to look at us.

And another happy day was had by all!

. . .

My brother and I had a wonderful time that holiday, even though it might sound ghastly now. When we got home, I couldn't wait to tell Grandmother about the bus ride to Scarborough and the boarding house room. And I believe I was even excited about my new pumps as they were so 'girlish'. We were poor, like most northern mill worker families, and when you had nothing, even the smallest aberration from the norm was exciting. I can still picture the faces of my Mother and Aunt as they chastised my brother. But wonderful brother that he always was, he never took offence.

One lovely spring Sunday, on the way to Mass, my brother and I were told we would be going to visit Auntie Mary and Uncle John later that afternoon. Oh gosh, I was so excited on hearing this as I absolutely adored Uncle John, not least because he always took me to visit his horse which was stabled in a nearby field. My Uncle worked for the Co-op grocery and sold provisions from a horse and cart. I remember I could hardly keep myself in check that morning. Visiting my Aunt and Uncle was always a special occasion and I was feeling so happy.

After lunch, we began to prepare ourselves for the trip. My Father, who didn't always go to Mass on Sundays, especially if he had worked a Saturday night shift, was now busying himself getting washed and shaved at the kitchen sink. My brother and I were sitting on the settee like coiled springs, waiting to dash out of the door. I could hear my Mother quietly whistling to herself. We were all so happy! Suddenly, my Father broke off from shaving and said, 'One of you, and I don't care whose turn it is, but I want one of you to bring up a bucket of coal so I can stoke up the fire before we go out.'

Straightaway, Michael said, 'It's your turn, because I brought up the last lot.'

I was immediately incensed as I certainly didn't think it was my turn for the coal. 'No, you didn't bring up the last lot, I brought it up,' to which Michael replied, 'No, you didn't.'

On and on it went until, without warning, my father's voice broke into the squabble and, turning to us both, said, 'I'll give you two minutes to decide whose turn it is. We're not going out until someone brings up some coal and I'm certainly not doing your job for you. It's the only thing either of you is ever asked to do.'

And there it remained, both Michael and I being stubborn, digging our heels in.

I really hated bringing up the coal, particularly if my brother was in the house, as he could put the fear of God into me by whispering scary stories about bogeymen waiting to pounce on me as soon as I rounded the dark corner at the bottom of the steps. I would usually be so spooked that I would rush down and rush back, hardly putting any coal in the bucket, and then being made to go down again to complete the task.

But this time, neither of us would concede. We both stuck to our guns.

It must have been hard for my father at the time. Maybe he was trying to show us that in life, everyone had a person in charge above them, and children needed to learn this lesson. I can picture it now. He stopped shaving and slowly began washing the razor under the cold-water tap.

Everything went quiet. Too quiet. I felt we had done something more than simply disobey my Father; that this was going to be a defining moment and that something unpleasant was looming.

My father turned around from the sink and in a quiet, controlled voice filled with anger, he told us both to go upstairs to bed; that we'd had our last chance and we wouldn't be going out that day. I panicked and said I would get the coal. But I could tell by my Father's face that it was already too late.

It was early afternoon when we went upstairs and, not only did we miss going to see my favourite Aunt and Uncle that day, but we also missed our evening meal. My father didn't allow us to go back downstairs. I was utterly heartbroken and cried for hours, being upset both with myself and with my brother. I was still convinced that it hadn't been my turn which added to my distress. The unfairness of it all. But, of course, it was to be a taste of life in general.

That spring day was the day I made a promise to myself. I vowed that I would never look forward to anything with such intensity, such desire, ever again. I would never allow myself to have reason to feel as unhappy as I felt at that very moment, thus I would never again have to suffer such regret. It just broke my heart.

And I'm sorry to say that I have mostly kept this promise to myself during my lifetime. Perhaps that's the reason I have never been very badly disappointed about anything. It may seem gloomy but, in the end, it has worked in my favour as, many times over the years, absolutely wonderful things have happened to me when I have not been looking; when I have been least expecting them.

'Kitty, Kitty, Kitty, Kitty.'

Mrs Bedford, the old lady who lived in the rooms below ours, was standing in the yard at the bottom of the stone steps, bellowing the name of her cat at the top of her voice.

'There she goes again. Why doesn't she keep the damn cat inside instead of waking the neighbourhood, calling its blasted name every night?'

It must have been a Sunday evening as Dad wasn't working and had probably been to the pub for a few beers. Needing to pee, he was standing in the corner near the sink and about to 'use' the bucket that was hiding between the sink and the gas washer. Despite the heavy cream net curtains, he could see outside. 'It's every bloody night now. I'm getting fed up with her.'

Calling in the cat had become a nightly ritual for the old lady, and she would continue calling, 'Kitty, Kitty, Kitty' until eventually the cat appeared. Meowing, it would run towards the steps and bypass the old lady, running into the open door of the downstairs house. Following the cat inside, she would slam the door closed to make sure all her neighbours knew she had heard their silent voices of disapproval. Mrs Bedford was a forbidding old lady, and most of the children in the street, including me, were a little afraid of her. She always dressed in black from head to toe, even wearing a black headscarf indoors.

The nightly Kitty-calling ritual had continued for a number of years until one day we noticed that Mrs Bedford was no longer calling for the cat in the evenings and we presumed Kitty had died. My dad was counting his blessings, of course.

The Bedford's had a lovely old Jack Russell dog, but it was so quiet we hardly knew it was there, only seeing it when Mr Bedford took it on its nightly walk down the road.

Then, one cold December morning, the loud noise of an engine alerted us to something happening outside our window. This was unusual as the only transport to come up the street normally was the coalman.

My mother was curious. Carefully moving a small portion of the curtain to one side, she was just in time to see two men, carrying a stretcher, coming out from our passage into the yard and on towards the open doors of a waiting ambulance parked in the street. Unsurprisingly, every door in the vicinity seemed to open at the same time, each doorway crowded with familiar faces trying to see what was happening. Our door was no exception.

'Who's ill, then?' Mother muttered to no-one in particular.

The grey blanket covering the patient had been pulled up so tightly around the poorly person's neck that it was impossible to see who was lying there.

The two ambulance men lifted the stretcher onto the guide rails inside the ambulance, pushing it towards the front of the vehicle, then, closing the doors, they climbed into the cab and the ambulance reversed down the street and out of view.

We were still in the dark as to who was ill. Was it Mr Bedford, or was it Mrs Bedford?

Sadly, it was Mrs Bedford, and news quickly spread that she had died shortly after the ambulance had arrived at the hospital, leaving Mr Bedford on his own with his beloved dog, Nellie.

I started visiting Mr Bedford regularly after his wife died. He was a small, plump man with very grey hair and a thick moustache which, as with most old men, usually had a few ginger-brown hairs around the edges, dyed by the pipe tobacco. He was smart for a man of his age, and even in his tiny, two-room house, he always wore a grey three-piece suit with a fob watch tucked into the breast pocket of the waistcoat, a thick gold chain hanging down, heavy with medals.

One day when I asked him about the medals, he told me that he had been a 'budgie fancier' in his youth, and when I asked what that meant, he explained he had hand-reared budgerigars and entered them into competitions. The medals were prizes for his 'girls', as he liked to call them.

With bony fingers, he would pick out a medal and proudly tell me the occasion when his budgie had won it. Each budgie had a name, though he always stressed they weren't pets, and he would describe each one in turn with feeling. He was a passionate man so far as his budgies were concerned, and he loved telling me about the 'girls', though his thoughts would often disappear into the dark chambers of his mind when he wasn't talking about them. Once he was quiet, I knew there would be no more stories that day and should leave him in peace, climbing the steps to my own home.

I loved to hear his stories, but my father was not very happy about my 'downstairs' visits. The house was very dirty having not been cleaned for years; even when the old lady was alive, she rarely shook her rugs outside. Of course, no-one had even heard the words 'vacuum cleaner' in those days, so we all 'shook our rugs'. The downstairs house was also infested with fleas and one would inevitably migrate with me to a new home on my return upstairs. But visit I did at every opportunity, with my mother's blessing, I have to say.

My brother, Michael, who was now ten years of age, had his own life with his own friends and this life didn't often include me if he could help it. 'No, she can't come with us,' was the usual cry from him if he was asked to include me in his games. To make sure I couldn't join them, Michael and his friends would disappear into the quarry to play, knowing their games were often too rough for me to enjoy. Even if I did follow them initially, I would eventually leave them to their rough games, and either visit the caravan lady or return home to play on my own, usually playing 'shop' on the pull-down table of the kitchen cabinet, pretending the small boxes of mustard, baking powder, yeast, bottles of cochineal, almond colouring, and other goods were sellable items in my 'shop'.

It was at around this time that Miss Ledbeater approached my mother to suggest that, as Michael was about to sit his eleven-plus examination, she would happily coach him. Miss Ledbeater had once been a teacher at a private school and, although in her eighties, was still as sharp as a new pin. Mother was very happy for Michael to concentrate more on learning than playing cricket in the quarry, and gladly accepted the offer, but she wondered if perhaps I might benefit from some extra tuition too, so made the suggestion to Miss Ledbeater that maybe she would like to take both of us. Thereafter started a brief nightmare for me!

My brother was a bright boy (though extremely mischievous, as I've already shown) who had no problem understanding the lessons and the homework he was given, even thriving on it. I, on the other hand, being so shy and nervous, would worry about everything. I reddened at the merest admonishment from Miss Ledbeater and was always anxious about what she would think of me, particularly when I wasn't able to remember something told to me a few minutes earlier. It was a traumatic experience for me, and I was so glad when, after only a few weeks, it was decided I was probably too young and would benefit from extra tuition a couple of years later. Thank goodness I never did go back.

Michael passed his eleven-plus examination with no problem, whether in spite of the extra lessons from Miss Ledbeater or because of them, and was excited that he would be going to a grammar school.

There were long discussions between my family as to which school my brother should attend, my mother deciding on a Catholic grammar school in Bradford. Auntie Mary said our cousin, Stephen, attended the same school and he was doing very well. However, there was a grammar school much closer in the next town, though it wasn't a Catholic school. But this was completely discounted as we all knew that Grandmother Bridget would have brought the priest to the house if she thought her grandson was being sent to a Protestant school. My father didn't seem to have an opinion about this either way, so my mother took the initiative, knowing it would keep everyone concerned quiet.

That first day at school I so envied Michael. My brother looked so smart in his green blazer, long grey trousers and green and gold tie. As was the custom for all boys in that era, he had worn short trousers until the age of eleven, and it was almost a rite of passage to progress to wearing long trousers from twelve onwards. For Michael, it was a double thrill, as he was wearing long trousers earlier than usual and also wearing a brand-new blazer as, like me, several of his clothes came from the rag mill. However, to get fair wear and tear out of the blazer, Mother had bought it a couple of sizes too large, which meant that she had to turn the sleeves under at the wrist and neatly tack them into place. My brother's thin frame made him look emaciated as the jacket was too large in every sense. But our mother didn't have the money to spare to constantly replace clothes as we grew. She probably knew, of course, that the jacket would be a perfect fit by the time he was fourteen though unfortunately, by then, it would have holes in the elbows and the edges of the pockets would be ripped into isosceles trapezoid shapes rather than in the neat squares they were meant to be when the garment was new, therefore the jacket would be so worn as to need replacing anyway.

For the first year or so, Michael actually seemed to enjoy being at the Grammar School, and occasionally brought friends back to our home. But his enthusiasm for the new school quickly began to wane and, as he told me in later years, he soon found that being disobedient at the school, even slightly wayward, meant there was no mercy from the teaching Brothers who, he thought, seemed to enjoy inflicting punishment. Sadly, he blamed our Mother a little for his lack of ambition, having convinced himself that, had he been sent to the local grammar school with our neighbour's son, he would have been better equipped to deal with life. By his mid-teens, Michael had decided there couldn't be a God if these Catholic Brothers were the role models. (Sadly, he died an Atheist, in 2010).

AT THAT TIME, EVEN THOUGH MY BROTHER WAS ELEVEN AND I was nine, we were still four of us living in two rooms. So, whether I was encouraged by my mother because we were growing up in a very cramped house, or whether it was because I enjoyed being there I don't remember, but at around this time, I started staying more often with my grandmother Bridget. Most weeks I would stay with her from Friday night until Sunday afternoon, and this seemed to work well for everyone as it gave my parents chance to have their weekly bath in the tin bath, in peace, in front of the fire. With a quarter of the family missing at weekends, it must have seemed to mam and dad that they were bathing in comparatively clean water (after my brother, of course who would have then gone to bed).

I loved being at my gran's house: it was full of fancy things we didn't have at home. She had two rooms downstairs and three rooms upstairs, which I thought was wonderful. In the back kitchen, holding pride of place on the wide windowsill, was an aspidistra plant. It was potted in a large, green ceramic container decorated with small white flowers, and around the middle, dancing maidens daintily waived flimsy scarfs. I wonder what happened to it!

The day my Aunt Alice visited us carrying a small, jet-black kitten is etched in my memory. I wonder now if she chose the time to arrive knowing my father would be in bed, having worked a twelve-hour shift the previous night.

The kitten, curled up into a ball, looked so fragile that, at first, I was afraid to touch it only gently daring to move a finger across its soft fur. My aunt was telling my mother that the people who had the kitten had been on the verge of drowning it; their cat had recently given birth to six kittens which they didn't want. She thought we would like it!

Michael and I were excited and immediately wanted to give it a name, making various suggestions which were instantly discounted by first one of us and then the other. But my mother was quiet for some reason.

By the time my father got up my aunt had already left. Noticing the kitten lying on my lap, he asked why it was there and mother briefly explained what had happened. My dad was furious, particularly as no discussion had ever taken place as to whether or not we wanted a kitten, or any other animal for that matter, and he berated my aunt for assuming it would be all right to dump this little body onto us.

Mother tried to pacify him, but he wouldn't have it, insisting we take the kitten straight back to Aunt Alice who, of course, still lived with Grandma Bridget on The Hill.

With a heavy heart and two crying children in tow, mother put the kitten into a large paper bag, having first punched some holes through, and we walked the half mile to my grandmother's, where we found a furious row taking place between my grandma and Aunt Alice, with Uncle Cormac standing on the side-line, shaking his head.

'What on earth made ye think I wanted another cat? Ye must be out of yee'r head. Ye've seen what it's like when I have to drown 'em – I hate it! But it's always left to me to do.' My grandmother's face was red with fury. Aunt Alice responded in the same tone and grandma shouted back.

Mother took Michael and me out into the yard to wait for the shouting to subside, knowing that she herself would soon be adding to the anguish. We had begun crying and, interspersed with our noise, was the meowing of the little mite in the paper bag.

Having gently pushed my brother and me as far away from the door as possible, my mother re-entered the house carrying the paper bag and broke into the ongoing row, adding her problem that my father had not accepted the kitten either. She told my aunt that now, not only did she have an irate brother-in-law and sister, and a distraught nephew and niece, but she also had an angry mother. And all because she wanted to please a stranger.

We were standing outside, listening to the shouting, when suddenly my aunt came rushing out of the door sobbing, her distress plain for everyone to see as she hurried past us and out onto the street. I had never before seen my lovely aunt crying and it unnerved me.

My mother appeared at the open door, looking shaken and still holding the paper bag. Seeing the look on our faces, she must have decided that this crisis had gone on long enough, so passing the bag to Michael, mother quickly followed my aunt who, by now, had stopped walking but who was sobbing into her blouse sleeve.

'Look, Alice, let's stop this rowing and go back into the house. We don't want all the neighbours to know our business. Let's just go back inside and sort this thing out. I'll take our cat back and maybe you can find another home for the one you brought here. What's done is done, but nothing can be worse than all this upset. Come on.'

Putting her arm around her youngest sister's shoulder, my mother gently guided her back up the hill, ignoring the twitching curtains of the neighbours. Once in the yard, mother told Michael and I to take the kitten and go across the road to the neighbour, Clara's, house and stay there until she came for us. Clara's door was already open and, good friend that she was, she had had the sense not to interfere or even show she had been listening. Closing the door against any further noise, Clara asked us to sit down and, offering us one of her home-made buns, asked us about school, which I now know was a safe subject. A short time later the door reopened, and mother appeared, her face red with the exertion of trying to placate two opposing sides, but placate she had managed, and the noise had abated. After thanking Clara, we started off for home, still carrying our package, Mother now rehearsing what she was going to say to my father. It might mean another row, but she was a tough northern woman who would expect to eventually get her own way. Which she did!

The next time I went to see my grandma everything seemed to have been smoothed over and no mention was made of the cat or the row. As usual, I played in the back kitchen, pretending my grandmother's sewing machine was a tool at the post office. My gran had found an old needle to attach to the machine arm, and with an old copy of the Catholic Herald newspaper, I 'sewed' small stamp-sized squares, first making columns one way then the other. It was very therapeutic to make the squares and more so when I had finished and could tear the imitation postage stamps off the sheet. It was easy for me to get immersed in such a solitary game, as in some ways, I acted very much like an only child, even though I had a brother, and particularly so now he no longer wanted to play with me, having his own friends.

Later that year, on my usual visit one weekend, I noticed that my grandmother was continually going down into the cellar; although it was winter, the fire was blazing merrily, and we didn't seem to need any more coals. On one occasion, my grandma even had some bread in her hand which seemed odd.

'Grandma, where are you going?'

She appeared surprised I had noticed. 'I though ye were playin'. Why don't ye ask Uncle Cormac fer some money fer some sweets, and then ye can go to Margett's which should still be open? Wrap yerself up well now as it's cold outside.'

But I preferred to know why my grandma was acting so strangely.

'But grandma, I thought I heard a noise earlier, coming from the cellar. Is someone living down there?'

She laughed. 'No, no, it's not a 'someone', it's a 'somethin''. Come on wi me then and ye'll see what I mean.'

I still wasn't sure what to expect but followed my gran closely down the stone cellar steps as she lit the way with a candle. It wasn't a very large cellar and was divided into two sections – one for the coal and one for storage of buckets, brooms, and things like that. I noticed on the stone shelf in the corner there was a large wicker basket, and inside it something was stirring. Moving over to look, to my amazement I saw that caged inside the wicker basket was a live turkey trying to get out of the container! I was in awe.

'Now, don't ye touch it,' said Grandma Bridget as she held out her hand to feed the bird.

'But won't it be cold down here?' I asked, not realising that much, much worse than being cold was the fact that it was far crueller to leave it caged in the dark!

'Oh, sure, it won't be here fer long,' said my grandmother as she headed back towards the stairs. 'Come on wi ye now before ye catch a cold.'

I took one last look back and then followed the light up the stairs, leaving the bird in the dark once more. Back in the kitchen, I resumed my play and forgot about the poor turkey.

On my visit the following Sunday, I noticed Grandma was still going down into the cellar with food. My gran didn't appear to give any thought to what she was doing other than feeding up a bird so I, in turn, didn't feel much empathy for the bird at the time either. It was just something my grandmother was doing.

Another week passed and, on the Friday night, I turned up as usual. The following day, Saturday, was Christmas Eve, and my grandmother indicated that she needed to start preparations for Christmas Day. Although she had invited every family member, she knew that only she, Aunt Alice, Uncle Cormac and I would be celebrating Christmas Day with her. But she still had things to do and told me to stay in the scullery out of the way and play, saying that she herself was going to be in the kitchen for a few minutes. I did as I was told but was curious as I saw her heading for the cellar, returning a few minutes later carrying the turkey in the wicker basket. It was complaining terribly, so I could hardly ignore the event.

'What are you going to do with the turkey, Grandma?' I asked.

'Now, never ye mind. Ye just do as I say an' stay here near the fire where it's war'em.'

Grandma Bridget carried the bird into the back kitchen and pushed the door closed, leaving me alone in the scullery. Aunt Alice was working, and Uncle Cormac was out. I didn't want to be alone, not when my gran was in the next room; also, I could hear the bird protesting about something. So, I went over to the door and quietly opened it. Peering inside I saw my grandmother sitting, with the body of the bird between her thighs, and the neck and head of the bird hanging down over a bowl. It was struggling fiercely, and my gran was having a problem keeping it still whilst she tried to grip its neck to twist. She heard a noise and, looking to her side, saw me in the open doorway, my eyes probably like saucers. My gran had just managed to get a good grip of the bird's neck, so she continued twisting hard while shouting at me to go out, but it was too late. I had seen everything.

The bird stopped struggling and was now limp in Gran's hands. Then, without a second glance at me, she picked up the knife and, cutting off the turkey's head, held the neck down towards the large bowl on the floor which began to take on the colour of blood.

I decided I didn't want to see any more, so I went back into the scullery for a while. The piano was at the back of the room; I went over and started playing Tiddly Om Pom Pom and Oh, Can You Wash my Father's Shirt? tunes my Aunt Alice had taught me.

Eventually, Grandma Bridget came out from the back kitchen with the dead bird in her arms. Ignoring me, she washed it in the sink in cold water then, picking up the pan of boiling water that had been slowly simmering on the fire, poured it over the warm dead body of the fowl. The task completed, she headed back towards the rear kitchen carrying the bird, telling me she was going to pluck off its feathers. Intrigued, I controlled my anxiety and followed her back into the outer room watching, mesmerised, as she pulled the feathers from the bird's body, occasionally stopping to give me a 'special' feather. It was a hard task, and by the time she had finished, she was perspiring heavily. Just one last thing to do. She took the sharp knife and cut off the bird's feet, which she handed to me. Remembering the dismembered feet my mother sometimes gave me from the hens she bought from the nearby farm, I sought the tendon that was just inside the sliced foot and, on finding it, pulled it, and was once more amazed to see the dead bird's toes open and close. A special toy for a child with no toys!

Leaving Grandma's that afternoon, I set off on the walk for home just before it got very dark and I soon forgot about the turkey. After all, it was Christmas Eve and I had other things to think about. I knew by now that there was no such thing as Father Christmas, but I loved Christmas, nevertheless.

I arrived home in time to help make new Christmas decorations. My mother and brother were in the process of cutting coloured paper into rectangles, and I helped by threading each one through a previous one, gumming its two end pieces to make a loop. We continued until there was a long chain of coloured loops. These were hung loosely onto opposite walls, taking in the gaslight fitting in the middle of the room. The process continued until there were enough long chains to brighten up the dingy room.

I didn't even mention the turkey to my mother, so engrossed was I in my work with the decorations. (Time clouded my memory of this until, many years later, when my memory bank became full and its recall recommenced, I once more saw and felt the pain of the poor bird held between my grandmother's thighs). The following morning after Mass, I sought out my Aunt Alice and went back with her to Grandma's to spend the rest of Christmas Day with them all. I had already opened my Christmas presents at home; this year, I had been given a storybook, the adventures of something or other, and a 'sweet shop' made from cardboard which contained three tiny bottles of tiny sweets. Although my mother knew we didn't believe in Father Christmas, she still put our meagre presents in a pillowcase, adding an apple and an orange to bulk them out.

My grandmother had banked up the coal fire the night before and had put the turkey in the oven to cook before she went to bed. She had woken twice during the night, and each time had gone downstairs to check the oven heat adding more coal to the fire when necessary. It was still cooking nicely as she prepared for early Mass that morning and had calculated that we would be eating Christmas Dinner at around 3 p.m. that day.

The turkey did taste good. I only ate fowl on special occasions, and this certainly was one of those!

WE RELOCATE

1952 was an unusual year.

On 6th February, King George VI died from lung cancer at the age of fifty-six and was succeeded by his twenty-five-year-old daughter, Princess Elizabeth, who ascended the throne as Queen Elizabeth II.

On 26th February, Winston Churchill announced the United Kingdom had the atomic bomb.

On 21st May, a post office van was held up in the West End of London and £287,000 was stolen. It was Britain's largest post-war robbery, and the robbers were never caught.

On 5th October, tea rationing ended after thirteen years.

On 5th November, we moved from our tiny two-room house to a three-bedroom council house.

On 25th November, Agatha Christie's play The Mousetrap opened at the New Ambassador Theatre in London and, in 2021, it is still running, having eventually transferred next door to St Martin's Theatre.

Unfortunately, that was also the year I failed my 11-plus examination, though I was to take and pass the Entrance Examination to a grammar school in Leeds. There would be a significant fee each term, but Grandma Bridget immediately offered to take on the mantle of paying as she was still working. Whether she did this because of her guilt at not allowing her son Cormac to attend grammar school when the nuns had offered to assist, or because she had mellowed a little with age, I don't know, but I was very happy as I would still be with my friends from junior school, those who had passed their 11-plus.

In early September 1952, at the start of the school term, feeling special in my new blazer, skirt and hat, also paid for by my grandmother, I met my friends at the bus stop in town and, together, amid much talk and laughter, we travelled to the big city on the top deck of a bus, then caught the tram to a stop near the grammar school. This was the route that was to be the norm for the girls for the next seven years, but for me, I was to take the journey for only two terms.

. . .

For a number of years, my parents had been pushing the local council for a government-assisted house to rent, being told on each enquiry that we were getting to the top of the housing waiting list. The situation was fast becoming serious as my brother and I were getting too big to be sleeping in the same bedroom as our parents, so it was with great relief when we received the long-awaited letter making the offer of a house in the next town. I believe future council tenants could refuse up to three of the accommodations being offered but if none of these was accepted, then the future tenant would go back to the bottom of the waiting list. However, having seen the house we were being offered I imagine my mother would have almost bitten the hand off the council employee in her bid to get the keys. It was lovely.

On 5th November 1952, which was my Grandma Bridget's seventy-second birthday, our happy family moved from our little rented house to a lovely council house in the adjoining town. Unfortunately, no-one celebrated my gran's birthday, but then, no-one ever celebrated anyone's birthdays at that time. Nonetheless, that year, I imagine my parents did celebrate their newfound good luck.

Michael and I squabbled about which bedroom we were going to sleep in, but the dispute didn't last long, and I was ecstatic when I was given the larger of the two choices we had been given. On that first night, after we had dispersed our meagre furniture to the various rooms, we all had separate baths in pristine clean water. Michael was thirteen and I was eleven. It was the first proper bath either of us had had in our lives.

The end of 1952 autumn term test results at the grammar school for me were quite poor, but as usual were good for Michael. I tried hard not to think about school over that Christmas holiday and had an enjoyable break that year.

After much discussion between Father and Mother, my grandmother was invited to have Christmas dinner with us, but I worried that my mother would end the day having to knock heads together. My father did his best to be amiable, even to the extent of having a conversation with Bridget, but the air was still heavy, and he quickly disappeared into the kitchen to do the washing up after the meal, leaving the rest of us sitting talking in the room beside the fire.

On returning to school in January at the start of the spring term, I found myself isolated from my friends. From the second term, the children were being educationally streamed, and now I found I wasn't in the same class as my old school friends who, being brighter than me, had been put into higher streams.

I became very lonely. I didn't find it easy to go up to any of the girls in my new class, who all seemed to have 'special' friends already. I stayed on the periphery of groups, flitting from one to another, sometimes being included in their games, but my introversion became worse to the point that I didn't want to be at the school anymore, feeling inadequate most of the time.

The only lesson I even remotely liked was English. My inability to grasp some of the other subjects, such as French, Latin and chemistry, made me feel more doubtful of my ability with anything. I wonder now, in my dotage years, if it was just that the teachers were too uncompromising towards the children who were slow learners. Even geography was an alien subject to me, at least at this particular school. I did a detention one day after school because I couldn't get the gist of the compass. I spent half an hour drawing the image from the blackboard onto my book, but it didn't help.

Having completed the detention, I was once more in panic mode. It was winter, it was dark, and I had to find my way alone through a bombsite to the tram stop, which would take me to my bus and eventually home, eight miles away. Once home, I believe it took my brother only five minutes to explain the compass to me, and I never forgot it!

The weeks went by, and the days began to get longer; by late February, it was light enough for me to stay back after school for reasons other than detention. On Friday afternoons, I would leave school and walk alone down the open ground past the derelict (bombed out) houses and into the city centre, where I would visit the Marks and Spencer store in The Headrow. My mother always gave me a written list of things to buy, even though the order rarely varied: 2lbs of Worcester Permian apples, 1lb Conference pears and four oranges. At that time 'self-service' hadn't reached the fruit and vegetable section of the store and the produce was stacked along four sides of a rectangle counter, which had a small opening on one side to allow the sales assistant to a central point from which to serve. She would select, weigh, bag and take payment for the purchases.

This particular afternoon, as I glanced at the array of fruit on sale, looking for the type of apples my mother had written on the list, I perceived a man standing at the opposite side of the counter looking over at me and smiling. I was eleven years of age. Why would he be smiling at me? I dropped my eyes and moved further down my side of the counter. But when I furtively glanced over again, the man had also moved down his side of the counter and was again smiling across at me over the stack of fruit! I tried moving once more but with the same result. Fear took over and I began to shake, my heart was pounding out of my chest, I needed to escape. But if I ran outside, he might follow me. However, I did run, and it was fortunate for me that the well-dressed man in the suit, wearing a badge making him look official, who I did run to, was the shop manager. In tears, I explained what had happened though I wasn't sure if I was expecting to be believed. But, to my surprise, the man I was speaking with instantly hurried over to a colleague and together they went to search for my 'villain'!

He wasn't found, of course, but presumably the man had seen me reporting him and had left the store. I was still shaking with fear when I was eventually taken by a member of staff to a back room, where I was seated on a chair and given a glass of water. I remained there for a while, though it occurred to me, as I was waiting, that I had another worry; my mother would be getting anxious, knowing the time I normally arrived home on a Friday night.

After a discussion, it seemed the staff thought it was safe for me to leave, and the person looking after me assured me that the man had, by now, totally disappeared. I must admit that I looked over my shoulder many times on my dash to the bus stop, and it goes without saying that my mother didn't get her Worcester Permian's that Friday night!

My end of term exam results in April were very bad, and I pleaded with my mother to let me leave the grammar school. She knew Grandma Bridget was finding it a problem putting aside the money to pay the school fees, and the fact that she was in her seventies meant she couldn't possibly be relied upon to continue working for the next five years. Thankfully, mother was agreeable for me to leaving the school; in fact, it was probably a relief all round.

The local girls' Catholic secondary school found a place for me, although the class for my age group, eleven to thirteen, was already oversubscribed. This meant I had to go straight into the final year – the class for girls who were leaving at fifteen. Being a secondary school rather than a grammar school, it was not enrolled for GCE examinations, and merely provided basic educational needs, leaving girls to embark on their lifetime careers without any qualifications.

To my eternal relief, I immediately fitted into the relaxed system, and was given plenty of time to settle down. I was allowed to shadow a lovely girl named Maureen, who was the head girl. She was fourteen, in her final months at school, and was presumably intelligent enough to assist the headmistress in her day to day duties. This headteacher also taught the final year group of girls, but her administrative duties often seemed to take her away from this part of her responsibilities. She delegated many of the minor jobs to Maureen, and by association, to me, and for the very first time in my whole life, I really loved going to school.

At this time, I was also being trusted with the house key, so that I could go home for the ninety-minute lunch break, the school being only a ten-minute walk away. Once there, I would prepare a sandwich for myself and sit listening to Music While You Work, a popular radio programme of the time. Life was good, and I was so happy. A bonus was that I could also wear my own clothes and not a frumpy school uniform.

Although that first term helped me to assimilate into the new school, unfortunately the actual lessons were almost non-existent which at the time seemed wonderful but, I now know, was not good for children on the verge of adulthood. The headmistress was so busy that often she only had time to set us work to do before rushing off to do her own essential administrative work. This would leave us with plenty of time to sit talking to each other as, having done what had been asked of us, it didn't enter our heads to do that little bit extra of our own accord. Our limited intelligence at the time gave us no expectation of ever getting a 'super' job when we left school, so what was the point of studying? Every single person in the class was a failed eleven-plus girl. We understood that shops like Marks and Spencer only took grammar-school girls and knew we didn't need to be Einstein aspirants to work in a factory, a mill or the local butcher's shop!

From time to time, a teacher from another class would come and remonstrate with us for making noise, threatening to tell the headmistress, who, of course, happened to be the person who had left us alone, and we would quieten down for a while, or until the headmistress returned. It was a relaxed atmosphere which beautifully suited my temperament at the time. However, I now think the lax attitude continued far longer than it should have done for me personally, as I still had nearly three years' education ahead of me, whereas most of the girls in the class had only weeks before they were due to leave, to probably work in the woollen mills beside their mothers.

All the girls in the class were down-to-earth, solid Yorkshire girls with hearts of gold but, like me, had very few aspirations at the time. Yet, somehow, the two terms I spent at grammar school gave me a slight head start and, with hindsight, it would have been far better for me had I had been placed in the lower class, enabling me to continue studying. There was still a lot for me to learn. In fact, by the time I left school aged fifteen years and two weeks, I had had very few formal lessons since I left my junior school in 1952, four years previously. Like a lot of people of my age now, I have gained my knowledge through the hard knocks of life.

Nonetheless, at the time I was young, and enjoying this manner of schooling.

Part V

1960-1969

Bridget's Final Years

Bridget had taken the death of her only son very hard. How would she survive? Eventually, she had no more tears to shed and her body shrivelled to a shadow of her former self. She was now continually drinking heavily, which worried Winnie a great deal fearing she would have a heart attack whilst in one of her stupors. Knowing her mother needed help, Winnie tried to make sure that she visited once or twice a week, often taking a cooked meal along with her.

Although she had a key to get into her mother's house, she always knocked before reaching for the door handle to open the door, thus allowing her mother to feel she still had some authority, some dignity, some power over whom she allowed into her small home. Yet time and time again, finding difficulty opening the door, Winnie would discover her mother comatose on the floor between the door and the stairs. Often, she would have drunk the best part of half a bottle of Irish whiskey, but her small, thin frame was unable to soak up the alcohol. At times like this, it was difficult to get any sense out of Bridget and the only thing left to do was to put her to bed.

Bridget's bedroom was next to that of Cormac, but neither Winnie nor her mother had been able to go into the room since he died. Everything was exactly as it had been on the day he left the house for the last time: his grey metal comb – the only type of comb that could persuade his wiry hair to look neat – was still lying on the bedside table, and his shoes, as he must have taken them off for the last time, were neatly placed, toes first, beneath the chest of drawers. His now empty wardrobe, partly ajar, displayed his absence of vanity; his best, and only, suit having been given to the undertaker to dress him for his final journey.

By the time Winnie had disrobed her mother of layer after layer of clothes, Bridget would sometimes have wet herself. But Winnie never expressed her frustration to her mother about the condition she was in, as her own heart was breaking too. At least Bridget was in oblivion for a while. Strangely, Bridget would usually go to work on the day following her drinking bout if it happened on a weekday, showing that her life-force wasn't completely dampened; just her ability to cope with it.

To make sure she ate a decent meal, Winnie was occasionally able to convince her mother to stop off after work and eat an evening meal with the family. The first time she accepted this suggestion, her discomfort was very noticeable. She arrived from work whilst Winnie was in the kitchen preparing the meal, so had no choice but to sit on the settee near Reg, who continued reading the evening newspaper. Anne was ushered out of the kitchen where she had been helping with the meal and was told, in a whisper, to 'entertain' her grandmother.

Not an easy thing to do. By now, Anne and her grandmother didn't have very much to say to each other. Anne was a teenager and she an old lady. Somehow, the connection they had had when she was young was now severed. Sadly, Anne had no need of her gran's stories anymore. Maybe she had also overheard her parents complain about Bridget too often and now believed her to be a cantankerous old lady.

Before sitting beside her gran, Anne switched on the TV, keeping the tone low so that it didn't unnecessarily annoy her father, and she was glad when her mother eventually called them into the kitchen to eat. Naturally, Reg didn't follow, instead continuing to silently read the newspaper.

After they finished their meal, they sat at the table and talked for a while, but Bridget was like a cat on hot bricks and couldn't wait to get away from the house.

'Ah well, sure, I'd better be on me way then,' she said, putting on her dirty, old, black work coat and headscarf, having quietly intimated to

Anne that she wanted her coat from the hook at the bottom of the stairs. Picking up her shopping bag, she headed for the front door.

'Wait a minute, Grandma, and I'll walk down the street with you.'

Winnie gave her daughter one of her looks as she went to get her own coat from a peg behind the door. There was no hugging or kissing or even a goodbye and, as Anne opened the door, her grandmother stepped past her muttering under her breath. She didn't hear what her grandmother had said, nonetheless she knew the gist of it: 'that devil of a man'. Anne felt sure her gran would have stayed longer had her father been more civil; as it was, he hardly acknowledged Bridget's presence.

As soon as they were out of the gate, Anne took hold of her grandmother's left arm which was permanently bent hanging from her side like a jug handle, and she gently manoeuvred her down the steep pavement. Safely reaching the bottom of the street, they slowly walked the short distance to the bus stop.

Feeling some embarrassment at being seen with her grandmother in her work clothes Anne hoped no-one she knew would pass by. Bridget smelled of dirty clothes and looked very much like a tramp-character from an old black and white movie. As they stood silently waiting for the bus, she glanced at her gran noting that, even during summer, she wore the same black pinafore dress which almost touched the floor, and on top of this, she wore a much shorter black coat. Everything was too big which made her look as though she had been seriously ill and lost a lot of weight. On her head she wore a headscarf fastened so tightly beneath her chin that there was only enough space for a few grey hairs to peep out.

When the bus finally arrived, people stared through the windows at them both, no doubt thinking what an odd pair they looked. Taking her gran's arm once more, Anne helped her up the step onto the bus platform, passing her over to the bus conductor who took hold of the arm and gently lowered her onto an empty seat.

Bridget's mouth was set; she looked neither left nor right, not giving her granddaughter a second glance. Anne stood waiting until the bus left in case her grandmother should turn and waive to her, but as the bus sped off she watched her gran's profile disappear from sight.

. . .

'Did your grandmother catch the bus all right?' Winnie was calling from the kitchen.

Anne had run back up the street eager to tell her mother about her thoughts. But when she looked through the kitchen door, her mother had her head down, absorbed in a Mills and Boon book, a cigarette between her fingers lingering like a deformed fifth finger. So she didn't bother to say anything. What was there to say now? Between the time Anne had left to take her grandmother to the bus stop and her return home, her father had managed to eat his evening meal and was now getting ready to catch his own bus to work.

Once he left the house, everyone took a deep breath. The tension had flown out along with the two people who so often collided with each other.

Over the next few months, Bridget's drinking became more extreme, and the situation came to a head after it became necessary for the family doctor to be summoned to the house one evening after a neighbour had found her comatose on the floor of the outside toilet. She was bleeding from a cut on her head and, although it looked more severe than it actually was, it was the final straw and culminated in the decision between the three daughters that their mother couldn't now live alone and should live with one of their families.

The most obvious place was with Winnie as she had the largest house, although they only had three bedrooms so Bridget would need to share a double bed with Anne. Winnie had a hard time trying to convince both Reg and her daughter that everyone needed to take some share of the burden, and that it was their turn now. Yet even as she was stating this, in her heart Winnie knew it was a futile attempt to make her mother happy. She didn't expect the stay to last very long, and it didn't. It lasted just one week.

Bridget had put a spanner in the works even before she moved in, by declaring that she intended to continue working. This had initially caused a row, as Winnie had expected that at nearly 80 years of age, her mother would want to quietly sit by the fire and read a book. How wrong could she be!

. . .

However, after the row, the more she thought about her mother continuing to work the more Winnie took to the idea. Spending less time in the house would mean that her mother wouldn't be knocking heads with Reg so often.

Nevertheless, each evening Bridget came back from work smelling of muck, and she would pointedly ignore Winnie's suggestion that perhaps she should change out of her work clothes. Added to this, her incessant talking and meddling irritated not only Reg, but Winnie too.

She would somehow manage to be in the kitchen at the same time that Reg was shaving getting ready for his night shift work, and she would begin running cold water onto the greasy plates, using the soap flakes that he had brought home from work to wash his dirty overalls. If the plates didn't have a coating of grease on them after she had finished washing them in cold water, they would be covered in a thick film of soap.

Reg would complain loudly, throwing things about to add to the effect, and with only the small kitchen and a scullery, it was impossible to get away from the shouting match that would ensue between Reg and Bridget. Michael and Anne would look at each other despairingly, waiting for the shouting to reach a crescendo, after which they would quietly head for their respective bedrooms, Anne's bedroom being shared of course.

It was apparent that Reg had been unhappy with Bridget for many years, so the chances were that it was never going to work between them, but the breaking point came when, one day, he found her false teeth soaking in bleach in his tea mug. He couldn't take any more.

After a week of arguments, both sides called a truce and separated. Bridget moved into Alice's house, and Reg and the rest of the family settled back into their everyday, predictable, quiet routine.

CHANGE OF SCENERY

1960 was the year JFK won the US presidential election; the year Chubby Chequer began a new dance craze - The Twist, and it was also the year Bridget decided to leave the world of the sinners and move into a Catholic care home in Sheffield.

. . .

Bridget only managed to stay with Alice for a few months before the arguments began and it became too much for both of them. Deciding she would be better off away from her family and in a residential home, and without discussing it with her daughters, Bridget had a word with her parish priest, who suggested a good care-home in Sheffield. Consequently, she arrived at Winnie's house one day to ask, without any preamble, if Winnie would go with her to look at the care home, with the aim of her living there if it was suitable.

Although Bridget had many times threatened to 'live as far away from ye as possible, because I know ye don't want me', the potential arrangement had come as quite a shock to Winnie.

After talking it over with Alice and Mary, it was agreed they would go together to look at the accommodation and the next weekend, the three daughters took their mother by bus to Sheffield. Everything must have passed inspection because Bridget moved into the home the following weekend, taking a few personal possessions with her. (It was at this time that the only photograph of Nicholas was mislaid, as no-one ever saw it again).

However, within a very short space of time of her being in the Home, Bridget began to look melancholic although, at first, when Winnie asked how things were, she was hesitant to complain probably not wanting to upset her daughter. The upheaval of arranging her relocation had been almost too much to bear for Winnie, who was still working long hours at the mill and was constantly exhausted. She had warned her mother that this was her 'last chance saloon', as the whole situation had become intolerable.

Anne usually offered to accompany her mother on the visits, even though she didn't like the atmosphere at the residential home. It was always quiet in the main sitting room, where visitors customarily met their family members. Residents without visitors would be found sitting silently on chairs arranged along the four walls, all facing into the room. No-one spoke unless spoken to by one of the passing nuns and, even then, it would be in hushed, reverential tones. The lonely residents seemed to spend their time sitting, staring into space.

Bridget shared a room with a quiet lady suffering from the early stages of dementia, who was now so introverted that she didn't even appear to notice Bridget, who took it as a snub when the quiet lady didn't always respond when spoken to. The woman would sit for hours nursing a doll and talking to it as if it was a baby, which probably caused Bridget much disquiet, her own psyche reflecting only hardship and work, with never a time in her life for such things as dolls, not even as a child. Winnie tried to explain to her mother that sometimes the body was strong, but the mind was weak, and such a person would often do something they wouldn't dream of doing if they weren't sick. But Bridget didn't understand, or at least she didn't appear to understand.

On their weekly visits, Bridget's daughter and granddaughter would take her for quiet walks in the lovely gardens which were beautifully laid out. The high beech hedges surrounding the gardens offered lots of shade from the warm sun, which was glorious that year even in October, and sometimes the small group would sit on a garden seat talking about 'the olden days', which must have seemed a million years ago to Bridget.

As the weeks went by, Winnie became aware that it was getting more and more difficult to leave her mother who would get very upset as they were leaving.

'Now, why don't I come back wi' ye? Sure, I won't be any trouble at all.'

But Winnie would ignore the comment until she was out of her mother's sight, then she would lose her temper. 'How in God's holy name can I take her back with me? Ha, she won't cause any trouble indeed! That's what she's done all her life – cause trouble. Why can't she be like the genteel old lady in her room and just smile at life? She's always complaining, nowhere is right for her. Well, if she doesn't stay there, she's going to have to go to Mary this time. Because I've had enough.'

This vein of thought would continue all the way back home, causing great anxiety to her daughter.

SHEFFIELD

Wednesday

Dear Mrs Shirley,

I got your letter and am glad ye all are well, considering the cold. It is cold here but nothing to grumble about the winter. I just got a letter from Alice and told her she has to come for me on Tuesday or Wednesday, that is a fortnight today. I should be home two months ago but putting it off getting a house now it is Michael's wedding. I do not know what will be next. If she cannot come, will ye tell Michael if he can come for me, I will pay him, so after this if nobody can come, I will go out myself. I am fed up with excuses. I do not want anything from any of you. Why ye have all despised me, I wish I knew. I have nothing to do with Oakenshaw. That is it, so I hope ye will try to do something. I am working here with nothing for it and my £2 kept from my pension. They won't part with me if they can keep me, but I am going out this time or else I will be carried out in a box if I stay here much longer. No excuse this time. Also tell Alice if she is coming to bring that big bag, it will hold all I have. Don't write after next week. With God's help, I think that is all. I hope to be there for the wedding. Do not bother about it you – it is her mother's place, not yours. Who bothered about Mary's or yours? I had it to do, not our Mary, silly, if you start it, you will have it to do.

Write soon.
Your mother,
God Bless.

THE ABOVE RAMBLING LETTER, A VERBATIM COPY OF THE original letter, caused much consternation to Winnie when it arrived as, at this time, she was in a crisis of her own with her son.

A month or so earlier, Michael had suddenly announced he was going to get married but that he wouldn't be marrying in the Catholic Church. His future bride wasn't a Catholic and he now admitted that he hadn't been going to Mass for years and didn't see why he should be a hypocrite. He was adamant about this, and Winnie was having a terrible time accepting the situation.

Bridget was only adding to the burden: 'Why the hell doesn't she just stay where she is? I can't take any more worries and, in any case, why does she think she should go to the wedding in the first place?' This was being said to Alice, who was keeping her own head down lest her sister should once again suggest that their mother move back in with her.

In the end, things turned out all right as they usually do. Michael eventually agreed to marry in the Catholic Church and his future wife seemed not to have a problem with that, dutifully taking 'instructions' from the parish priest for the accepted time. But Michael was so young – only twenty-one – yet he wasn't prepared to wait a few more years before marrying, even though there was no apparent reason for the hurry.

As had been demanded by Bridget, she left the home in Sheffield and moved back in with Alice for the third time, with the assurance from her three daughters that between them they would find her a little house to rent nearby.

Michael's wedding arrangements were going well; the invitations had been sent out, the wedding dress chosen and bridesmaid dresses in the process of being made. But Bridget turned awkward: 'I'm not goin' to the weddin'. If they can't come and ask me in person, then I will not be there. His only grandmother, now wouldn't ye think he would come and ask me personally? Well, I'm not goin'. Is that all I'm worth, a card through the post?'

Winnie didn't immediately react to the threat, hoping she meant it. But Bridget was there in the end, wearing her best coat and hat, solemnly glaring out from the wedding photographs, looking for all the world as if she had been shanghaied and was there against her will.

Tears sting my eyes as I look at the picture hanging on my office wall of my lovely brother Michael, who died from cancer in 2010. I remember arranging to meet him in a restaurant a few days after his third session of chemotherapy. I arrived first and took a seat facing the door. Even now, I can see him walking towards me, pulling out handfuls of grey curls from his head, a lopsided grin on his face. I still have those curls safely hidden away in a locket. My brother's nickname with his friends had been 'Busby' because of his mass of unruly, curly hair and, though it must have hurt him to know he would soon be bald, his view of life was to take whatever came and make a joke of it. I do believe Michael bore a great resemblance to Grandfather Nicholas but, with no photograph, I am unable to compare the likeness.

By this time I was nineteen, and had relinquished the bond I had had all those years before with my grandmother. I don't think this was because I was taking sides with my father so much as that I was now grown up and didn't need my gran anymore. I had my own life, and I was selfish enough to think things should revolve around me and my feelings. I didn't realise at the time that it was more important than ever to continue seeing my grandmother, particularly as she was growing older and lonelier, and nearing the end of her life. I must have broken her heart.

Although I probably went to see Aunt Alice a few times during this period, sadly, I can only remember going once to see my grandmother in her new home. I have no memory at all of the inside of the house.

In 1963, I got married and moved away from the immediate area, going to live in the city where I worked as a secretary. At the same time, my new husband was commencing a three-year training programme to become a science teacher. Between us, we developed a routine, me visiting my parents once a week, and my husband seeing his family and friends at the same time. We had quickly grown from teenagers to adults; I was twenty-two and my husband was twenty-three.

We spent the next three years working hard towards an idea that had been formulating in our minds for some time and, in 1966, we left Leeds City Station for Southampton, on a warm day towards the end of August, and from there we travelled by ship to Cape Town, South Africa, arriving on September 12.

It was to be the start of an adventure that would take us out of our safe cocoons, where we were to some extent cushioned from the realities of life, and into the real world where we were to witness amazing things and meet amazing people. What we saw was an absolute culture shock, but that is another story and another book.

My husband had a three-year contract to work for the Malawi Government as a science teacher and, at the end of the contract, in May

1969, we returned to England, again by sea, bringing with us our baby daughter, Linda, who had been born on March 10 that year.

By now I had not seen my grandmother for a number of years nor, to my shame, had I written to her personally assuming my mother would pass on my letters to everyone in the family, including my grandmother, which I'm sure she did.

During those three years I was overseas, my grandmother had become frail and unable to take care of herself. She agreed to be admitted to The Little Sisters of the Poor, a Catholic care home for the elderly in Leeds where, once more, after only a short period of time, she again became miserable and depressed. She wrote letters to my mother on a weekly basis, begging to be brought out of the home, promising she wouldn't be any trouble to anyone. But there was so much hostility now between my mother and grandmother that it was impossible for them to live together again and, besides, my mother had her own problems. My father was now retired and my parents, finding themselves together for twenty-four hours a day with no distractions, were having their own domestic troubles. They realised that they didn't get on and, sadly, probably never had. Having children, as well as the daily slog of working, had covered the negative feelings they now felt for each other.

ON 26TH APRIL 1969, AFTER A SHORT ILLNESS, AT THE AGE OF 89, my grandmother, Bridget, died. This was seven weeks after our daughter, Linda, was born in Malawi, and just a few weeks before we arrived back to England in May.

SADLY, MY DAUGHTER NEVER GOT TO MEET HER GREAT-grandmother, Bridget, but I started this book with the intention of giving her an idea of what life was really like for her. Reading it back now I feel it has also become my own celebration of her life.

Although my grandmother had already died by the time we returned to England, I feel eternally remorseful that I didn't think about her once. We were bringing back with us our beautiful daughter, granddaughter, great-granddaughter and niece for everyone to see. I felt so happy with my life, I was blessed. My only regret at the time was that we didn't have our lovely Siamese cat, Sam, with us, as he had died in England in quarantine whilst we were on our long sea journey back from Africa.

I AM NOW IN MY EIGHTIES AND HAVE PLENTY OF TIME TO ponder. I think of Bridget often and wonder what she would make of the world as we now know it. Her house on The Hill has long since been demolished and, in its place, a modern housing estate has been built with all its anonymity. The ghosts have melted into the black soil and cinders, and new generations walk on the souls of the past. I feel I was lucky to have known such a woman as my grandmother, and happy that I inherited some of her spirited genes which I have been able to pass on to my daughter and two granddaughters.

Although Bridget couldn't change the cards she had been dealt in life, she nonetheless had the strength of character to cope with all the hard knocks. Yes, she was a tough, unyielding lady, and her domination left its mark on almost everyone she came into contact with. But, as a child I never felt anything but love from her.

If I look closely in the mirror, I see her in my features; her eyes, her nose, her mouth. But closing my eyes and picturing her, I now realise I never saw her smile, not once. So sad.

I learned from her that in life you should work for what you want and not expect it to be given; that you should give a good day's work for a good day's pay, and that stealing your employer's time was the same as stealing his goods, his pencils, his pens, his money. Happily, this work ethic still lives on in the next generation of our family.

Oh, Grandmother, riding along on this journey, I kissed your shadow as I passed over it.

There are six things you cannot recover in life:

A stone after it's thrown
An angry word after it's spoken
An occasion after it's missed
Time after it's gone
Trust after it's lost
And a person after they die.

God bless you, Bridget.

Afterword

Whilst I knew Bridget, my grandmother, for a good deal of my life, nonetheless I didn't know her for the greatest part of hers. Although most of this story is an account of true happenings, other events have been created and dramatised based upon the reminiscences of some of the characters named.

- Anne Shirley
November 2022

Printed in Great Britain
by Amazon

14347965R00149